Presented at
The American Friends of The Ghetto Fighters' Museum
2006 Gala

*"The world stands on three things:
on Torah, on Service and on Acts of Loving Kindness"*

Pirkei Avot, 1:2

With the compliments of William Ungar

IN TRIBUTE

TO THE INNOCENT VICTIMS
WHO PERISHED

TO MY FELLOW SURVIVORS
WHO WILL FOREVER
BEAR THE SCARS

TO VLADKA AND BENJAMIN MEED
PIONEERS IN THE CAUSE OF REMEMBRANCE
OF THE HOLOCAUST

Justice and Righteousness
Shall Triumph!

WILLIAM UNGAR

DESTINED TO LIVE

WILLIAM UNGAR
with David Chanoff

UNIVERSITY PRESS OF AMERICA, INC.
Lanham - New York - Oxford

Copyright © 2000 by
University Press of America,® Inc.
4720 Boston Way
Lanham, Maryland 20706

12 Hid's Copse Rd.
Cumnor Hill, Oxford OX2 9JJ

British Library Cataloging in Publication Information Available

Library of Congress Cataloging-in-Publication Data

Ungar, William.
Destined to live / William Ungar with David Chanoff.
p.   cm.
1. Ungar, William, 1913- 2. Jews—Poland—Biography.
3. Holocaust, Jewish (1939-1945)—Poland—Personal narratives.
4. Poland—Biography. I. Chanoff, David. II. Title.
DS135.P63U54 2000 940.53'18'092—dc21 00-057752 CIP

ISBN 0-7618-1806-5 (cloth:alk.ppr.)

⊖™ The paper used in this publication meets the minimum
requirements of American National Standard for Information
Sciences—Permanence of Paper for Printed Library Materials,
ANSI Z39.48—1984

ACKNOWLEDGMENT

I would never have written my memoirs without the help of my wife, Jerry. Her encouragement inspired me to express my tragic and painful experience during the Holocaust. Her good nature, love and dedication, brought this project to fruition.

I appreciate the countless hours spent by my wife, Jerry and my daughters, Florette, Joan, Denise and Rita in the editing and proofreading of this book.

I thank Kate Kelly for her professional expertise. Her comments and suggestions were of great value and enhanced my memoirs.

I am grateful to Arthur Klebanoff for his advice and assistance, which contributed greatly to the publication of this book.

I express my appreciation to Chris Johnson and his staff for readying this manuscript for publication.

In addition to my wife, the love and devotion of my four daughters have prodded me for many years to document my past. My legacy to my children and grandchildren is to remember the Holocaust and to transmit its history to future generations. It is a legacy of painful memory but also of optimism and faith, a legacy of pride in the heritage of our people.

To the memory of my loved ones
who perished during the Holocaust

and

To my children and grandchildren
who will honor their memory

INTRODUCTION

According to Jewish tradition King Solomon, the wisest of all men, was the author of three of the 24 Biblical books—"Proverbs," "Ecclesiastes," and "Song of Songs." The Rabbis were certain that each had been written at a different stage of the great King's life, but uncertain which was the book of his youth, which the work of his middle age, and which the statement of his final years. The three books are so very different in tone and in content.

"Proverbs" suggests wisdom, perhaps accumulated over time, the hard-won truths chiseled into our being by life, clearly the work of an aged King—or perhaps not. Perhaps the book reflects the sharpness of a young mind so certain of his truths, so poignant in his insights, so convinced of his knowledge, filled with the kind of certitude that only the young can feel—or perhaps not. Those in mid-life have predicated their lives on the truth they live. They seek the certitude of wisdom because they must risk their wisdom in the daily conduct of their lives.

"Ecclesiastes" is a cynical book, debunking every known source of authority, every accepted truth. It is clearly the work of a young man overturning authority or of a middle age man suffering through some mid-life crisis. Or, is it the work of an old man, who has seen it all and remains unconvinced, cantankerous, unyielding?

And what of the passion of the "Song of Songs," the work that Rabbi Akivah called the Holy of Holies. Frankly, I well understood the Rabbinic argument that this was the work of the young Solomon, whose passions were deep and whose lyrical eroticism could be considered by some, sexual, and by others, mystical. Perhaps it could have been the work of a middle age King, the husband with a thousand wives, who seemingly could give full expression to each of his deep passions in practice, but expressed what he could express in writing with poetry. I could not be convinced that an aged Solomon could write a book of such passion, until now.

William "Wilo" Ungar's, *Destined to Live*, is a passionate ode to the love of his youth, Wusia, the bride of his twenties, whom he married before the Holocaust took root, when the world was dangerous but still had some semblance of sanity. She seems to have been murdered in Belzec along with 600,000 other Jews—and along with their son, Michael. It is also a loving homage to Michael, one of the more than one and a half million Jewish children who are numbered among the Nazis' victims. Perhaps such passion is inevitable for the love that flourished and never withered, the blazing flame of youth that was never allowed to simmer by the normal passage of time and the ordinary tests of life itself.

As I read of Michael, I was particularly touched because I was holding in my arms my young son, Joshua Boaz, the third of my children, fully two decades younger than his next oldest sibling and the son of a father more than two score and ten. Any husband will weep as he reads of the loss of Wilo's wife, and every father will shed tears at the death of the young child, but the younger the child the more uncontrollable the tears, especially for one holding a young infant son in his arms. The younger the son the greater the injustice, the more the child was deprived of life, robbed of the opportunity to give joy to his parents, but also of the sorrows and the anguish that make children, children, and parents, parents.

I read survivors' literature often. I read it because I feel close to survivors. I read it because survivors make the history come alive; they are the history incarnate.

I also read survivors' memoirs to pierce the silence, which was my first encounter with the Holocaust. When I was a child, the Holocaust was unspoken but ever present, as I saw teachers with fists but no fingers, teachers with tattoos on their arms. Words were whispered, ominous words, which we did not understand—concentration camps, murder, ghettos, death and children. But the Holocaust remained inarticulated and survivors did not speak. They did not speak, perhaps because they could not speak; they were too close to the Event, the loss was too near to them. They felt the presence of absence. All energy had to be concentrated on the future. To look back on the past was to be paralyzed by grief.

More importantly, perhaps they did not speak because they intuitively understood that no one was ready to listen. In the countries where they found refuge, primarily in Israel and the United States, when survivors first told of the past, they were quickly informed: That was then and this is now. In Israel, the Holocaust was the story of exile and now the survivors were home, to build and to rebuild. In the United States, they came from Europe—everyone who came from Europe was escaping a past they wanted to leave behind, whether it was the famine of the Irish, the poverty of the Italians, or the persecution of the Jews. America was forward looking. We did not look back.

And when they spoke, they were asked an unanswerable question, "Why did you survive when no one else did?" For men the question beneath the question was "Whom did you betray?" and, for women, "Whom did you sleep with?" This was not a strange question to survivors; it was *the* question that haunted their sleep that tormented their waking hours. There was no answer then. It was too soon to offer an answer.

William Ungar can now answer that question by the quality of the life that he has led, which transformed survival into witness, an act of witness to the past, an offering to our collective future. He can answer the question by the deeds he has performed to build his personal future and ennoble the collective Jewish future.

The Master of the Good Name, The Baal Shem Tov said: "In remembrance is the seed of redemption, in forgetfulness, the root of exile." I am perhaps slightly less optimistic than the great Hasidic founder. Forgetfulness is the key to self-exile, remembrance may not yield redemption or self-liberation, but it is the key to moving forward with integrity. One cannot undo the past—especially so evil a past as the Holocaust—but one can transform the future, and offer the ashes of the past as a spark for that future. And this William Ungar has done in *Destined to Live*.

Professionally, I have been engaged in two great tasks to give voice to the unspoken secrets of my youth and to bring the silence of survivors to the American people and the world. The first project was the creation of the United States Holocaust Memorial Museum in Washington, D.C.. The second is the work of the Survivors of the Shoah Visual History Foundation, which in five years has recorded more than 50,200 testimonies in 57 countries and in 32 languages. The Shoah Foundation, established by Steven Spielberg after the filming of *Schindler's List*, has compiled more than 116,000 hours of testimony that would require more than 13 years 6 months and 17 days to view, if one worked 24 hours a day, 7 days a week.

I read survivors' memoirs with considerable trepidation not only because of what I read but also because of the burden that this literature must bear. It must be adequate to the task of describing the indescribable, revealing the concealed. And they must do justice to a life lived with such anguish, filled with such pain. I read William Ungar's book with even more concern because I am fond of him as a person and I so respect all that he has done. So, as the work unfolded, the courtesy of reading a friend's work loomed so small as the work loomed so large.

A word about the history William Ungar lived: When the Germans invaded Poland in 1939 to begin World War II, they did not act alone. A few days before the war, precisely at the moment when Ungar's memoir begins, a pact was signed between Germany and the Union of Soviet Socialists Republics. The consequence of the Ribbentrop-Molotov pact would soon be apparent. Germany invaded Poland from the West and the USSR invaded Poland from the East, dividing the country. More than two million Jews came under German control and more than one million came under Soviet domination. Between 1939-1941 Germany and the USSR were allied and then, in June 1941, the Germans attacked the USSR in Operation Barbarosa and unleashed a wave of killing by *Einsatzgruppen* [Mobile Killing Units]. Thus, there were two periods of wartime adjustment for Wilo; as a Polish soldier, he fought the Germans and then after the surrender he had to go over to Russian-held territory to rejoin Wusia. He then had to adjust to the conditions of Communism, which overturned the existing social order. After June 1941, the Germans arrived and with them the still evolving policies of the "Final Solution to the Jewish Problem." In German-held Polish territory, the movement was from ghettoization to annihilation in death camps. In former Soviet-held territory, most especially in the territories of the former Soviet Union, Mobile Killing Units were followed by ghettoization and then the "liquidation" of the ghettos—deportation to death camps.

A word about the book: There is a modesty to William Ungar's prose that readers will come to appreciate. Few words are used, they must bear the burden of many. For example, Ungar describes his parents' home: "In my house a pat on the head was an event." So much more could be said. So much is contained is these eleven words, especially when we sense his effusive love for Wusia and Michael.

His observations are keen. They are also completely without polemic. Few who read this work would forget his first awareness of anti-Semitism, when as a wounded Polish soldier while others are treated he was shunted aside because he is a Jew. He is even without anger when he describes the anti-Semitism of an ordinary family he encountered. They opposed the German occupation, but supported the German efforts at imposing the "Final Solution," the systematic destruction of European Jews. Speaking of the Germans, they said: "Pray God, they won't be around for long. But as far as we're concerned, they can stay long enough to take care of the Jews."

Ungar observes, "These were kind people in a way. Normal middle class, Polish Catholic people, with books in their bookcase." He describes the pervasiveness of anti-Semitism and its commonness, even among those suffering under the German occupation.

His anger is expressed carefully and precisely. Thus, Ungar writes of the native population's response to the deportation of Jews, "Paying off the superintendents, they'd ransack the newly vacated apartments like vultures feasting on the leftovers from a lion's kill. You would see them loading furniture and other possessions and driving through town, their wagons piled high with the belongings of condemned Jews."

But he is never blinded by the anti-Semitism he experienced to the goodness that saved his life, time and again. The hero of this book is a man who gave Ungar the life support he needed and who asked for nothing in return. Wilo became Edward Wawer, a Polish Catholic who gave him his identity papers and his story and, because Wilo looked

Polish—not Jewish—and spoke Polish without an accent, he was able to pull off his acquired identity. The gesture was at once magnificent and simple. The asking price was simple. Just do not stay in the same town, Lvov, Waver asked. A reasonable request that protected the lives of both men. But even when it was necessary for Ungar to violate the request, he was offered hospitality and haven.

Simple gestures saved lives. One did not have to be a hero for long—just long enough to provide an evening's shelter, a place to hide, a piece of bread. Nobility could be achieved in a single moment, in a small deed. And throughout this book, we read of such people, read of them without exaggeration or mythic dimensions, but with gratitude.

Wilo wrestles with himself, his morality and integrity, most especially after Wusia and Michael are deported. Notice how carefully he observes his feelings, how open he is, how he writes without self-pity, with such unusual candor.

I had to save my life for the day when Wusia and Michael and I would be reunited, but I also wanted to save my life. Was my mind making excuses for my will? Was I finding justification for my own determination to survive even though they were dead and gone? It could be. For the first time since my father died I felt fragile, battered. I knew my inner life was coming apart at the seams. I was shaking all the time. But my instinct to survive pushed me to safety.

When we train interviewers at the Shoah Foundation, we ask them to be hesitant in asking survivors about their feelings after moments of extreme loss or even moments of extreme tension. The reason is simple. Speaking of the loss of his wife and son, Ungar writes: "I can't recall much. A haze seemed to come over me, making me numb." How did he feel, numb and dead. He anesthetized his feelings and did not permit himself to feel anything intense until it was safe. Perhaps, this was one key to his survival.

Ungar is careful to describe his capacity to numb his feelings of danger. After a knock on the door by the police in the darkness of night, he writes:

> *The strange fact was I was so sure of that ID and so pacified by the cozy warmth of the bed and the little gurgling sounds Michael was making that I dropped back to sleep myself.*

Sometimes major historical events are mentioned in passing. There is no area of Jewish behavior that is more controversial than the behavior of the Judenrat, the German-appointed Jewish leaders of the ghettos who faced an impossible dilemma. To the Germans they had to represent Jewish interests and to provide for a captive population under the most difficult of conditions. Raul Hilberg, the distinguished historian of the Holocaust, suggested that we view their function much as a Mayor and City Council, but under the most dire of circumstances. They had to provide food, shelter, sanitation, and other necessary municipal services. To the Jews, the Judenrat had to enforce German decrees, dangerous decrees, difficult decrees, and even lethal decrees. They had to decide when to be cooperative, when to stall, when and if to resist, when to sabotage by inaction. And they were in danger of their lives, held personally responsible for the execution of German wishes. Some scholars see these Jewish leaders as pathetically ineffective, reluctant co-operators, if not even collaborators. And yet there were other leaders of the Judenrat who refused to compromise and therefore paid with their lives. Wilo describes how Dr. Joseph Parnas died a martyr's death. His successor was quickly appointed and he could be under no illusions as to his options. He must have well understood his status.

Ungar was an optimist, most especially at the beginning. Perhaps it was the hopefulness of the young who are very much in love or perhaps it was a failure to perceive the dangers that enveloped his environment. Writing of a time just months after the German invasion, Ungar said, "We both took it for granted that the future was bright." Or, "The idea of not circumcising him [Michael] never entered my head. Trying to look back at that time, not with the wisdom of hindsight, but through the eyes of those days, the truth was that even with Jewish blood being spilled daily, Wusia and I saw in the future not death and destruction, but survival. I hadn't the slightest doubt that this child of ours would flourish and that we would be there to nurture him."

Of course, circumcision was an indelible sign of Jewishness and endangered every male Jew from infancy to old age.

He is careful to present us with what he knew at the time. Never the omniscient narrator, he tells us what he knew at the time, seldom does he elaborate. Thus of Belzec, the death camp in which 600,000 Jews were killed in 1942 including in all probability Wusia and Michael, Ungar describes what he heard. "Nobody who goes to Belzec comes back. Nobody escapes. No one gets messages out." Indeed, there were only a handful of known survivors of Belzec.

There is much you will not read in this book. Ungar is modest about his considerable achievements, modest about the life he has led, the wonderful woman he married, the family he raised, his success in business, his generosity in philanthropy. I have observed these achievements from afar and have seen his graciousness and generosity up close. But of that, he will not speak.

Surely the book of "Job", the Biblical work of anguish ends with the restoration of new possessions and a new family. One life is linked with the other, connected to the other, but surely not balanced by the other. The past is past, but not fully so.

And Ungar saves his deepest truth for his last words. Thinking of the options of the life he led, thinking of how he could have become Edward Wawer, he writes:

"How puerile such a life would have been. How devoid of the meaning that comes with grasping your people to your heart no matter what and accepting the full weight of your own history, and theirs."

MICHAEL BERENBAUM
President, *Survivors of the Shoah Visual History Foundation*
Los Angeles, California

POLAND POLITICAL DIVISIONS UNDER GERMAN RULE
1944

MY TRAIL IN SEARCH OF SAFETY!

1. *Lwow to Tarnow; Tarnow up to Kutno.*
2. *Kutno up to Gostynin; Gostynin back down to Kutno.*
3. *Kutno down to Rzeszow; Rzeszow to Przemysl; Prezmysl to Lwow*
4. *Lwow down to Krasne; Krasne back up to Lwow*
5. *Lwow up to Warszawa; Warszawa up to Nowy Dwor;*
   Nowy Dwor back to Warszawa
6. *Warszawa down to Lublin; Lublin back down to Lwow*

"Hope in the Lord,
Be strong, and let your heart take courage…"

Psalm 27

IN THE JESUIT GARDEN

August 27–28, 1939

I often wondered why it was called the Jesuit Garden, especially since the Metropolitan's Palace was right up the hill. Andrei Sheptytsky lived there, the Ukrainian archbishop who tried to save Rabbi Yeheskiel Lewin and did save Rabbi David Kahane, though those events happened later and I don't want to get ahead of myself. Historically the Jesuits weren't always great friends of the Ukrainian Church, and definitely not of the other religions, so there was some irony in the name. But when I was a young man their Garden, at least, was enjoyed by everyone—Orthodox, Ukrainian, Protestant, Catholic and Jew. It was quite simply the jewel of Lvov, a city famous for its magnificent parks.

Stately oaks and spreading beech trees shaded the Garden, along with tall white pines. Here and there little intimate areas were set off by azaleas and flower beds, with benches where you could enjoy your privacy or have a quiet conversation with a companion. On the night of August 27, 1939 I was sitting in one of these private places with Wusia Rosenman on what we used to think of as "our" bench. Wusia's hand was in my hand and I could feel the warmth of her shoulder and the flesh of her arm pressing against mine. We'd been talking nonstop all the way from the Rialto where we had just seen the new Jadwiga Smosarka movie "Longing for a Second Youth." When we ran out of things to say about the movie, Wusia told me all about her new bookkeeping job, but what she really wanted to talk about was Warsaw, where I'd been for the last month with Chaim Rosen.

Chaim and I were taking the teachers' certification course, which we needed for our jobs as instructors at the Korkis Technical School. Wusia laughed when I told her about Chaim's attraction to the nightlife in Warsaw. With a quick smile, sparkling blue eyes and rosy cheeks, Chaim had a special zest for life that aptly matched his name, which means "life." Chaim was my best friend.

In late August the air in the Jesuit Garden gets heavy with pine resin and you can smell the perfume of the scented fall lilies. As we talked, I moved a little closer and put my arm around Wusia's shoulder. When she leaned towards me I could feel the soft rise and fall of her breathing. "You and I," I said to her, "we're like the two convicts who've done nothing but talk to each other for years. When they're released and walking down the road one says, 'Look, there's a rock. Why don't we sit down and talk a little.'"

Wusia laughed that contagious laugh of hers. Then she looked up at me. Neither of us could speak. We were so close I felt dizzy. I'm sure it was because I hadn't seen her for so long. There was an unusual silvery light from the full moon, which made the leaves glow a dark phosphorescent green. Wusia's pale skin seemed translucent. All I could think of at that moment was, "This is *bashert*, Wilo, it's destined." I had a sudden, very clear conviction that Wusia could feel everything I was feeling, that she could hear every single word that was forming in my heart. What I wanted to say was, *Don't we feel that we're one already in spirit? That our souls are one? Now it's time for us to make our lives one.*

I didn't say those things, which I regretted bitterly afterwards. But at that moment I just wasn't able to. Instead I chose other less explosive words. "Do you know the Talmudic legend about babies?" I asked her.

"No," she said, "what legend?"

"They say that before a child comes into the world a match is made in heaven and the child is shown the other child he or she will be paired with on earth. The two children see each other's faces. But then, just before they're born, an angel pokes them in the middle over the upper lip with his finger, right under the nose, which is why everyone has a little indentation there. The poke makes them forget the face they've seen. But they still keep a faint memory of what happened. I think the two of us were paired in heaven."

I switched from Polish, which was what we usually spoke together, to Yiddish, which had the right words for it. "A pair made in heaven." I felt her lips on mine, like a promise sealed. I put my fingers up to touch the tears that were forming at the corners of her eyes. "A pair made in heaven," she whispered back, "A pair made in heaven." She paused a moment. "Wilo, I hope God will bring us together soon."

I held onto her as tight as I could. My hands caressed her bare arms. Then I forced myself away. It was after midnight, August 28th, a new day. We knew her parents, worried as usual, would be waiting and listening for her arrival. Holding hands, we walked across Jura Square to the apartment house at Sheptytsky Street 5, where she lived with her mother, father, and older brother Sunio, an engineer's draftsman. When we stopped out front she kissed me again, then she went in. I watched through the glass panes as she raced up the steps toward the second floor and disappeared from my sight.

I was so completely lost in thinking about what had happened that I was hardly aware of walking toward the Korkis School where I shared a room with Jake Hirshfeld on the fifth floor. You could say that I was deliriously happy, but I was also exasperated, which was how I often felt after an evening with Wusia. As I walked a familiar conversation was replaying itself in my head. *Fool!* the frustrated voice said. *You almost told her. You almost asked her to marry you. You were right on the edge of saying what you truly felt in the depths of your heart. Then you pulled back, like you always do. You opened your mouth to say something real and all that came out were stories and fairy tales.*

At last the voice of reason returned, not that it made me feel any better about my shyness with Wusia. *Does it really matter?* this voice asked. *Isn't it obvious she feels the same as you? For the first time in your life you have someone to share your feelings with, what's deep in both your hearts and minds. You'll be together soon enough. In time, you'll go to her parents and ask for their blessing. You can't just tell them you decided to get married. Who could do such a thing? You have to be patient and control your impulses. You have to be a mensch. Then it will happen, practically by itself. You'll see. Your lives will be tied into one life. You'll become one person with one future. Because it's destined, Wilo, destined.*

When I got to the school I unlocked the front door and ran up the five flights to my room, without even noticing the stairs. Wusia had said, "I hope God will bring us together soon." They were beautiful words, mesmerizing words. I was savoring them as I opened the door and saw Hirshfeld sitting on his bed looking at me with sad eyes. I knew instantly it was something bad.

"I got a note from Badian," Hirshfeld said—Badian was the Korkis School director. "He wants to talk to you."

"Okay," I said. "You know about what?"

As a teacher at the Korkis Technical High School in Lvov, 1938

"He wants to talk to you now."

"Now he wants to talk? At midnight? Why does he want to talk to me at midnight?"

"He'll tell you," Hirshfeld said, as if he knew something he didn't want to have to tell me himself. "He said for you to come down, whenever you get in, it doesn't matter. You should go right down immediately."

Badian lived in a large apartment on the ground floor with his wife, Maria, and their second son, Julek. Their oldest, Grzesio, was in school at that time in England. Badian was expecting me. He was wearing a dressing gown over his pants and shirt, yet he still conveyed an impression of power. He was about average height, but solid in the middle with broad shoulders which he threw back slightly in a military way. During World War I he had been an officer in the Czar's army, which gave an added touch of authority to the respect he enjoyed as director of the school (though given what happened afterwards there were obviously a few who didn't feel that way). Despite his commanding demeanor, I always felt comfortable with Badian. Even though he was somewhat remote, I thought of him as a friend. Mrs. Badian, Maria, had taken a liking to me from the first time I arrived at Korkis as a student seven years earlier. She had even arranged tutoring jobs so I could earn extra money, which I needed desperately, first for myself and afterwards for my mother.

"Please sit down," he said, waving me toward the sofa. Badian was known for his directness; with him there was no beating around the bush. "Unfortunately, I have bad news for you," he said. He handed me a document that had the government seal on top. Underneath I read my name and date of birth—Wolf Ungar. January 21, 1913. Place of birth: Krasne, Province of Tarnopol. "The above named reservist," it read, "is ordered to present himself for mobilization at the 5th Regiment, PAL (Field Artillery), 50 Grodecka St, City of Lvov, on August 28, 1939 at 8 a.m." I glanced at my watch. Eight a.m. was seven hours and thirty minutes away.

I wanted to get up from the sofa, but my legs didn't seem to have any strength. My mind had gone completely blank too, except that I could actually feel my happiness slipping away, making me slightly nauseous. Badian was speaking, but the words sounded like they were coming from a distance. "We're going to war with Germany," he was saying. "That's what this is all about. I thought maybe Beck"— (Poland's foreign minister at the time) "could keep us out of it. Obviously I was wrong."

Badian was staring at me through his rimless round glasses in this disconcerting way he had, "You should know," he said, "this is something you have to prepare yourself for completely. Do you understand what I mean by completely?"

I didn't have any idea what he was getting at.

"You have to be brave, of course. That's your duty. You can't let yourself be afraid of the consequences. But Ungar," he paused to emphasize the point. "I urge you seriously, please, take a cyanide capsule with you, in case you fall into German hands. Better to commit suicide than let yourself suffer their atrocities."

I was no stranger to what Badian was talking about. I had read the articles in *Der Tug* and the *Chwila*, the Polish language Jewish newspaper; not that I paid much attention to them. After all, what was there to learn? By now everyone knew about Hitler and his *Mein Kampf*. Everyone knew about the Nuremburg anti-Jewish Laws. But to me, at that time, it seemed mostly propaganda. Back in 1933, Hitler talked as he did for domestic consumption, because he wanted to get himself elected. Now he wanted to stay popular. And what easier way to stay popular than by attacking the Jews? Besides, there were plenty of anti-Semites where we were. To my mind the Ukrainians weren't much different, and neither were the Poles. Grabski, the prime minister, with his "No physical violence, but economic boycott, absolutely!" Or the National Democratic Party with their murders and "No Jew" days at the schools. If you were looking for anti-Semites, who needed to go to Germany?

Of course I had talked to Richter, a student whose family had escaped from Austria at the time of the *Anschluss*. He knew first hand about some of the things that were going on. There was also a new school administrator who told horror stories about what had happened to him and his wife along with thousands of other Polish Jews living in Germany. The year before they had been rounded up and shipped out of the country in boxcars. And then the Warsaw government had refused to let them back in, leaving them stranded at the border. Newspapers had reported that it was the son of one of those Jewish families who shot the German third consul in Paris, which had led to *Kristallnacht*, the "Night of Broken Glass."

But through all this, I never allowed myself to get swept away with anger. It was terrible for the German Jews, and for Polish Jews who lived in Germany, but that was what pogroms were. In Krasne, my village, older people often spoke about Petlyura's Ukrainians, who had murdered their way through our region during the Polish-Russian War, less than twenty years before. And Jews always remembered Khmelnytsky's Cossacks from the catastrophes of the 17th century. I didn't see how these new troubles could be any worse than what we had already experienced.

In particular, I couldn't see how what was happening in Germany might affect me personally. It certainly wasn't going to distract me from my main preoccupation of the last two years, Wusia. She was all I could really think about. When could we meet? Where could we meet? How often could we meet? What would we talk about when we did meet? What would she wear, and would she give me a kiss when we said goodnight? Next to matters like these, Hitler and his rantings hadn't made that much of an impression upon me.

"I'm sure you think you know what's happening there," Badian was telling me. "I know you've talked to Richter. But believe me, you don't know. What they're doing to Jews there is unbelievable. I'm completely serious about the cyanide, Ungar. Take a capsule with you. God forbid you should need it, but take it along."

When I got back upstairs I told Hirshfeld I'd been mobilized. "Badian thinks it's war," I said. Then, since I didn't want any discussions, I got into my pajamas and went to bed. But I couldn't even think about sleep. I kept replaying what had happened that evening, our long walk, the strange moonlight in the Garden, the scented air, Wusia's face, her laugh and the warmth of her lips. I tried to relive the elation I had felt when I was with her. But I couldn't do it. It had taken me about ten minutes to walk from her house to the school. For those ten minutes I had enjoyed a happiness more powerful than anything I had ever imagined. Now, suddenly, it was being torn away from me.

I got out of bed at dawn feeling exhausted. I hadn't slept at all. In the gray light from our window I put on my clothes and gathered two pairs of underwear, a towel, a sweater, my toothbrush and razor and put them in my little bag. Hirshfeld heard me moving around and got out of bed to say good-bye. We shook hands and kissed each other's cheeks. "Talk to Wusia," I told him "Explain what's happened. Tell her to meet me at the old Austrian armory on Grodecka."

Despite the warmth of the previous night, the morning air was chilly. Walking toward the armory I began to think that maybe the situation wasn't as bleak as it had seemed while I was tossing and turning in bed. Mobilization didn't necessarily mean that Wusia and I would be separated. When I was in the army for basic training, three years earlier, they had let me out after six months, which I hadn't expected. Right now it looked like war would break out. But maybe it wouldn't. Maybe they could still find some way to resolve it peacefully. At least I was mobilized in Lvov, not Kalish where I was last time, which was hundreds of miles away. Actually, Grodecka Street was practically around the corner from Wusia's house.

The armory was a great squat brick building set back from the street, which allowed the pavement to form a kind of shallow courtyard. Its only other distinguishing feature was the sentry standing in front. Although the Austrians had built it when Lvov was part of the Empire, it didn't have any of the Viennese architectural embellishments that distinguished the railroad station and the opera house. I had walked by that armory a thousand times. It had never looked uglier.

I showed my mobilization order to the sentry and went in. There was nobody to tell me where to go, but off to one side of the cavernous interior was a group of young men in civilian clothes who also turned out to be mobilized reservists. Before long there were twenty-five or thirty of us, most of the others obviously peasants from the villages around Lvov. Without being conspicuous, I began searching for signs of Jews, which was something I did automatically. I checked eyes, noses, hair color, and complexions. I watched for a certain way of shrugging the shoulders, a slightly cocked head, the crinkling of the eyes, a slight lifting of the palms. I listened to the talk, hoping at least to hear a guttural or one of those inflections that gave away most Yiddish speakers when they spoke Polish. But after a few minutes it was clear that I was the only Jew, so I settled into my Polish identity. Back then I had blond hair and blue eyes. There was nothing Jewish about my facial features either, and I spoke pure country Polish and Ukrainian, having grown up in Krasne where there were only a few Jewish families. Passing as a Pole had never been a problem for me.

=12=

Before long a sergeant came over. I had never seen him before, but he had the same bull neck and sloping shoulders I remembered from the sergeants during my basic training, even the same temperament. The first thing we heard was "Shut up!"

"First off," he said, "in case you're interested, you're here because the Army wants you here. Second, get your uniforms and gear from the quartermaster. Third, listen for your names to get your room assignments and your duties. I'm only going to say them once. Understand?"

We all said, "Yes, sergeant!"

"Not 'yes, sergeant,'" he barked. "I want to hear 'Absolutely yes, sergeant!' Understand?"

"Absolutely yes, sergeant!" we all shouted.

"That's better," he growled. "Now listen for your names."

Ungar, my last name, isn't Polish, but it isn't necessarily Jewish either. Ungar could be a Pole of German origin, or even a Hungarian, which is what the name means. Wilo is a good Polish first name. Then I remembered that the mobilization order didn't have "Wilo" on it, but "Wolf," my birth name, which was not a name used by anyone except Jews.

Towards the end of the list I heard, "Ungar, Wolf." When I said "Here, sergeant" two small, cold eyes stared at me. I could practically hear the word *Zhid* running through his head—"Jew," but with a negative connotation, more like "dirty Jew," or "kike."

"You, Ungar," he said. "It says you're qualified for lead rider on a cannon team. Too bad, we got all the lead riders we need. You'll ride an ammunition wagon. Meanwhile report yourself to the blacksmith. You can be his assistant until we move out."

In basic training, three years before, I had been a top horseback rider. I had had a lot of practice earlier in my life, unlike most of my platoon mates, peasants whose only experience had been with plow horses. We were an artillery unit, but we were expected to master the riding techniques of the cavalry. The general principle in the Polish army at that time was that a cavalryman, or in our case even an artilleryman, had to be prepared to fight the enemy from any imaginable position on a horse.

I loved riding. When I was growing up I used to ride whenever I could at the big estate near Krasne where my brother-in-law David was the manager. I loved to race through the fields and the forest, feeling the wind on my face and nothing but air under the galloping horse. But the army's cavalry training was like nothing I had ever dreamed of. Imagine, for instance, riding a horse while you're standing up. I don't mean in the stirrups, I mean on the saddle. We'd all dismount next to our horses and the sergeant would yell, "Run the horse." The horses would start cantering with us running alongside. Then he'd shout, "Up on the horse!" When you hear that you grab the saddle and swing yourself aboard. "Stand!" You pull yourself up on the saddle into a squat, one leg, then the other—by now the horse is running pretty fast. And suddenly, if you've got good balance and your legs are strong enough, there you are, standing up like a circus performer.

Even harder, think about turning around completely in the saddle while the horse is galloping at full speed. To do this you grab the saddle on either side and support your weight on your hands like a gymnast. Then you execute a quick turn, which leaves you facing backwards over the horse's rear end so you can see whoever's behind you to shoot him with your rifle.

Hardest of all was jumping hurdles. When you're galloping straight at a hurdle the only thing you have in your head is pure, unadulterated fright. Your brain is screaming at you to pull on the reins hard so that the horse won't jump. To counteract that instinct they trained us to drop the reins completely. When the horse jumps, you lie flat against his neck, your arms down at his sides, squeezing with your knees, heels down, feet up, then straightening yourself up as the horse comes down. If you should be sitting straight while the horse is going up, he'll throw you backwards. Sit too far forward when he's coming down, and you go flying over his head.

You might ask yourself exactly what all this had to do with being in the artillery. We certainly asked that of ourselves.

The only answer we could come up with was that horse riding was the glory of the Polish army. Training had always been done that way and they weren't going to change now just because we were in the fourth decade of the 20th century.

I only fell once, not jumping hurdles but on the training field. The whole platoon was riding in a circle while the sergeant stood in the middle giving orders. He had a long horsewhip in his hand so that if someone did something wrong he could give him a hard crack. I made a mistake, and the horse, who had plenty of experience already, knew what to expect before I did. As the sergeant snapped the whip towards me the horse jumped to the side and threw me off, which caught my boot in the stirrup. Fortunately for me, the heel of the boot broke off, otherwise I would have broken a leg, to add to the several broken legs we already had in our training group.

Back then, because I never fell except that once, I was made a lead cannon rider. Six yoked horses pulled our 60-mm howitzers and my job was to sit on the right side lead horse and control the team. Behind me rode the assistant lead, and behind him was the third rider. Two-horse teams pulled ammunition wagons, with a lead rider and two soldiers sitting on the wagon's front bench. Riding the bench was the lowest job. They always made the least competent ones ride the ammunition wagon.

Now, there was no question as to why the sergeant assigned me to the wagon. "Wolf" told him everything he needed to know. But I wasn't complaining. Riding the wagon might be the lowest job, but it was also the easiest. You just sit there waiting until you get to your destination, nothing like the hard work of controlling six big draft horses.

I got my clothes from the quartermaster's and located my bunk in the barracks on the second floor. Then I went down to the blacksmith's forge at the back of the armory, next to the stables. Up to that point every artillery piece I had ever seen was drawn by horses. It's not that the idea of a mechanized army was completely foreign to me, but I had never given matters like that any thought. I had heard there was such a thing as tanks—*czolgi* in Polish. But the word didn't bring anything concrete to mind. In basic training we had been told that even if there was a tree in the way a *czolgi* could run it over. But exactly what such a contraption might look like I had no idea.

When I got to the forge, the blacksmith, a short, stocky Ukrainian with a thick mustache, was banging on a horseshoe with a heavy hammer. Sparks shot from the red hot iron. A huge horse was tightly tethered by leather straps on both sides of his bridle, watching the smith with big, nervous eyes.

I stood there until the smith eventually noticed me and looked up with an annoyed expression. He didn't say anything, just stared. Finally I said, "They told me to report to you. To help."

"Ever shoe horses?" he grunted, as if he was sure of the answer already.

I shook my head. A few times at home I had watched the blacksmith at my brother-in-law's estate. But it had never occurred to me that this was a skill I might need someday. The smith looked disgusted, but didn't seem surprised that they would send him someone who would be more trouble than he was worth.

Pick up his front leg," he said, pointing at the horse. "Hold his hoof up so I can fit the shoe."

I did what he said. The artillery horses were draft breeds, powerful, but with sluggish, unexcitable dispositions. It only took a pat on his neck and a few soft words to calm this one down. I watched the smith grab the heated shoe with his tongs and eye it against the hoof I was holding up. Then he pumped the leather bellows with his foot, stuck the shoe back in the fire until it glowed again, lifted it to the anvil, and beat it with his hammer. Then he tested it against the hoof again.

I spent the rest of that day and the next holding hooves in position and watching the smith. What I learned was that although horseshoeing seems crude, in fact there's an art to it. Starting with a cold shoe, the smith measured it against the hoof. Then he heated and hammered the shoe on the anvil to conform to his mental image of the hoof. Sometimes he needed two or three tries beating the shoe into the proper shape, but just as often he did it on his first attempt. When he was satisfied, he knocked the fitted shoe into place with six horseshoe nails, three on each side, angling them off toward the edge so they would stay in the horny material of the hoof and not penetrate to the muscle and tissue beneath. Finally he snipped off the protruding nail points where they emerged from the side of the hoof and filed down the stubs with a big rasp.

After his first flurry of words, the smith didn't speak to me at all. When he wanted me to lift another hoof or bring another horse he grunted and pointed. I didn't say anything either, since I couldn't think of anything to talk about. Instead I counted nails, six to a hoof, four hooves to a horse, horse after horse as we worked our way through the entire herd. We were preparing them for war against the Germans, in exactly the same way the Polish army had been doing it for the last five hundred years.

2

THE WIENER BANHOF

August 28, 1939

The next day Wusia came to see me. Hirshfeld had been to her office that morning to give her the news. After that she looked at her watch every few minutes waiting for lunchtime so she could run to the armory. She didn't know if they'd let her in, but when she got there the front doors were open and people were going in and out as they pleased, as if it was some kind of visiting day. There wasn't even a sentry on duty. Wusia said she couldn't have imagined it would be so relaxed if there was going to be a war. She thought maybe they had called it off and had sent me home. But since everyone else seemed to be going in, she decided to come in herself and see if she could find me.

It was lucky we met. I was hoping she would come and at lunchtime I walked from the blacksmith's forge to the main area where there were a lot of people milling around, some in uniform, and some not. When I saw her standing there looking lost, I wanted to run to her and hold her, but there were too many people around, so I didn't. When she saw me her face lit up and she held her hands out for me to take.

At first neither of us could speak. All the hopes we had, and now for no reason at all, they were suddenly smashed. "Look at me," I said finally, stepping back so she could see how dirty my uniform was from the work. "They made me into a smith's helper."

"I can see," she said, trying to smile. Then, so quietly I could barely hear her, "We were so happy."

"Don't," I said, putting my hand to her lips. I couldn't bear it. "Who knows what might happen? Maybe there won't be a war. No one here has any idea what's going on. They don't even know if we're staying in Lvov or not, so it doesn't make any sense to jump to conclusions."

It was one of those conversations where you say things because you want to talk about anything in the world except the one thing that matters. I told her what had happened when I got back to the school from her house, how Hirshfeld was waiting up for me with Badian's message and how I went right down to see him. I told her how grim Badian's mood had been, although I didn't say anything about the cyanide. While we talked I had a hollow feeling in my stomach from thinking that if there was a war anything could happen. It could even be that we would never see each other again. We must have been standing there for about fifteen minutes, but it seemed no more than a moment before she had to go back to work.

"Come tomorrow." I said. "Who knows, everything could change by then."

The next morning the sergeant's voice dragged me out of a dead sleep. "Up, up you Polish heroes," he was roaring. "Up! Today's your chance to show 'em what kind of soldiers you are. Dress uniforms, hats, rifles, and fixed bayonets. We're going on parade!"

An hour later the whole regiment was lined up in the back of the armory, listening to an officer whose rank was so high I could only guess what it might be. I had never seen anyone like him before. He had three rows of medals pinned across the left side of his jacket and a red sash trimmed with white draped diagonally across his chest. Gold braid looped down from his right epaulette and he wore a stiff-brimmed hat with a thick gold encrusted band around it. I thought he must at least be a general. "This parade is for the people of Lvov." His voice was shrill and high, like a blaring trumpet. It echoed through the armory. "Now they will see the kind of fighting men Poland breeds. You are the spirit of the Polish army, an army that has never hesitated to spill its blood in defense of the Fatherland. You will show them how ready our brave army is to drive back the Prussian dog. We will not give them an inch of our holy soil nor a button of our uniforms. You are the warriors of Poland. You fight for God, Faith, and the Fatherland. You are the soul of the nation. Long live Poland!"

Afterwards we practiced marching. The last time I had heard cadences and marching orders was three years earlier in Kalish. From the way some of the other reservists marched it looked as if they had done their regular service even longer ago than I had. They were having trouble with the left, right, left rhythm of it and often seemed about to trip over their own feet. During rest breaks everyone talked, although no one mentioned the general or his patriotic speech. Mostly people wondered how fast France might get into the war. Poland had a tradition of allying itself with France and the French army had a good reputation.

"France has the toughest army and the smartest generals, a corporal announced. "Once they come in it'll be over in a day."

"They know we fought alongside them last time," someone else said. "They used to say, 'Play the Poles a patriotic song and they'll attack mercilessly.'"

"Now maybe we should play *them* a patriotic song," another broke in. "Hey, is it true Madame Curie was married to a Pole?"

"What do you mean, married to a Pole? She wasn't married to a Pole, idiot. She was a Pole."

"Napoleon's cavalry was Polish too," an innocent looking farm boy said. "We have his picture on the wall at home."

I listened, wondering if the French would really come in. I knew there was a treaty, but what that meant I wasn't sure.

I wished I had kept myself better informed. Some of the men were joking, but underneath the jokes there was a feeling of uneasiness. Looking around, I saw little knots of Ukrainians talking among themselves. They weren't making any secret of how much they hated the idea of fighting for Poland. I didn't know any of them, but back in Krasne I had many Ukrainian friends. For the most part, life in the village went on harmoniously; there were even a lot of marriages between Ukrainians and Poles. But the Ukrainians in eastern Poland had a long history of hating their Polish conquerors. I was sure most of them would have been much happier taking revenge on the Poles instead of fighting for them.

Exactly at noon the big front doors of the armory opened and we marched out onto Grodecka Street. You could tell instantly from the cheering what kind of an impression we were making, what with the sun glinting off our fixed bayonets and our freshly polished, high, cavalry style boots. I was staring into the neck of the soldier in front of me as we turned onto Legionowo, but out of the corners of my eyes I could see crowds on both sides of the street pushing to get a better look. There seemed to be a forest of red and white banners and standards with white Polish eagles against a red background. Along the curbs children were waving miniature flags and throwing flowers.

At first all the cheering just sounded like loud noise. But when I got used to it I began to make out words and phrases.

"Long live the army!" "Long live Poland!" "No to the enemy!" "Down with the Prussians!" The crowd was going wild and the regiment seemed to pick up their excitement. Everyone started to straighten up more and step smartly in unison, a minor miracle given what the practice marching had looked like. I had always hated parading, but it was impossible not to get caught in the excitement. I was thinking that this was what parades must have been like under Emperor Franz Josef.

From somewhere I could hear people singing the national anthem.

The Germans will not
Spit in our faces
Or Germanize our children
So help us God
So help us God.

In front of us to the right a giant banner was waving with a slogan in foot high letters:

NOT AN INCH OF OUR SOIL NOR A BUTTON OF OUR UNIFORMS.

August 31, 1939

The next afternoon during her lunch break Wusia came to see me again. It was another bright, warm day that showed every sign of turning into what they used to call a "golden Polish fall." We stood facing each other on the wide

NOT AN INCH

OF OUR SOIL

NOR A BUTTON

OF OUR UNIFORMS.

Mobilized into the Polish Army, 1939

sidewalk in front of the armory. As usual Grodecka was bustling with people walking and talking. Soldiers were going in and coming out and here and there families and other couples were saying their own farewells. Last night we had gotten word that we were moving out.

Wusia and I stood close, almost touching, neither of us aware of the people pressing by us. "I'm going," I said. "I don't know what the outcome might be." I knew how weak that sounded. I wanted to say something more. I wanted to tell her how much I loved her and how the thought of leaving her was torturing me. But the words wouldn't come. Wusia's face and her eyes conveyed what she was feeling. I couldn't stand the thought of making this more painful than it already was. For a moment she searched around in her pocketbook for something. Finally she found it and put it in my hand. I held it up to see. It was a small photograph of her wearing a school uniform and a beret with her school badge pinned to it. "It was when I was fourteen," she said. "But it's still my favorite. I gave it to my mother as a present, but last night I asked for it back." I turned it over. On the back she had written, "To my dear mother from her dear daughter, 1935."

"You have to remember our initials, Wilo," she said. That night in the Jesuit Garden, it seemed like an eternity ago, we had laughed about how our first initials were the same, Wilo and Wusia, and how our last initials might be the same too. As if we were still in the privacy of the Garden and not out on a busy street, we put our arms around each other and hugged each other for dear life. We kissed as though we both knew it might be our last.

"Remember our initials," she said. Then she turned and walked away, so quickly that after a moment I couldn't see her anymore in the hurrying crowd.

Early the next morning we assembled. When we marched out of the armory there weren't any crowds cheering—at that hour the streets were just beginning to fill with people on their way to work. Still, most of the regiment was in a good mood. Yesterday's nervousness, with all the talk about the French, had evaporated. I could feel how eager they had all become. Lvov was the first big city many of the peasant boys had seen. Except for their military training most hadn't been beyond their farms and villages. Now they were beginning to think that they were on the way to the greatest adventure of their lives.

The Lvov train station, the *Wiener Banhof*, was built in the Viennese style. It was as big and grand as a nobleman's castle. From here we would be traveling west toward a world with cities even bigger than Lvov, whose names we had only heard of. Standing on the platform waiting for the order to board the long troop train, someone started a soldier's lovesong in a clear, longing tenor. "The buds of the white roses are blooming/Return, Jan, from the war, return." Other voices joined in, "Return and kiss me like you used to." By now half the regiment was singing. *Wroc ucaluj jak za dawnych lat bywalo.* "Return and kiss me like you used to."

I loved singing, and the song was a beautiful, tender one, but I couldn't see that there was anything to sing about. All I felt was gloom. I already missed Wusia terribly, and anticipated missing her even more. Besides, I was also depressed by the enthusiasm of the General and the effects of the parade yesterday, which had given such a false face to what was really happening. This reminded me of the old peasant story, the one about the grandmother whose grandson is going off to war. "Be brave, my boy," she tells him. "Kill a few enemies, then come back to us healthy and happy." It was as if they had all forgotten the second part of the story, the part where the boy says, "But grandma, what if the enemy kills me instead of me killing them?" The grandmother doesn't have anything to say to that. She hasn't considered the possibility.

While I was lost in these thoughts, I was searching the crowded platform for Jews. I'd been looking ever since I arrived at the armory, but so far I hadn't found any. I wasn't expecting to, but if there was even one other Jew among the regiment's thousand or so Poles and Ukrainians it would have made me feel a little less lonely, even if we never would have said hello to each other.

I was startled from my thoughts when the boy in back of me suddenly shouted, "Look there!" I looked to where his finger was pointing. Off in the direction of Sknilow airport I saw six or seven airplanes flying toward us just above the height of the station. By now other fingers were pointing and the crowd was buzzing with excitement. I knew the air force kept a squadron of fighters at Sknilow, although I had never seen one. Actually, I probably hadn't seen more than a couple of airplanes in my life, even though I had read articles on their aerodynamics and knew something about them. Watching the black shapes approach, I admired their sleek outlines and their speed. They seemed miraculous, powerful mechanical birds soaring through the heavens. I would never have called myself a patriotic Pole, but I felt a surge of pride that Poland's air force possessed planes like these and skilled pilots to fly them. I was genuinely moved that they had come to give this patriotic farewell as we went off to fight for Poland.

Many of the boys were waving at the planes, their faces beaming with childish delight. Then we noticed small black objects detaching themselves from the planes' bellies and skimming down towards us. It took a moment before we realized that we were being bombed. In that moment there was a dead stillness. Then the platform erupted into noise and movement. I had the idea that I should get on the train fast and I lunged for the door of the car nearest me. People were shouting and pushing and I was aware that some were trying to crawl under the train and others were running down the platform. As I shoved my way toward the door I saw people flattening themselves against the concrete with their arms clasped over their heads.

I was just at the door when the explosions started. To my left came a string of blasts, one after the other like a series of thunderclaps. I could hear screams and cries as I grabbed the stairwell railings, catapulted myself inside the car, and dove for cover. Then the screams were blotted out by an ear-shattering roar as the planes hurtled overhead, rattling every window and door in the car.

As the roar trailed off the screams came back. I crawled into the passageway and pulled myself up to look out the window. People were rushing around the platform and Red Cross squads with stretchers were running toward where the bombs had hit. The station roof had five or six smoking holes in it, their edges jagged and broken. Craning my head out the window I saw bodies sprawled on the platform in unnatural postures. Other soldiers were sitting on the ground dazed. A few were crying.

From what I could see leaning out the window it didn't look like any of the bombs had hit the train itself, only the station and platform. Outside officers were shouting orders and everyone on the platform was climbing aboard. More Red Cross workers were running to help with the dead and wounded. I pushed into the first compartment with four or five other soldiers and hoisted my pack up on the rack.

I was still in shock from what had just happened when the engine gave three blasts of its whistle. A minute later the car lurched slightly, then began to roll.

As we picked up speed I listened to the couplings squealing and the wheels clacking over track joints. Wusia would be worried sick, but I knew she'd be able to find out that I wasn't hurt. It was amazing the bombs hadn't done even more damage and that despite all the scrambling I hadn't felt scared. I wasn't even nervous about what lay ahead, though I knew this was probably just a taste of what we could expect at the front. Like me, the others in the compartment were silent, so subdued by what had just happened that no one said a word for a long time.

3

THE FOREST

For some reason the train seemed to be moving at a snail's pace. It took hours before we crossed the River San at the old city of Przemsyl, which was only about 50 miles from Lvov. I watched the landscape roll past, undulating hills and farmers' fields broken by copses and swaths of forest. The thatched roofs and whitewashed farmhouses made me think of home, where every few months we applied a new coat of whitening to keep things looking clean and new. Often the train pulled onto a siding and stopped for hours, though nobody seemed to know why. We understood there was a great battle going on in the west, but those in charge didn't seem in any hurry to get us into the fight.

At night we slept in our seats, waking up sometimes to find that the train had stopped again. The next day we crossed the Wistok, which had shrunken to a sluggish creek in the summer drought. Later we came to the Wistoka river, and soon after we passed through Tarnow on our way north toward

Kielce. Now rumors were circulating through the cars. We heard that German planes had bombed other cities at the same time that we were bombed in Lvov. Somebody heard that the Polish cavalry was fighting German tanks. Riders were climbing on the steel monsters and prying their hatches open so they could spear the Germans inside. I had no idea where the rumors came from, especially since none of the soldiers was getting off the train during its numerous stops. We couldn't tell which stories might be true either. They all sounded plausible.

Sometime during the third day we heard a new word, *Blitzkrieg*, though nobody was sure what it meant. Someone said it was a new way of fighting with planes and big numbers of tanks. I could imagine the planes well enough, but not the tanks. I was still thinking about how the bombs at the station had hit in such sudden quick succession, and how sad and unnatural the dead had looked sprawled on the platform.

Dozing on and off I fantasized about war. I remembered the legend of how before one great battle between Poland and Germany in medieval times the German general had told the Polish general that Germany's wealth was so great she could never be defeated. According to the story, the Polish general threw his gold wedding ring at the German and said, "Let gold go to gold and iron to iron. We'll see if your gold is stronger than our iron." That had happened at the Battle of Gruenwald, the most heroic in Poland's history.

The Battle of Gruenwald was in 1410. If you thought about it, it seemed like Germany had always been trying to invade Poland. Every schoolboy knew that battle. I had learned it before I was expelled from Polish school in fourth grade for accidentally damaging a picture of the Polish kings. During that battle, the Prussian Teutonic Knights (*Krzyzacy*, the Poles called them, "cross bearers,") had attacked Poland. I had seen pictures of them, encased in gleaming armor with white capes and black crosses. They rode great metal-sheathed war horses and carried long lances and shields with a black German war eagle.

At Gruenwald the *Krzyzacy* had crashed like battering rams into the Poles. But the great King Wladislaw Jagiello never lost courage. His army was beaten and bloody, but he refused to give up. Time after time the knights smashed into his troops until finally they had exhausted their strength. Then Wladislaw let loose his boyars and they killed them all, including the *Krzyzacy* grandmaster. I don't know if that's an accurate version of what happened, but that's the way we learned it and that's how it appeared before me on the movie screen of my imagination. I pictured how the boyars had cut them down at the end and how afterwards King Wladislaw hung the Prussian battle flags from the great cathedral of Krakow.

It was no mystery why the Poles hated and feared the Germans, "Prussians" they still called them. I wasn't a scholar of history, but I knew the Germans had been marching into

Poland for at least 500 years and probably longer. There was that unbelievable line from the national anthem, like an expression of the Poles' racial will. "The Germans will not spit in our faces or Germanize our children, so help us God!"

I wondered if anyone else's anthem could have a line like that in it. Maybe what was happening in this war would be similar to what happened at Gruenwald. To beat the Prussians you might have to suffer terrible losses. But after that you could begin to grind them down.

On September 4, four days after we started, the train stopped beside a forest near the town of Gostynin, not far from where the Bzura and the Wistula rivers come together. Here we were ordered to disembark and unload the horses, wagons, shells, and howitzers from the special cars at the back. The forest was quiet and dark. There were no people, no farms, nothing, and not a hint of war. It seemed like we had arrived at some kind of enchanted dell, a million miles from whatever fighting might be going on.

We couldn't believe our luck, although it turned out to be an illusion, of course. Later I understood that our secluded little forest was a temporary haven formed between the two arms of the great German attack that was just then surrounding and crushing Poland's armies. To our north the Germans had already cut the Corridor to Gdansk. In the south they had taken Czestochowa and were on their way to Krakow. Though we had no idea of it, their tanks were already speeding toward Warsaw, 70 miles to our rear. During the period between September 4th and 13th in every area but ours, the west of Poland was burning. But of these events we knew nothing at all. We waited for orders, but none came. One warm, sunny day followed another, then another and another, as if we had been blessed by a guardian angel.

Once we set up camp there was nothing to do but lie around and play cards or talk about the latest rumors. Many of these were about the *Volksdeutsche*, Poles of German descent who considered themselves Germans even if many of their families had been living in Poland for generations. We heard that the *Volksdeutsche* had formed fifth columns and were shooting Polish soldiers in the back. Some said that the *Volksdeutsche* had scouted out everything in the country so that the German army knew exactly what to do and where to go. We also heard that about Polish Ukrainians. Supposedly whole groups of them had mutinied and had been lined up and shot on the spot. I didn't know if that one was any truer than the others, but it fit with what I knew about Ukrainian feelings. That rumor was unsettling, though, given how many Ukrainians we had in the regiment. It made everyone nervous.

I spent a lot of time alone, writing in my diary so I wouldn't forget the details to tell Wusia when the war was over. By now I had also become friendly with some of the others, including a young Ukrainian corporal. One day while this corporal and I were sitting by ourselves he suddenly said,

"You're a Jew, aren't you?" There wasn't any hostility in his tone; it was more a statement than a question.

"Yes," I said, already on guard. I wondered how he had guessed, whether it had been some opinion I expressed, or maybe some mannerism I wasn't aware of.

"I knew it," said the Ukrainian. "I thought I could talk to you. Listen, do you have a girlfriend?"

That startled me. I had just that moment been daydreaming about Wusia, though I wasn't planning to talk to him or anyone else about her. But it turned out he wasn't even interested. What he wanted to talk about wasn't Wusia, but his own girlfriend.

"I've got a girl," he said, pausing, as if he expected me to ask about her. When I didn't, he said, "She's Jewish." He looked to see my reaction. I nodded, trying to convey neither approval nor condemnation. Although I didn't say anything, he must have felt that we had established a bond. He had a Jewish girlfriend. I was Jewish. We had things in common. Then he said what I think he wanted to tell me all along. He looked around, and keeping his voice low even though there was nobody nearby, he said, "I hate these Polack bastards. I hope the Germans really give the sons of bitches what they deserve."

Given the circumstances, it seemed a strange thing to say. But I understood the sentiments. Several times around

Krasne while I was growing up, Ukrainian peasants had set huge fires on Polish-owned estates, burning down whole fields of wheat. I had a distinct memory of clouds of black smoke billowing over the forests. Afterwards Polish soldiers had beaten people and taken them away somewhere.

"Look what they've done to us," the corporal said, biting the words off and shaking his head in anger. Did I know, he asked, that the western Ukraine was supposed to get its autonomy after the big war, that this had been promised at Versailles? Did I know that Poland had given its solemn word to the League of Nations?

"So what do they do?" he said. "They bring in their damned settlers and steal our land." His voice was a rough growl. "They've always used us as slaves and serfs. We ought to do to them what Khmelnytsky did. When it comes to Poles, the Cossacks had the right idea."

The corporal was so angry he had started speaking Ukrainian, a kind of mantra the Ukrainians spoke. *Perebulismo pansczynu/Perebudimo Konstitucju*—"We lived through serfdom/We'll live through the Constitution." The "Constitution," being their term for the Polish government. "Someday we'll have our freedom!" His voice was rising before he caught himself and looked around again.

I didn't say anything, but underneath I was shocked that he would bring up Khmelnytsky. "When it comes to Poles," he said. What was that supposed to mean? But not when it comes to Jews? Bohdan Khmelnytsky was the Ukrainian national hero. But his Cossacks had butchered Jewish communities from the Dnieper to the San. In Jewish memory that name is written in blood, never mentioned without a prayer that it should be blotted out forever. Of course, in his revolt Khmelnytsky had also slaughtered all the Poles he could get his hands on. After his death the Ukrainians had risen many more times, but each time the Poles had suppressed them without mercy.

And now this corporal was facing death as a soldier for Poland. What a terrible irony, I thought. But was it that much less terrible for me? What Jew would willingly go to war for anti-Semites? I wasn't violently angry like he was, but if anything I wanted to get out of there even more than he did. Not because I hated Poles. I didn't hate Poles. All I wanted was to get back to Wusia.

That night I couldn't get the discussion with the corporal out of my mind. I lay on my mat listening to the snores of the men in our tent, my head filled with images of Cossacks, Poles and Jews. The wrinkled face of Judith Kleiner floated across my consciousness. She was an old, stooped woman who had lived in Sadzawki, the village next to ours. Her husband had been murdered in a Ukrainian pogrom, but she had saved herself by pretending to be the Ukrainian maid. I imagined Khmelnytsky leading his wild Cossack horsemen. I tried to picture what Berko Jusselovicz must have looked

like; Jusselovicz, the Jewish hero who a hundred and fifty years
after Khmelnytsky had raised a regiment of Jewish cavalry and
perished fighting the Prussians under Kosciuszko. I had read
somewhere that Kosciuszko had seen Jewish soldiers when he
was a general in the American Revolution and that had given
him the idea of letting Polish Jews have their own regiment.

I had never seen a picture of Berko Jusselovicz, but I
knew very well what Kosciuszko looked like. He was the main
figure in the giant circular battle panorama that filled the
special museum in Lvov's Kilinsky Park. This panorama was
unique, half painting and half tapestry, the two parts blended
so artistically that the casual observer couldn't tell how it was
done. Fifty feet high and a hundred yards around, it celebrated
the famous battle of Raclawice in which Kosciuszko had
defeated the Russians who were trying to block his advance to
Warsaw. I had marveled at this panorama many times, not just
at its wonderful artifice but at its huge size and the
innumerable painted figures of warriors who had fought in the
battle. Then too, the Polish soldiers had been poorly armed, a
citizen army fighting for the nation's freedom from the
Germans and Russians. At Raclawice, Kosciuszko's peasant
auxiliaries had won the day, charging into the guns with
nothing but their scythes and pitchforks.

Soon, though, my thoughts settled down to where they
did every night before I slept. Wusia's face was always there,
not just at night, but during the day when at odd moments she

would come to me and I would be distracted from whatever I happened to be doing. It was almost as if her spirit was haunting me, a sweet haunting. I longed for her and would have spent most of my idle time writing to her, except that there was no way to send letters. Instead I thought about her, going back again and again to the times we had spent together. I talked to her too, carrying on monologues in my head, telling her what I was doing and how I was feeling. Lying there that night I decided to relive just how it was that I had begun to love her.

4

THE AMMUNITION WAGON

September, 1939

Three years before, right after I finished my basic training, and before Badian hired me as an instructor, I worked at Appel's, making radios. I was looking for a place to live when I heard about a room for rent in the Jewish quarter located behind the Solski market. It wasn't the most luxurious neighborhood, but on my salary I couldn't look for luxury. An elderly widow had two bedrooms in her apartment, with one to rent. It was clean and convenient, so I took it. I never dreamed that little room was going to change my life.

I wish I could remember the first time I saw Wusia, but the truth is I wasn't paying attention. The old woman had two daughters who lived with her and a married daughter who visited often, sometimes bringing along her own daughter, a high school girl. Whenever they showed up I'd close my door so their talk wouldn't bother me. Then one day I was in the kitchen when the granddaughter came to visit, by herself, and the widow introduced us.

From that moment I started paying attention. Wusia was one of those people who made an impact. She looked at you with an openness you didn't expect, which was slightly unsettling. But it wasn't only her looks, it was the air she had of self-assurance combined with innocence. She seemed completely unaware of her beauty. That was a big part of her attraction, I admit. Here was a striking young woman, with finely sculpted features combined with liveliness and modesty, yet she seemed utterly unaware of the effect she had on others—on me, for instance. I could hardly speak, just managing to choke out a few polite words. Then I pretended I was busy and went back to my room. After that, whenever Wusia visited her grandmother, I left my door open so I could listen to them talking.

I can't recall anything specific they said to each other, other than the grandmother urging her to believe in God and to listen to her parents. It wasn't what Wusia said that attracted me, but how overflowing with life her voice was, bubbling over with enthusiasm about the things she was doing. Maybe it was because my own nature was watchful and reserved, even secretive, that I was so drawn to her vitality. She had no complaints, this girl, there was no whining about her. Her entire being was positive. Maybe it was just that she didn't have anything to complain about, I thought, after all, she was only in high school. But sitting on my bed and listening, I was sure there was more to it than that. I think that what I sensed was how good her heart was. Occasionally

I'd peek out to catch a glimpse of them sitting at the dining room table. While they talked Wusia would hold her grandmother's hands, a gesture that revealed so much of who she was. Underneath the physical beauty and self-assurance was an essentially down to earth person, a kind and loving human being.

Before long I made it a point to meet Wusia when she came to visit, unobtrusively, of course. She'd come in and instead of staying in my room and letting the grandmother monopolize her I'd say hello and start a conversation. We had things to talk about. She was the youngest of three. I was the youngest of six. She had a brother in Argentina, so did I. Her brother in Argentina wanted to bring over his fiancée, as did mine. In fact my brother Herman was hoping my mother and I would go there as well, but I didn't tell Wusia that. Wusia said she was planning to become a bookkeeper when she graduated next year. Her father was an accountant and could help her get a job. I told her about being in the army, about how I had learned to shoot cannons and stand up on a horse.

It was very comfortable talking to Wusia at her grandmother's. But our pleasant conversations came to an end when Badian gave me the teaching job at Korkis. In addition to the salary, he offered free accommodations on the fifth floor, which meant moving out of her grandmother's apartment. That put an end to our casual meetings. Now, if I wanted to see Wusia, I had to make special arrangements.

That was how we started going out on Saturdays, every couple of Saturdays at first, but soon every Saturday. Often we went to the movies. Smosarka was our favorite actress, and we liked Wallace Beery who played in *The Champ* and other American movies. It was at the movies that we started holding hands. I'm still not sure how it happened and how the attraction we felt for each other began to turn into something more. After the movies we'd walk to the park and sit there, feeling each other's closeness. It is said that the eyes are the window of the soul, but what happens when you look into each other's eyes and see at the same time both another soul and your own image, until you can't tell one from the other? You can feel your hearts beating in identical rhythm. You breathe the same air. You kiss and the sweetness stays on your lips. You embrace and the feeling of it lingers. Afterwards, you look back, when you are alone, thinking about the few happy moments in your life, and you know with absolute certainty that this was one of them.

Wusia's parents, of course, adored her, their youngest child and only daughter. They showered her with love and did their best to shelter her from danger. At first they weren't sure of me. They were suspicious of my motives, especially since she was seventeen and I was seven years older. One night, after the movies, Wusia and I walked to the Italian ice cream parlor and then went to sit in the Jesuit Garden. We got back late and the next time I saw her, Wusia told me her father had sent her brother Sunio out to look for her.

He was horrified that maybe I had taken her up to my room at the school.

Of course they didn't know me then, so I didn't blame them. They couldn't know how seriously I took things like that. In Krasne I had always been friendly with the girls. I especially loved to dance at the get-togethers we used to organize. Whirling them around in polkas and mazurkas, feeling their bodies swing and glide in our arms—not like our parents, who always danced separately, men with men, women with women. I had a good time with the Krasne girls, Blima Zeftel, Ettel Chatchkes and the others. And they liked me. But it never entered my head to have a sexual relationship. Such a thing was so far beyond the pale that no one could even think it.

My mind drifted to other memories of our times spent together. Once I caught a purse-snatcher. One evening after a movie we went to our favorite ice cream place. When we got our cones we went back out to Zamarstynoska Street mingling with the crowds of people making their usual evening promenades. Suddenly Wusia shouted, "Wilo, Wilo, my pocketbook," and I saw someone sprinting down the street. I took off instantly, trying to keep him in sight as people stared and jerked themselves out of the way. Nearby was the Solski market. The huge square was dark and deserted now. During the day it was always packed with shoppers looking for bargains among the rows of second hand stalls and tables of cheap goods. The thief tore into the square and disappeared down one of the aisles into the blackness. With my heart pounding, I sprinted down the next aisle.

Even in the dark I knew the market, Solski was one of my favorite places. For years I had been coming here to watch the shoppers, the peasants bringing in their goods, the three card monty players preying on the gullible. I knew that with an extra burst of speed I could get to the end of the aisle before the thief and cut him off. I felt like I was flying. An instant later I was out with the snatcher just a step ahead of me. I lunged and grabbed the back of his shirt collar, jerking him to a stop. Then I swung him around and stripped the pocketbook from his hand.

We were standing there face to face, both of us gasping. I still had a fistful of the thief's collar, but before I could think what to do next a figure stepped out of the shadows and shouted, "You, let him go!" I was angry, but I had to consider that now there were two of them and I did have the bag. "I'll let him go," I yelled back. "He can go to hell!" Then, just as I let go of his shirt, the pocketbook opened and a small cascade of objects scattered on the ground. I bent down to gather them, and when I looked up they had both vanished.

As I walked back to Zamarstynoska I saw that many people were standing around looking in my direction, waiting to see what had happened. When I came out of the darkness they all started to applaud, clapping loudly as I walked up to

Wusia and handed her the pocketbook. It was embarrassing, but I also felt very proud. Later, when we were alone, Wusia said, "Wilo, weren't you afraid? It was so dark in there."

"I'm used to darkness," I told her. "I grew up in darkness. In all of Krasne we didn't have a street light." No one had electricity there except the flour mill, which owned its own generator. I told her how I used to play in the forest when I was a child. At night it was pitch black, but I always felt at home. The dark, for me, had never harbored evil or frightening things.

The truth was that I had no idea how brave I might be. I was pretty certain I wasn't a coward, although I had never really been tested. I hadn't hesitated to go after the thief in the dark, and I hadn't felt any fear even when the second person stepped out of the shadows. Of course I hadn't had the time to think about being frightened, so maybe it was still an open question. Anyway, the crowd thought I was a hero, and so did Wusia, which was even better. I had demonstrated my courage to her, at least, and I felt good about that, really good.

September 13, 1939

I woke up in my tent the next morning with a dream fragmented, just out of reach, a good dream, something about Wusia. It had seemed so real, yet as hard as I tried I couldn't quite remember. It was Tuesday, September 13. We had been camped in the woods for almost a week and a half. For the last few days now, we knew we were in a war. Our illusion of living charmed lives had dissolved the instant we realized that the barely audible rumble in the distance was artillery, not thunder. Over the last couple of days the sound had gotten louder and more ominous. At night explosions lit the horizon, flaring, receding, then flaring again. Now the guns sounded like an avalanche not too far off, except steadier and more insistent. Even with the battle so close, we still knew nothing about it. No hard news reached us, nor orders; nothing but rumors.

It was obvious that the army was being pushed back. We didn't need anybody to tell us that. The fighting was coming toward us, moving from west to east, yet we had no sense of impending disaster. Whatever was happening, we were being held in reserve, waiting. Other units, near us no doubt, were also waiting to be thrown forward. Behind us, three days march away, was Warsaw and the great bend in the Wistula where our resident military experts declared the main reserves must be poised to strike. Of all the regiment's soldiers and officers, I am sure no one thought that the thread of his life might just then be stretched out on the sharp knife of fate. Some of us were going to die in the coming battle, there was no denying that. But not me, each one reasoned. Why would it be me?

Only years later did I find out what really happened. The fact was that our regiment's experts were wrong in practically every particular of their assessment. While we were waiting, the great German pincers rushing by us to the north and south were wrecking everything in their path. But between those two pincers were developments the German generals somehow failed to notice.

Directly to our west, where Polish Posnania bulged out into Prussia, a Polish army group had managed to hold on. General Tadeusz Kurtzeba's Poznan Army was battered in the initial fighting and he had considered retreating to reinforce the Warsaw garrison, which would have taken him right through where we were camped. But after the first few days, when he didn't feel any more pressure, he changed his mind. Instead of running, he shifted deliberately eastward, gathering the survivors of decimated units from other Polish forces and building his divisions into a powerful strike force. Meanwhile, the Germans were so eager to close their pincers and take Warsaw that they didn't pay attention to an army that they thought was already dead. Then, on September 8, four days after we arrived in the woods, General Kurtzeba's cavalry scouts reported that just below the Bzura they had come across the extended and vulnerable flank of the German southern armies.

On September 9 General Kurtzeba finalized his plans. On the tenth he struck—it was his guns that we had first heard. Kurtzeba's army smashed southward across the Bzura in an attempt to cut through the southern pincer. On the first and second days they bit deep into the German flank. For a moment it looked as if the Poles might succeed, but the Germans recovered quickly. They pulled back from their assault on Warsaw and threw all their tanks and mechanized units toward the battle. By September 12 they had stopped the attack's momentum. Unable to keep going, General Kurtzeba swung his forces eastward, hoping now to reach Warsaw. All around him the Germans gathered like wolves. On the 13th they closed the trap.

That's what was going on when I woke up that morning trying to remember my dream of Wusia. We knew nothing except that the fighting was getting closer, until our lieutenant called us to assemble in the early afternoon. As usual, some of us were playing cards, others were gossiping, and one or two were napping in the sun. I was sitting under an oak tree making notes in my diary. When we lined up, the lieutenant seemed excited and I was sure we were going to get some news.

"Men," he began, "I'm happy to be able to tell you that our forces are winning a great victory. Right now, as I am speaking to you, they are defeating the German invader who has been stupid enough to think he could march on Warsaw. Our artillery at the front needs ammunition and we've been ordered to resupply them. I'm asking for volunteers. Anyone who's prepared, step forward."

I thought fast. I hadn't found another Jew in the regiment. Of course very few knew that I was Jewish. Other than the Ukrainian corporal, the sergeant, and no doubt some officers, maybe no one knew. But really, it didn't matter how many knew. *I* knew. At that moment I understood that it just wouldn't be right if the only Jew showed himself to be a coward. Already two volunteers had stepped in front of the line. "I'm prepared," I said, and I took a step forward.

Fifteen minutes later I was sitting on the front bench of an ammunition wagon creaking through the forest behind two broad beamed horses. On the right one, directly in front of me, sat the rider, talking softly to the horse and prodding its flanks with his heels. A few yards behind us came a second wagon, followed by a third. Our entire little convoy was headed for the road that lay to the north of the woods.

As we emerged from the trees I saw instantly that the lieutenant's story about the great victory was nothing but a lie. As far as I could see in both directions the road was packed with refugees, some walking, some riding wagons or sitting on farm horses. Many carried babies or young children, others had pots or bits of furniture from their homes. Along the margins of the road infantrymen marched, looking haggard and beaten. The traffic flowed in one direction only—east. There was absolutely no doubt what we were looking at. If there was artillery ahead that needed shells, it could only be to cover this huge flight.

Pulling onto the road, the wagon slowed down as refugees and soldiers moved aside to let us through. From where I was sitting it looked like the Red Sea, a tide of humanity parting before the two lumbering horses. After half an hour or so we left the forest behind. Now on both sides of the road, fields spread out, looking as if they had just been plowed, probably for winter wheat. No doubt the farmer and his family were among the refugees. After all that work it was too bad he'd never get to harvest that crop. Up ahead cannons boomed and for the first time I could distinctly hear the chatter of machine guns.

From the north two planes suddenly appeared. They streaked low across the sky, dipped their wings and rolled toward the road. I could see their guns spouting bursts of flames. All around us refugees and soldiers were shouting and scrambling into the shallow ditches that separated the road from the fields. Farther off I could see other planes. They seemed to be cavorting in the sky, twisting and diving after the first two. Ahead of us a hail of bullets lashed the road, sending up puffs of dirt. On either side people were running crazily across the fields trying to get away. The horses trembled violently, snorting and tossing their heads in terror. In another moment it might have occurred to me to jump down and run away from the wagon, which was loaded with more than a ton of high explosive artillery shells. But just then the horses bucked to the side and bolted over the little embankment, jolting the wagon through the ditch and onto the plowed field.

I gripped the bench with all my might and hunched forward as the wagon bounced me up and down. In front the rider jounced wildly in the saddle, struggling to keep his seat. Planes sliced through the sky, their machine guns hammering. As they howled overhead the air seemed to vibrate. Bombs hurled up huge clods of earth. Then there was a flash and a violent blast of hot air slammed me backwards just as the wagon jerked abruptly to the right and threw me into space. I hardly felt the impact as I landed on my back. But for a split second I was aware of axles and wheels and I knew the wagon was about to run over me.

5

THE PRISONER OF WAR HOSPITAL

September, 1939

That instant is frozen in my memory. There's no sound, no pounding hooves or racket from the wagon. I don't feel any pain. But I am exquisitely aware of the granular and crumbled texture of the earth as the wagon wheels grind me into it.

The whole summer had been dry. Under the hot sun the ground had baked and hardened. Then the war came, which kept many farmers from plowing. But the man whose field I was lying in had stubbornly, or optimistically, prepared his land. When I opened my eyes an instant later I was half buried in the tilled soil.

I could just make out my wagon careening across the field. Turning my head, I saw another wagon rushing toward me and I wondered idly if this one was also going to run over me. As it came closer, though, I could see it wasn't out of control. I knew I had been crushed, though how badly I couldn't tell. I couldn't feel any blood or wounds, but my chest was on fire and something was seriously wrong with my legs. I tried to shout, *Pomotz! Pomotz!* "Help, help me." I don't know if they heard or just saw me, but the wagon pulled to a stop and the two riders jumped down.

They dug me out with their hands and lifted me onto the floorboards in front of the bench. As we started rolling I tried to understand what had happened. I knew the wheel had run over my chest, I had actually seen it. Breathing hurt. When I tried to inhale, a dagger stabbed my ribs. Inside somewhere a throbbing ache had started. I had the unsettling feeling that my upper body had gotten compacted and thinned out. By now I knew it wasn't both legs that were hurt, just one, but I couldn't feel that one at all.

At least you're alive, my mind kept saying, *at least you're alive.* But I was confused. What was I doing on the floor of this wagon when I'd never been sick or injured in my entire life? I'd never even had a headache, so how could this have happened to me? One moment I'm as strong and healthy as an ox and the next I'm bouncing along at the feet of two wagon riders on my way somewhere. It was a big mystery which I needed to focus on, except the fire in my chest wasn't letting me. I couldn't imagine what had happened to my right leg so that I couldn't even feel it.

I don't know how much time passed, it wasn't much, and then we were again in a forest, at a kind of first aid station. Medics with Red Cross armbands were walking around and the ground was littered with wounded soldiers. The two wagon riders lifted me out and put me down with the others. There were no stretchers or tents, just people lying on the bare earth. Some of them were moaning, others screaming in agony, which made me even more confused. Just a little while ago I was sitting under a tree on a beautiful sunny afternoon writing in my diary, and suddenly I had been transported to this grove of pain. Now that I was stretched out on the ground, I could see that one of my neighbors had a blood soaked bandage covering his eyes and another was pressing his hands over his stomach where his shirt had turned into a wet black mass. The boy lying at my feet was whimpering "Jesus, Jesus, Jesus, Jesus." When I looked down I saw that his pants were shredded and the bottom part of his bloody leg was twisted strangely out from his knee, as though the torn pants were the only thing still connecting it.

I tried to calm myself. I felt I had to concentrate. Two questions lodged in my head. Was I going to live? And if I did, would I be a cripple the rest of my life? Some of the boys were crying for St. Mary or Jesus. Others cursed or called on their personal saints. I didn't call any saints. I didn't call anybody. I felt myself, my hands running over my chest and down toward my leg. I couldn't feel anything wrong with my ribs, but I hurt deep inside and each breath still cut like a knife. With the tips of my fingers I tried to probe my leg, but it was too painful to touch. I could feel it swelling up and I knew something was wrong with the bones.

I can't stay here, I thought. I should get up and do something, but how, when I can't move? I always had a high tolerance for pain, but this was something completely different. What would they do to me? Would they amputate my leg? And then what would become of me? I wondered why none of the medics were coming to treat me. I couldn't see that they were taking care of anybody else, either. This isn't a first aid station, I thought, it's a waiting place on the road to hell.

They finally came to move us at dusk. Until then German planes were flying overhead, we could hear their engines and the rattling of their machine guns. Then six or seven of us were loaded into an open farm wagon and taken into the town of Gostynin. By the time we got there, night had fallen.

The converted school they took us to had long, half-lit hallways that smelled of blood. In the corridors stretchers were laid out end to end. A hum of moans filled the air, punctuated now and then by a sharp cry or a curse. By this time I was moving quickly from bewilderment to self-pity, although I wasn't complaining or crying out loud like many of the others. Inside, though, I was bitterly bemoaning my fate, asking someone, I don't know who exactly, I don't think it was God, what happened to me? Do I deserve this? Why me? Wusia's face and words came to me in flashes. "Remember our initials Wilo." "I hope God will bring us together soon, Wilo." But she wouldn't stay. I slipped into unconsciousness and saw myself back in my room at the Korkis School immersed in a dream. I had never paid much attention to dreams, but this one, from many years ago, had remained in my head. In my dream, I was very ill, dying. I knew what it meant because I remembered my father when he was dying. In my dream I started to plead, "How could this be my time? I'm the only one who can help my mother. I promised I'd help my mother. If I die, who will take care of her?" I was talking to someone, but I couldn't see who. How is it possible that I should die when I have such an important mission? I can't die, somebody else maybe, but not me! I started to cry, to plead. I prayed for my life. I was crying in my dream, tears coursing down my cheeks, I who never cried, but now I was crying, pleading. Let me live.

I came out of the dream with the strange feeling that someone was hovering over me. I opened my eyes. A priest was kneeling down, speaking to me in Latin. *In nomine domine et filio et spiritu sanctu...*words linked themselves together in a singsong drone. For a moment I thought I was hallucinating. Then I realized the priest was flesh and blood and he wasn't speaking to me, he was giving me last rites. When he saw my eyes were opened he looked at me sorrowfully and made the sign of the cross.

A priest making a cross in the air over me was the last thing I expected. I was drowning in my own misery and sorrow, in pain, and a priest wasn't someone I wanted to see at that moment. I wondered if I was really so near death that I needed the last rites? I raised my hand and motioned for him to stop. The priest looked at me, his eyes widening slightly, surprised that I would interrupt him in the process of saving my eternal soul.

"What's the matter, my son?" he asked, putting his ear down near my mouth. Are you in great pain?"

"No, Father."

"Then what's wrong, my child?"

"I'm Jewish, Father."

He looked into my blue eyes. "You're Jewish, my son?"

"Yes, Father."

"I'm truly sorry, my son."

"I understand, Father."

Then he stood up and walked away.

A few minutes later two orderlies picked up my stretcher and carried me into the examining room. The doctor was just starting to take my pulse when another orderly came in and whispered something in his ear. I had noticed this man before, standing behind the priest during our brief conversation. When the orderly finished whispering the doctor let go of my wrist. "Take this one out," he said. "I'll get to him later."

I knew instantly that he had learned I was Jewish. The orderly had obviously overheard me telling the priest, and now he had told the doctor. I couldn't believe it.

They carried me back to the hallway and put me down again with the others. Here I am, I thought, fighting for their country, willing to sacrifice my life by volunteering for the mission. Why are they treating me like this? They don't even know what's wrong with me, if I'm going to live or die. One Jew more or one Jew less, what's the difference, is that how they see it? I don't think this was anger talking—I am someone who rarely gets angry. Anger is not my specialty. What I do believe is that at that moment, while they were laying me down again in the corridor, I was shaken to my soul by the first tremors of a profound disillusionment.

That may sound strange. Several years later I would think back on my reaction to that doctor as naïve; after all, a Jew in Poland could not grow up without feeling marked. With Poland's history how could it be otherwise? But with all of it, until that moment I was at heart an innocent. Prejudice, like the armory sergeant assigning me to the ammunition wagon, was something I noticed, then forgot. It rolled off my back. With my Polish appearance I usually didn't draw a second glance from anyone. I had never stood out as a target. For all my Jewishness, I had never in my life thought of myself as a victim.

I considered myself fortunate to have grown up in Krasne, which in Ukrainian means "beautiful." Nestled against the Honeyridge Mountains, surrounded by fruit orchards and deep hardwood forests, the village was so lovely that even those of us who were born there could see it. Krasne was beautiful spiritually too. I'm not speaking only of the few Jewish families all of whom were followers of the famous Kopyczynicer Rebbe. I mean the harmony that existed between the Jews and their gentile neighbors.

At the age of 17 relaxing in the garden of my home in Krasne

Krasne had two priests, the Orthodox one who lived in the nearby town of Grzymalov but included Krasne in his parish, and the Ukrainian one, who lived in the village and was friendly with my father. Neither of them were Jew haters, as many priests were. Both Father Hankiewicz and Father Leszczynski mainly preached the loving kindness of God. Because of the priests' behavior, the peasants didn't bear a grudge against Jews. They didn't set their dogs on us or attack us in the street. In Krasne we had no pogroms.

The result was that I had the unbelievable good luck of growing up without either hatred or fear. My playmates were Ukrainian and Polish children and no one ever insulted me or tried to beat me up. I looked like them. I spoke their language. Of course they knew I was Jewish, the son of Mechel the tavern keeper. But they considered me one of theirs.

I had lived life in a kind of double key. I knew what it meant to be a Jew, yet in the inner reaches of my mind I was untroubled and secure. Jewish, but never a victim. It was this innocence that the doctor in the converted school violated. I probably should have thanked him for bestowing on me the beginnings of wisdom, but I didn't think of it. Lying untreated on my stretcher, I was too stunned by the revelation that not only was there a Jewish problem in general, but there was a Jewish problem in particular, for me, Wilo Ungar, and if I wasn't careful, it might kill me. I honestly cannot recall if a flitting shadow did not cross my mind in that instant, a stray thought whispering an evil question about my life and my Jewishness. Were the two truly one, as I had never doubted, or, just perhaps, might the one not be separate from the other.

I lay in the hallway that night among the wounded, listening to their suffering. By now the stabbing in my chest was almost gone, but the pain in my leg was worse. The leg seemed to be swelling to a grotesque size. The skin felt stretched tight. I wondered if they planned to treat every last one of the hundreds of wounded before they got around to me.

I was pretty sure I wasn't going to die, but I worried about my leg and whether I might lose it. I had never experienced anything but perfect health, but now it seemed as if my body was betraying me. I had never imagined such a thing could happen. It was an unexpected sensation, this feeling of helplessness. I thought about Wusia and my mother in Krasne. Would I come back to them on crutches with one leg gone? Would I come back to them at all? Finally I fell into a fitful sleep, awakened now and then by somebody screaming, or by the incessant pounding of my damaged limb.

The next morning, September 14, they picked me up and brought me to another doctor. He examined me carefully, then told me my ankle was broken, a severe, multiple break. My ribs were badly bruised, but he couldn't detect any cracks. The plowed earth had certainly saved my life, he said, after I described what had happened. Had the ground been hard, the wagon would definitely have crushed me to death. The doctor worked quickly, with deft hands. When he was done my chest was taped and bandaged and my lower leg had been encased in a plaster cast.

From the school they transferred me to the local hospital where I was put in a big room with five or six other soldiers. We knew that the fighting was still going on around

Gostynin; the sounds of battle came in through the open window. Other than that none of us had more than a vague idea of what was happening in the outside world. It was clear that things were going badly for Poland, but we couldn't get any specifics. Counting the time from when our train left Lvov, it had been almost two weeks since I had heard any news at all, and the others didn't know any more than I did.

The next day I woke from a nap to find a beautiful girl about Wusia's age sitting next to my bed. She introduced herself as Elza. She was Jewish, she said. She lived in Gostynin and had come to the hospital to see if there were any Jewish wounded who might want company or need something from the local community. She had cookies with her, and a newspaper. My name was on the patient list, "Wolf," so she had stopped by to talk.

None of the news Elza brought was good. There was not any doubt that Germany was going to defeat Poland completely. The government had already fled to Rumania, even though Warsaw and other places were still holding out. France and England had declared war on Germany a week and a half ago, but other than the declaration they had done nothing. They were just sitting there and waiting. Poland had been betrayed by her allies, which was the main reason why the Germans were gaining ground so quickly. Hitler didn't have to defend his country in the west, so he had thrown his whole army into the attack against us.

Elza came every day. But each day the news was worse. People were telling stories about violence against Jews by the Germans, not the regular troops, but a special kind called the SS. Then, on September 17, Elza brought news that the Russian army was attacking Poland from the east. The radio was reporting a secret agreement between Hitler and Stalin that gave half of Poland to Germany and half to the Soviets. Once again Germany and Russia were carving up the country between them, as they had in the past. Poland's army had been almost destroyed in the war against the Germans. There was no one left to fight the Russians.

It wasn't more than a day or two later that the cannon fire stopped. Whatever might have been happening elsewhere, in our area the war was over. Elza stopped coming. With the Germans in charge of the hospital now, civilians were no longer allowed to visit. We couldn't tell whether there had been any other changes. German officers looked into our room, hospital administrators the nurses said, touring the building. For the moment, at least, that was the only sign that things were different.

The hospital routine stayed the same as it had been. The nurses checked our progress and changed our dressings. Orderlies brought us our meals. But everyone was nervous, waiting to see if something would happen. With the German victory all the wounded had become prisoners of war. The question was, what were the Germans going to do with us?

No one thought that they would just let us lie here in peace, especially me. Elza's stories about the SS worried me, even though I wasn't sure the Germans could identify me as a Jew. My records said nothing about my religion and I didn't think it likely they would be able to make anything of my first name. I kept my anxieties to myself, but I wondered if maybe I shouldn't have brought a cyanide capsule along after all.

A week or so later the Germans made their move. It was something nobody anticipated or had any objections to. The hospital staff announced that Germany had annexed the part of Poland that had been taken from them by the Treaty of Versailles, including northwestern Poland and Upper Silesia. Gostynin was now part of the Third Reich. Since the Reich didn't want Polish prisoners on its territory, it had been decided to move the hospital to Kutno, a nearby city that wasn't part of the annexation.

Transferring that hospital, the planning and execution of it, was like nothing I have ever experienced. It was no wonder the Germans had won the war so easily. In a matter of hours they moved the entire hospital, patients, staff, equipment and supplies from one city to the other. We were told to be prepared to leave at nine in the morning, stretcher-cases first, then those who could walk. No delays would be tolerated.

At exactly nine o'clock in the morning, the procession started. There was no confusion. The stretcher cases went first, then the rest followed, vacating one room after the other. On the street a long convoy of trucks waited, with their numbers clearly marked. Before long the entire hospital was on wheels. Meanwhile in Kutno they had prepared the new hospital with the same efficiency. When we got there each patient was assigned a room number, and a little while later we were all in bed as if nothing had happened. Kutno was about 25 miles from Gostynin. The entire transfer, including the drive, had taken about four hours.

By now I wasn't thinking any longer of death, but I was preoccupied by the idea of being disabled. I had seen others with wounds far more terrible than mine. I had seen plenty of death too. But somehow those sights didn't make me feel less worried. I had never thought of myself as a patient, I detested the idea of being weak and dependent. And if I was so upset by being a patient, what would it mean to be an invalid, hopping on crutches the rest of my life? I was obsessed by it. You never notice something as ordinary as an ankle until you can't use it. Then you understand what it means. Before this happened I could run like the wind, I could dance every dance, and do all the things people take for granted. And suddenly I couldn't. I was faced with a dimension of thinking that I had never before considered. I had now become a sick man, with a sick man's troubled mind.

With nothing else to do, I lay in bed brooding. The hospital had no books or magazines. No newspapers came in.

No one organized any social activities. I worried about myself, and I worried about the Germans. A rumor was circulating that they were requiring Jews to wear special armbands on the streets and that they were planning to segregate Jews from non-Jews in hospitals. I was glad the Russians had taken over eastern Poland. The Soviets didn't like religion and capitalists, but at least they weren't anti-Semites. Wusia would be safe under them. So would my mother and the others back in Krasne.

My mother was on my mind a lot. Ever since my father died, seven years earlier, she and my sister Esther had kept our little tavern and general store going. Neither was good at business and they were finding it harder and harder to scrape by. I remembered scenes from years before when peasants would come in with some eggs or butter or a few zlotys wanting to pay off a debt. My father would study his ledger and tell them they didn't owe anything. But they would insist that Pani Ungar, Mrs. Ungar, had given them credit and they wanted to pay what they owed, whether it was in the book or not.

"Feige," my father would say later, "do you remember giving Sergei anything on credit?"

"Yes, I think so."

"*Nu*, so why didn't you enter it in the book?"

"I guess I forgot," she'd answer, even though they both knew it was a lie. She hadn't entered it because Sergei's wife was pregnant, his children were sick, and she didn't want to take his last kopek.

That was the kind of businesswoman she was, and Esther was no different. For the last three years I had been sending her part of my salary every month to help out. How could I send anything now? They had an extra burden too. A few days before the war broke out my brother-in-law David, the one who used to manage the estate, had come back from Argentina where he had gone to join my brother Herman. The previous year Herman had convinced David that there were great opportunities in Argentina, so David had left my sister Dvorah and their three children with my mother while he went to make his fortune with Herman. But life in Argentina was hard. Herman and David were peddlers. They carried their merchandise on their backs out into the countryside around Buenos Aires to sell to the peasants on credit. Then they had to go back and collect. That's how they started, not knowing the language, not having any friends, not knowing anything about the country.

Herman was younger than David and a very physical, strong person, so this kind of work didn't bother him - and in fact he eventually did extremely well. But David wasn't accustomed to hauling goods around on his back. He had been the director of a big estate. To leave his wife and children to become a peddler in a strange place made him desperately unhappy, so he decided to return. Toward the end

My parents, Feige and Michael; their four children: Dvorah, Herman (on Father's lap),
Max and Zalman (kneeling, from left to right); and their friend, Tema (standing, center)

of August he booked passage on the Batory, the last boat to make port in Poland, before the war broke out. So, now David too was living at our house, with his wife and children, but without a job. I knew he was back. We had talked when I called on the one telephone in Krasne to let my mother know I had been mobilized. I worried about how my mother would have enough money to support everybody.

My fraternal grandparents, Sheindel and Leib; and their three daughters: Rachel, Encia and Gusta (standing, left to right)

Most of all, I thought about Wusia. I was lovesick for her. Day after day I stayed in bed reliving the things we had done together, the movies we had seen, the talks we had had, starting with the last time we saw each other and going back in time. I imagined what she was doing now. I wondered what they had heard about the war in Lvov, and if any news had gotten back about our regiment. I took her picture out of my pajama pocket, where I kept it close to my heart. It was the photo she had given me when we said good-bye, and I held it up close where I could study her face. After staring a while I'd slip it back in my pocket, then five minutes later I'd take it out again. I wrote our initials on pieces of scrap paper with a pencil a nurse let me have. WW. Those were her last words. "Remember our initials." Before long scrap after scrap was covered with them, WW entwined and encircled in a hundred ways.

My great regret was the things we had not said to each other. Why hadn't we confessed our feelings for each other openly? Why hadn't we at least made our private vows to each other, even if we weren't quite ready to make them in public? What had we been afraid of? What had I been afraid of? We said to ourselves that life was uncertain, without having any idea what that meant. Now I did know—now, here in a German prison hospital while she was five hundred miles away, as good as on the other side of the world. I had squandered my chance to reveal my heart to her, to tell her how I ached for her and hear what I longed to hear, that her soul was as bound to mine as mine was to hers.

6

KUTNO

November – December 1939

At the beginning of November the anxiety level in the hospital shot up. Until then the Germans had allowed wounded soldiers to go home when they recovered. Suddenly the policy changed. There weren't any announcements, but word swept through the wards that they had started shipping healthy patients to unknown destinations, some sort of special POW work camps in Germany.

I was as nervous as everyone else was, even though I knew I wasn't up to doing any work. Six or seven weeks had passed, but I still couldn't put any weight on my ankle and could only get around on crutches. But enough time had passed so that the doctors decided to remove the cast anyway. When they did, the ankle looked normal. There wasn't any swelling. The leg had atrophied a little, but they said that wouldn't be a problem, the muscles would build themselves up when I started walking. But although the ankle might have looked normal, it wasn't. I could move it up and down, but not right or left. When I tried to step on my right foot, sharp pains shot up my leg. Without the crutches I couldn't even hobble.

The third day after they took off the cast I went for a checkup. In the hallway outside the examination room a male nurse watched me suspiciously. "Wait a minute," he said. "Your ankle's fine. Why are you putting on such an act? Drop the crutches and let's see you walk on your own."

If I had been a civilian I would have told him that I wasn't acting, that I really couldn't take a step on that leg. But I was still in the army, so I followed orders. I leaned the crutches against the wall, took two excruciating steps, and toppled over in a flash of pain. When I was carried to the examining table, the doctor took one look and told me I had broken it again.

I didn't know if I could tolerate the idea of having to stay in that hospital for six or seven more weeks. It was another barrier that was suddenly blocking my road back to Wusia. Already I couldn't sleep for not seeing her. On the positive side, I also knew this new break was a piece of good luck. If the ankle had healed, I might have been on my way to a labor camp, maybe worse if they found out who I was. Now as I thought about it, this was the second time fate had saved me, the first being when I landed in the plowed field instead of in an unplowed one. It wasn't something to get superstitious about, but I took notice.

The second cast came off in early December. I still couldn't walk, but they discharged me anyway. They had no reason to keep me and there was no point in sending me to a labor camp, so they just let me go. By that time I was desperate to get back.

Now, less than three months after the start of the war, Russia and Germany were both so happy with their new Polish possessions that they were having a kind of honeymoon with each other. One result was that they were allowing a free exchange of citizens. People who lived on the Russian side but whom the war had caught on the German side were permitted to return home; those with homes in the west but had been caught in the east could go back to the German side. We heard that many Ukrainians were going east and some Poles were coming west.

I was released, along with some others who were too sick or crippled to work for the Germans. In my uniform, with a small rucksack on my back, I hobbled on my crutches out onto the streets of Kutno and looked around. I had a pretty good idea of the city by then; I had made it a point to orient myself while I was in the hospital. My plan was that I'd somehow get to the railroad station and take a train to Przemsyl on the River San, the nearest crossing point between the Germans and Russians. From there I'd take a train to Lvov. I had rehearsed a thousand times how I'd go to Wusia's apartment and knock on the door, how she would be overwhelmed by surprise and joy, what I would say to her, and how we would fall into each other's arms. I didn't have a zloty for food or a train ticket, but I wasn't worried. Somehow I was going to get there.

Instead of immediately making my way toward the train station, once I was out on the street I experienced a tremendous rush of anxiety. I felt weak, disoriented, in the middle of crowds hurrying to get wherever it was they were going. All the movement and hustle bore down on me. I felt surrounded, closed in. I had been in the hospital so long that I hadn't given a moment's thought to how I was to survive. Without being aware of it, I had begun to regard hospital life as the natural order of things. Maybe I couldn't stand without crutches, but there were some who couldn't stand at all. I had a bad ankle, but one of the men in the ward didn't have any legs. No matter how bad it seemed, the soldier in the next bed had it at least as bad, and compared to the soldier across the hall we were both in good shape. But here, in the real world, there wasn't another invalid in sight, only healthy people. Out here everyone had two good legs, while I couldn't even take a step on my own. I stood in front of the hospital awhile, trying to catch my breath. Then I crutched off slowly, without even thinking about which direction the train station was. I didn't know how I was going to cope.

It was a cold mid-December afternoon. As I moved along, the crisp, chilly air began to have an effect on me. You'd better think positively, I told myself, or you'll never get back, and even if you do, why would Wusia want someone who acts doomed? A Jew always knows it could be worse, right? So get hold of yourself, Wilo. You should be thanking God that it's as good as it is.

Crutching my way through Kutno, I noticed that people on the street were looking at me with expressions of interest and sympathy. This was two and a half months after Poland's defeat, and their eyes were drawn to my uniform. There were no other Polish soldiers around. And here I was, not just a soldier but a wounded soldier, someone who had sacrificed himself for the nation. A passerby stopped me, excusing himself, and asked what unit had I been in and where had I been fighting. He had a brother who was missing, a Ulan, a calvaryman. Had I by any chance been fighting alongside the Ulans? Had I heard anything about any of their units?

People walking by slowed down to listen. Some stopped and tentatively asked their own questions. One had a husband who was killed at Lublin, another a son whom they heard had been captured somewhere in the south. Had I been in that area at all? Did I know what the Germans were doing with war prisoners? Had I heard something about where they were being held, or when they would be released? And me, they wanted to know, how I had been wounded? Did I need any help—maybe a meal, or a place to sleep? They would be honored to have me. They looked at me as if they were trying to learn something from my face. A few touched my uniform.

Others stopped for a moment to say a few words or just passed by with a kind look. One couple not much older than me were insistent about helping me. They weren't asking out of politeness, they said. They owed a lot to our soldiers, everyone did, and they would consider it an honor if I allowed them to do something for me. Where was I going, for instance. If it was somewhere in the area perhaps they could take me. When I said I was on my way home to Lvov they invited me to stay with them overnight. I could have a good meal and sleep in a real bed; tomorrow they would take me to the train station. The couple had a horse and wagon waiting a few blocks away, and the next thing I knew we were on our way to their house.

When we arrived, their two young children and a nanny were waiting. The house itself was nicely furnished in the typical middle class style of those days, heavy dark upholstered furniture, carpets, china in the cabinets, a small bookcase full of books and a few framed photographs. Here and there, prominently displayed on the walls, were paintings of Jesus and various saints, especially St. Mary. After almost three months of looking at the hospital's bare gray rooms and corridors, I felt positively immersed in warmth and domesticity. Dinner was wonderful, a rich beef stew with potatoes and white bread, and some kind of fruit soup for dessert. Next to the army rations and hospital fare this dinner seemed like something a king might eat.

Before the war I hadn't spent much time in western Poland. The stereotype was that people in this region were wealthier and better educated than people in the east, where there was a large Ukrainian population many of whom were illiterate. Westerners were supposed to be more patriotic too; the provinces of Great Poland, Little Poland, and Mazowsze were the original Polish heartlands. They were also more religious, which was evident with Jesus and the saints looking down at us from every wall.

After dinner we talked about the great tragedy that had befallen Poland. So many soldiers had died or were missing, they told me, it seemed as if half the country was in mourning. The German invasion had been so devastating and sudden that no one seemed to know exactly what had happened. Whole units had disappeared as if the earth had swallowed them. People had no idea if their loved ones were dead or alive, and if they were indeed alive, where they might be. It was known that the Germans had captured tens of thousands of soldiers, but many prisoners seemed to have vanished. There were going to be hard times in Poland. The previous partitions had been bloody and full of suffering. There was no reason to think that this one would be any different.

I told them where I was during the fighting, how it had taken us so long to get to the woods, and how once we were there we had never been ordered into battle. They had heard that this kind of experience wasn't unusual. The Germans had bombed the roads and railroad tracks so effectively that many units had never even gotten into battle. I told them about the great retreat I had seen, and how I had been wounded. I described what it had been like at the field medical station in the woods, and at the hospital later, though I didn't mention the incident with the doctor or anything else connected with Jews.

The discussion turned in that direction anyway. From talking about how the Germans were treating the Poles, it was just a step to discussing what they were doing to the Jews, and what they had in store for them. Other than saying that I hadn't heard anything about it during my stay in the hospital, I kept quiet, nodding my understanding every once in a while.

"Give thanks to St. Mary," the woman said. "We may have lost our freedom, but at least the Germans are teaching the Jews a lesson they won't forget." She looked at me for concurrence.

"Which they richly deserve," her husband broke in. "I don't know about Lvov, but around here they own all the big buildings, they own the stores, they own the banks. They take our money, and you can bet they make sure Poles can't get into businesses themselves. The one good thing that's come out of this is that the Germans are going to put a stop to it. You know they've started making them wear armbands. We heard that in some places they're even shooting them. It's just a matter of time now, and the sooner the better."

"Pray God the Germans won't be around here long," his wife said. "But as far as we're concerned, they can stay long enough to take care of the Jews."

I didn't object. It didn't occur to me to stand up and walk out or do anything else that might give me away. I was wary, but more than that, I was stunned. I could hardly believe what I was hearing. They had no idea I was anybody other than what I seemed to be, an ordinary Polish soldier, one of theirs. These statements weren't for some outsider's consumption, this was straight talk. This was how they truly felt about Jews. Their words were full of malice. It sounded as if they themselves were capable of murdering Jews.

I excused myself as soon as I could, pleading fatigue. The wife showed me to a bedroom. She was concerned about it being my first day out of the hospital and my facing a long, exhausting journey the next morning. The bed was normal sized, not a cut down hospital cot, with a thick mattress and a heavy white comforter. I couldn't relax after a conversation like that. I couldn't sleep. The worst of it was that these were kind people, in their way. They had taken me in out of sympathy and gratitude; normal middle class, Polish, Catholic people with books in their bookcase and saints on the walls.

I lay under the comforter, letting it sink in. There were currents of hatred here I had never imagined, a river of poison that somehow I had always managed to avoid. This is exactly what the doctor in the makeshift hospital was thinking when he sent me back. Who cares if they die? Let them. Suddenly my mind flashed back to my time in basic training, an event so absurd I hadn't thought about in years.

I had hated the army, not because of any anti-Semitism, but because it was so brutal and mind-numbing. Among other things, we often didn't have enough to eat. The canteen served plenty of food, but one of the tricks the sergeants liked to play was to have us get our food, then order us not to eat until just before the end of mealtime. Then they'd say, "Start to eat!" and a minute later, "I'm counting to ten. Whoever's finished is finished, whoever isn't isn't. One, two, three…" We learned to shovel it in, but half the time we went hungry, which contributed to our constant exhaustion. They liked to wake us up in the middle of the night. "Up!" they'd yell. "Up, you bastards. Mattresses on heads!" And we'd spend the next hour running around the training field carrying our mattresses on our heads, which might sound funny but wasn't humorous at all if you were the one doing the carrying. After ten minutes your arms were breaking. Another ten and it was your neck. Then you're going on pure will power and fear.

The result was that we were always so worn out it was a struggle to say anything unnecessary. The environment wasn't ripe for discussions of any kind, let alone something that required energy, like anti-Semitism. The faces of the boys I trained with had faded almost as fast as their names. But none of them had ever said a word about Jews, that I was sure of.

Which made it much more striking when one day while I was cleaning out the latrine I overheard a discussion among some of the sergeants and corporals who were lounging around in the barracks. Either they had forgotten someone was on toilet duty, or, more likely, they didn't care.

Their subject was Jews and the most effective ways of getting rid of them. The talk was so full of stereotypes that I thought they were joking at first; Christ killers, usurers, child murderers—the old standbys. "We have to find a way to get rid of them all," one voice said. "There's too goddamned many of them." Then came a serious discussion about how best to do it. Someone would make a suggestion and the others would start criticizing it, pointing out its various flaws, as if they were planning tactics. The one they seemed to like best was the idea of building a fleet of big boats with false bottoms. You could put the Jews on them, go out to sea, open the bottoms, and watch them sink. The whole thing was so bizarre and ridiculous that you wondered how they had enough intelligence to put their shoes on properly.

But there was nothing at all bizarre or ridiculous about my hosts. What made their talk so disturbing was precisely how normal they were. With the Germans in charge you sensed a sinister miasma settling over the country. If this was how Poles truly felt in their hearts, then evil was going to rise to meet evil. It wasn't something I saw in any kind of analytical way; in fact, rationally I didn't even accept it.

There was something deep inside me that rejected the idea that in the world's mix of good and evil, evil was the true driver. I had refused to deal with it, to take it in and examine its implications. But in Kutno, with that family, I began to feel it.

7

THE RIVER SAN

December, 1939

The next morning my hosts greeted me warmly, with solicitous questions: "Had I slept well? Was my ankle still in pain? Did I feel all right otherwise?" In the kitchen coffee was waiting, real coffee, and thick slices of white bread spread with butter. I ate and drank. I smiled, straining my acting ability. I couldn't wait to get away from there. After breakfast the wife kissed my cheeks and handed me a little bag of food for the trip. Then her husband drove me to the station. When the train came he held out his hand. I shook it, but it gave me a queasy feeling.

I got into a third class car, one of those with the straight-back wooden benches and narrow corridors. In the pocket of my pants I had my *besheinigung*—the discharge papers that gave me the right to travel home and my instructor's ID from the Korkis School. In the breast pocket of my shirt I carried Wusia's picture. I had no money, but it didn't matter. The conductor looked at my uniform and my crutches, touched his cap, and moved on.

I was retracing the route our troop train had taken almost four months before. But the landscape had changed. Instead of green fields and forests just touched by early fall colors, now I looked out the window at a gray, frost-bitten plain under a leaden sky. Trees silhouetted their bare branches against barren fields and frozen, colorless villages. Snow had begun to fall. I sat, stiff backed and uncomfortable and thought about Wusia. Hours went by. We passed through Lodz, then reentered the hypnotic countryside. But I wasn't looking anymore. My mind was on Wusia. I felt as if she was with me, sitting next to me, holding my hand, not here on this train, but back in our Jesuit Garden. The third class bench wasn't made for sleep, but I was in a waking dream, as I had been so often during those months in the hospital. There I would fall asleep dreaming, here every few minutes I jerked awake when my chin fell forward onto my chest.

Night came early and I tried to curl up on the bench. But finding a comfortable position was impossible and I slept in fits and starts. Morning brought the same gray monotone world passing outside. Before Tarnow I dozed off again, but as we pulled into Rzeszow I awoke with a start. Przemsyl was the next stop, where the Germans and Russians had set their border. And beyond Przemsyl lay Lvov.

Przemsyl was the ancient center of Galicia, predating the salt marsh city of Halych and even Lvov itself. In Przemsyl were renowned libraries, a famous Lyceum, and Catholic, Orthodox, and Uniate cathedrals. But from the moment I maneuvered myself off the train onto the platform, the only interest I had was how to get from the station to the bridge over the San.

I asked directions, then started off through the city, as fast as I could. The closer I got to the bridge the more excited I became. Lvov was less than 50 miles away. My mind was racing. I didn't know what the railroad schedule might be, but once I got a train in the Russian part of the city, across the bridge, it would take two hours, three hours at most. In Lvov I'd take a tram from the Wiener Banhof to the corner of Sheptytsky and Grodecka, a block from Wusia's house. I might not get there before evening, so probably the whole family would be at home. This meant that Wusia's mother was likely to answer the door.

I was still thinking about what I would say to her when I saw the wooden bridge that spanned the river, which didn't seem more than seventy-five or a hundred feet across. At the German checkpoint there was only one guard on duty, dressed in a heavy gray greatcoat and a steel helmet. I showed him my *besheinigung* and explained that I had been released from the war prisoners' hospital and was on my way home. He glanced at the paper without much interest, then raised the gate and let me through. "*Viel Gluck,*" he said, "Lots of luck," as though he thought I'd need it.

Przemysl, the border city between Germany and Russia, 1939

Standing at the bridge over the River San at Przemysl, 1992

The Russian checkpoint was twenty yards away. Already I felt a tremendous relief. Getting away from the Germans was like having a heavy weight lifted off my chest. In front of me lay safety. Two Soviet guards were waiting at the barrier, ready to open it for me. I was beginning to feel a little lightheaded. Every step was taking me closer. I'll speak to them in Ukrainian, I thought. I hadn't learned Russian yet, but the two languages were close enough.

"Dobry den," I said, "Good day, comrades. I'm on my way home to Lvov." The first Russian examined my *besheinigung*, then gave it to the second, who also looked at it carefully. I wondered if they could actually read German. Then the first one asked if I had any other papers. I dug out my Korkis School teacher's card and explained that this was where I worked, on St. Teresa Street in Lvov.

"Anything else?" he said.

"No," I said. "What else should I have?"

"If you want to cross here, you need a permit from the Repatriation Committee. Do you have a permit?"

"No, I've been in the hospital. No one ever told me about a permit. I never even heard of the Repatriation Committee"

"Well, you need a permit. Nobody crosses without a permit."

If I had had any money with me I would have tried to bribe him although I had no experience and would probably have botched it. Behind the two of them in their brown overcoats and tommy guns slung across their chests, eastern Przemsyl was strung out along the opposite bank of the river, so close I could touch it. I needed to be in that city so I could get the train.

"Look," said the Russian, "don't worry about it. The Committee registers all Poles who want to return. When you get your permit, you can come back here. There won't be any problem."

"Do you know the Committee's address? I asked. "Maybe I can go there right now."

"You can't," he said. "There's no Repatriation Committee in Przemsyl. The nearest one's in Jaroslaw. You'll have to go there."

I went back through the German checkpoint and into west Przemsyl. Jaroslaw was on the railroad line going back toward Rzeszow. I just passed through there an hour or two ago. It was already after noon. God knew when there would be a train. I was heading in the direction of the station to check the schedule when I realized that people were looking at me, exactly as they had in Kutno. The uniform and crutches were like magnets. Almost every face conveyed sympathy and interest. Before long a young man stopped and introduced himself. Had I had lunch yet? he asked. Could he possibly invite me to his family's house for a meal? His parents would be honored, and so would he.

When we arrived at his house a few minutes later, the young man's mother and father were both extremely happy that their son had found me and that I had accepted his invitation. While the mother prepared dinner—in Poland the midday meal was the main meal of the day—the father, the young man, and I talked. If I hadn't had that experience with the Kutno family, I would have assumed these were the kindest people in the world. But now I wasn't rushing to any judgments. Still, they seemed truly concerned about my physical condition, particularly when I told them I wasn't sure if I'd be able to walk normally again. They were deeply worried about Poland. What had happened already was a nightmare and they were nervous about what the Germans might be planning. I was hoping this wasn't heading in the same direction as the discussion in Kutno. So far there was no talk of Jews at all. If anti-Semitism was any part of these people's make-up, it wasn't showing itself. When they learned I was a stranger in town, they insisted I stay with them. I'd be happy to accept, I said, except that I had to get to Jaroslaw to see the Repatriation Committee, and I was in a hurry to return to Lvov.

When I mentioned Jaroslaw, the father told me there was a train later in the afternoon. He worked for the railroad, he said, and knew all the schedules by heart. When I heard there was an afternoon train I began to think that maybe I could get to Jaroslaw, get my permit, and come back, maybe even in time to take an evening train to Lvov, if there was one. I didn't want to waste a moment, so I thanked the family and got up to leave, even though they insisted I stay with them, that it would be so much easier and more restful if I would sleep at their house, then leave for the Committee the next morning.

I made the train with time to spare. But it went so slowly that it was obvious from the beginning that my plan for a quick visit to Jaroslaw wasn't going to work. It reminded me of our troop train, hauling itself along at a few miles an hour and stopping now and then for no obvious reason. When we finally arrived in Jaroslaw, it was already evening. There was nothing to do but stay in the station and sleep on a waiting room bench. I would have to wait until morning to present myself to the Soviets.

Jaroslaw isn't a big city, but the train station was crowded. The war had disrupted people's lives and sent them wandering, some to stay with relatives, others searching for loved ones, some looking for work or a place to settle after their own homes had been destroyed. Even now, months after the fighting had stopped, the wandering went on, an aimless, disorganized migration. Many of these people had no place to stay while they were waiting for the rail system to be repaired to take them wherever it was they were going, so they slept in the stations.

The empty seat I found was between a Catholic priest and a *Volksdeutsch* woman who turned out to be looking for her wounded husband. Before long we were talking about the universal topic—the war—and what was going to happen now between the Germans and Poles. But it was only a minute or two before they turned their attention to the Jews. The priest started. "I'm from Warsaw," he said, "and I can tell you that the Jews were the ones who stabbed us in the back. Not that it's any surprise to anyone. They stabbed Christ in the back. They'll stab any Christian in the back if they think they can get away with it."

The first words had me reeling. Even in Kutno I had never heard such a tirade. I tried to get the discussion back to the war, but it was like trying to stop a flood. Jews were what they wanted to talk about. It was as if the war had broken some kind of emotional dam, unleashing torrents of hate. They needed to find some reason this disaster had befallen them. And with no obvious targets, they lashed out against the people they were used to blaming for everything. The *Volksdeutch* woman's husband might have been hurt fighting the Germans, but at least the Germans were also oppressing the Jews. Anyway, she announced, everyone knew the Jews' real loyalty wasn't to Poland, it was to the Communists in Moscow.

The priest agreed emphatically. You couldn't say a single good thing about them, he said. They had killed Christ, they killed Christian children for their blood, and they stabbed their neighbors. In Warsaw there was a breadline where the

Jews had knifed the Poles so they could get all the bread themselves. This wasn't something he had just heard of, he knew the situation first-hand. He had seen it. On their Sabbath they trampled on Christ's cross. It was the only day of the week they weren't busy sucking money from the poor.

I sat there stone-faced. Did this priest really think Jews spent their Sabbaths trampling on crosses? How could he make up stories about Jews knifing Poles in breadlines, or killing children? I couldn't remember the last time I had really lost my temper, if I had ever lost it. Now I was coming close. I didn't know if I might just have to grab his neck and throttle him. He was like a wild beast spewing filth. I could feel myself trembling. You can't do anything, I was telling myself. You're not a Jew sitting here; you're a Pole. You're a Polish soldier. There are Germans all around you. They're shooting Jews here, understand? I fought to keep control, clenching my muscles to stop the trembling. I made my body rigid. I tried to look composed, put a serene look on my face, a Polish look, to show I was not bothered by any of this. Why should I be? A Polish soldier, not too concerned by some overheated priest. I nodded, I blinked, saying with my eyes, "I don't know, Father. You might be right, Father, Who's to say about these Jews, Father."

The next morning I found my way to the Repatriation Committee, which turned out to be three people sitting at a rickety table in a big drab room. No one else seemed to be around. From the moment I walked in I had a bad feeling about them. It occurred to me that the reason there weren't any lines was because no Pole would be anxious to be seen here, unless there was a necessity, like mine, or if they were Communists. Ordinary Poles wouldn't trust the Soviets an inch, even if they did want to get across the border. Why volunteer your name, your relatives' names, your address and theirs to a committee of commissars? Before the war everyone knew that many Russians had tried to escape to Poland. But you never heard of Poles trying to escape to Russia.

I sat down in front of the three commissars and answered their questions, which they asked with a kind of bureaucratic inattention. Where was I born? What was my rank in the army? Where was I during the war, and what did I do? What were the circumstances of my injury? Why did I want to go back? Ten minutes worth of mechanical questions.

"Give us your name and an address where we can contact you," one said when they had finished. "When your case is processed we'll inform you whether your application to be repatriated has been approved."

"When do you think that might be?" I asked.

"Every case is different," another responded. "Before a case is investigated, it's impossible to know what its nature is. At the right time you'll be informed."

I left the building knowing that I was never going to get an entry permit. If they wanted to let somebody cross, they would do it immediately. There was no reason not to. This wasn't a repatriation committee; these people were interested in denying repatriation. What possible reason would they have to allow Poles or Jews back into the territories they had occupied? More people only meant additional potential troublemakers.

Only then did I realize what had given me the bad feeling when I entered. These three exuded an air of unmistakable malevolence. They had looked at me, as I'm sure they looked at everyone, not in terms of human suffering they might rectify, but with the indifference a temporarily sated predator might have toward a prey animal. I had heard of the NKVD, and as I walked away from the building I understood that those people were its agents.

8

THE NKVD

December 1939, continued

On the way back to Przemsyl I was thinking furiously
about how I could get across the border. When I returned to
my new friends and told them what had happened, they began
to investigate possibilities. In fact, the son had already been
inquiring. His girlfriend lived in the Russian side of the city
and he was looking for a way to see her. In the process he had
met a young woman whose husband was in the hospital in
Lvov and who was intent on getting there to see him. Like
me, she had come away from the Repatriation Committee
without any hope of an entry permit. The three of us decided
that we'd find a way, and go together.

There was only one bridge, and since the checkpoints
were guarded twenty-four hours a day, that was out. But as we
scouted around, we learned that a brisk trade in smuggling was
going on. Since the war, thousands of Jews from southern
Poland had been trying to get into the Russian sector, and
many of them had found their way to Przemsyl. As a result,

a small class of smugglers had come into existence, people who made it their business to know the river. We heard there were some German border police who could be bribed; some might even turn their backs without a bribe. The Russians patrolled the far side, but the smugglers knew their routines and which places were likely to be unguarded.

It took a week or so to make our arrangements. My friends found a smuggler who would ferry us across and managed to bribe a German border guard. The crossing was to be December 21, the longest night of the year.

Late that night my friend and I left his home and met our companion. We walked through Przemsyl's streets doing our best to look inconspicuous and headed toward our rendezvous with the German border guard near the river. Although we had hoped for a dark, overcast night, a bright moon shone down on the city reflecting off the thin layer of river ice and the rippling stream that coursed down the San's unfrozen center. The guard was waiting for us, which calmed us a little. Now we had some cover, at least until we got across. Our plan was to meet the boatman at a certain time, but the German said it was too dangerous to go by boat. On a night like this the Russians would be watching the most likely boat crossing places. It would be much better wading across ourselves. He could take us to a spot upriver where the water was shallow. Crossing there would be a lot less noticeable than in a boat.

The three of us talked briefly about what to do, whether we should wait for a darker night or take our chances now. On balance it seemed better to take our chances. We had already bribed this border guard, and who knew when he might again be on duty? Another guard might not be amenable, and trying to bribe the wrong person could have dangerous consequences. The weather too could be unpredictable. We could wait a long time for a cloudy night and we had this guard right now who knew a safer crossing point. Getting across would be risky under any circumstances. This night was probably as good as it ever would be.

The German led us along the river bank until we were a distance from the city. He seemed to know all the crossings and as we went he talked in a low voice, about the depths and current. Sounds carry on the river, he warned. He was a Sudeten who had been drafted into a border guard unit after Germany attacked Czechoslovakia. "Ich bin nicht ein Ritter," he said. He wasn't one of "Hitler's knights." He felt badly that so many people had become refugees, and had helped many of them get over.

Finally we arrived at the spot he had in mind, a place where the bank was overgrown with bushes, leafless now, but which still offered some protection from anybody who might be watching from the other side. Here the river was completely iced over. The far bank looked barren, with bushes and withered vegetation, but not a light to be seen.

We watched for a few minutes, straining to catch anything moving in the shadows across the ice. "Go ahead," the German said. "It looks clear. Don't worry about anything on this side. Hopefully, you'll be fine on the other side too."

We stepped onto the ice gingerly and took a few tentative steps. It seemed solid enough to hold our weight. Afraid that the crutches might break through, I took both of them under my left arm and put my right arm over my friend's shoulders, letting him support me. Slowly we moved along, stopping every few feet to listen. The other side was quiet; there was no noise or movement. Then, a third of the way out, the ice crackled underfoot and made a soft little ripping sound. We stopped, not a muscle moving. A long moment later thin fissures appeared around us and the ice sheeted. Water started coming up through the cracks and I could see that the frozen surface was far thinner here than it was near the shoreline. Then the sheet we were standing on gave way and dumped us into the river.

The German had said it was very shallow in this area, but I had a split second of terror before my feet hit bottom. We were well out into the river, but mercifully the water was only thigh deep and there wasn't much of a current. My legs instantly became numb in the ice-cold water, stopping the pain in my ankle that had been worsening with each awkward step. We weren't in any danger of drowning or being carried away, which was a relief, but we couldn't move without making noise. There was no choice, though, but to move ahead. Ice seamed around us as we waded toward the far shore. It crackled and ripped as we sloshed through, sounding loud enough to wake hell.

When we stepped out onto the Russian shore we shushed each other and listened to the darkness. We heard nothing. Wet and shivering, we started off for town and the house of my friend's girlfriend.

We had only gone a step or two when the night was split by the sharp crack of a rifle. I dropped the crutches and fell, flattening myself against the snow. My friends were on the ground too. Another shot rang out, then two more almost together. I yelled into the darkness, "Don't shoot. We're not armed. We're here, we surrender. Don't shoot us." I lay still, hoping they'd come looking and not shooting. We heard noises in front of us, people moving through the snow and bushes. When I looked up, two Russians were standing over us, their rifle muzzles pointed at our heads.

After a moment one of them shot into the air a couple of times, and a minute later a jeep pulled up with three more Russians. The three of us crowded in with the driver and a guard and drove to what turned out to be a kind of interrogation center and prison. As we drove I rehearsed what I was going to tell them. They could see for themselves that I wasn't smuggling anything. I'd show them my *besheinigung* and explain that I was just trying to get back home. I was a wounded soldier, completely innocent. Once they heard my explanation, what more could they want from me? By the time we arrived, I had convinced myself that after I explained, the Russians would probably just give me some time to warm up and get dry. Maybe they'd even give me some soup. Then they'd let me go. How difficult would it be for them to see that my companions and I were completely harmless?

Once inside the prison it took me about a minute to understand that the Russians weren't in the habit of giving people a chance to explain. Instead of bringing us to someone who would listen to our story, they separated us and led me to a small cell. Even outside the cell I noticed an odor of unwashed bodies. When the guard swung the door open, a wave of stench hit me. Inside sixteen or seventeen prisoners had somehow been jammed into the cell. There were no benches and no room to sit on the cement floor. My entrance caused a small stir, obviously because of my uniform and crutches. There was a little jumble of talk and somehow my new cellmates shoved back and opened a little space on the floor, making enough room for me to sit down.

I sat there for a couple of hours, answering my cellmates' questions as briefly as I could and trying to focus on how I could get out of here. I was convinced that all I really needed to do was find someone who would listen. It was ridiculous that they would arrest me. I had just escaped from the Germans and all I wanted was to go home. Once they gave me a chance to talk to a person in authority, they'd free me instantly.

Several hours later, maybe at one or two in the morning, a guard came to the cell and called my name. I followed him through the corridor, thinking that at last this would be my chance. I'd be out of here soon, and then I'd find the railroad station, get some sleep on a bench, and catch an early train for Lvov. We came to a door, the guard knocked, then opened without waiting for an answer. Inside the room was a table, and sitting behind it were two men in military uniforms. One pointed to a chair facing the table for me to sit in, then without any further preliminaries, they began asking questions.

"Your name?"
"Ungar, Wilo."

"Father's name?"
"Mikhail"

"Birthplace?
"Krasne, province of Tarnopol."

"And where were you wounded?"
"Near Gostynin, in an airplane attack."

"And were you in a hospital?"
"Yes."

"Good, and tell us, Wilo Mikhailovich, why is it exactly that the Germans let you go?"

"I don't know. Probably because they had no reason to keep me and with my injury they couldn't put me to work."

"I see. But why let you go when so many Polish soldiers are still prisoners, including the wounded? Please tell us why that is."

This kind of questioning wasn't what I had in mind at all.

"Listen," I said, "let me tell you why I crossed the river. I'm trying to get back to Lvov..."

"Wait. Please, just answer our questions for a moment. Why is it you think they let you go?"

"I don't know exactly."

This was becoming more frustrating.

"Could it be, Wilo Mikhailovich, that they let you go so you could spy for them?"

My mouth opened. This was the most bewildering thing I had ever heard. In my wildest dreams I couldn't imagine that someone might accuse me of spying for the Germans. I dug out my besheinigung and my Korkis ID card.

"This is my ID from the Korkis School, where I teach," I told them. "It's a Jewish school. I'm Jewish. You can check in Lvov. How can you think that a Jew would be a spy for the Nazis?"

"You're absolutely right, Wilo Mikhailovich," the first one said. "A Jew would be the least likely person, which is exactly why a Jew would make the best spy, don't you think?"

"And knowing you're a Jew," said the other, "how come they let you go free? What makes you such a privileged person? They're killing Jews over there and putting them in prison. Why are you the exception? Not only that, but they brought you to the border. We know the Germans guided you to the crossing. Why would that be if you weren't working for them?"

This interrogation went on for about an hour. Whatever explanations I gave were disregarded. They seemed to be completely convinced that I was a spy. Even though they were polite, I somehow began to get the message that things would go a lot easier for me if I would admit to working for the Germans. I pretended I didn't understand the intimidation and kept answering the questions plainly and honestly. Finally, one called in the guard who escorted me back to my cell.

Throughout the night other prisoners were taken for interrogation. The guards only came at night, a cellmate said. Daytime they left you alone. For the most part I tried not to get into conversations with my cellmates. Instead I kept to myself and practiced being a Pole. I watched their body language when they talked, how they held themselves, what they did with their hands and their faces. I had grown up with it, so in a way it was second nature to me. But now I started to concentrate on it as something that might save my life.

Meanwhile, I couldn't figure out how I might get myself out of this predicament. The whole thing was inconceivable. Never in my life did I think I'd have to defend myself against an accusation that I was a German spy. I had no idea how to convince them that I wasn't.

The second night I was brought to the same room with the same two interrogators. This time they took a slightly different approach. Instead of accusing me and trying to get me to admit that I was a spy, now they just assumed that I was. "Listen," one said, "we know you're spying for the Germans, but we're not even concerned about that. However, there are some things that are very important to us. We have to know what your mission is. What instructions did they give to you? What do they expect you to do, and how are you supposed to get information back to them?"

I started to protest, but they cut me off. "Wilo Mikhailovich, please. You have to understand that you have nothing to be afraid of. We have no interest in keeping you here. All we have to know is what they want, so that we can take steps to counteract it. There's no reason at all for you to hide that. We don't want to make you suffer. Just tell us the truth and we'll let you out of here."

They were in no hurry. Again they kept me for about an hour, then sent me back to the cell, where I sat all day thinking about what they had said. The same thing happened the next night, and the night after. They never stopped being polite. It was as if they were trying to convince me that I could trust them, that for me they had nothing but good intentions. Still, they kept hammering away. They knew I was a spy, all I had to do was admit it.

Not having had any experience, I didn't completely understand what they were trying to do. In a way, maybe I was saved by my naiveté. Instead of deliberating what little thing I should make up that I could admit to, just to get out of there, I kept thinking: What a dialogue to have between Russians and a Jew! Why in the world are they doing this to me? Throughout the interrogations, I kept repeating the same things I'd been telling them. During the day, I sat with my cellmates, most of whom seemed to have been arrested for smuggling. Then at night I'd be back in the little room hearing the same questions, and giving them the same answers.

As the days passed I began to see that part of their method was sleep deprivation. Interrogation was at night. You couldn't sleep beforehand because you were too nervous about what might happen. You couldn't sleep afterward because you were thinking about what had happened, and what you might have to say to get them to release you. Of course, with the cell so crowded, there was no real way to sleep anyway. They seemed to have the idea that if they kept prisoners without sleep long enough and kept hammering into their heads that they were spies, eventually they might come to believe it themselves and confess.

I didn't feel hopeless. I couldn't understand what they would want with me. I wasn't a spy, which they had to at least suspect was the truth. I couldn't work for them, so there was no point in sending me to a work camp. As long as I stuck to my guns, eventually, they'd just have to give up and let me out.

Fortunately, I didn't get to really test the Russians' ideas about sleep-deprivation. After five or six days they decided I was a lost cause. Every night I told them the same things, and of course they had plenty of other prisoners, who might have actually done something. Every day new subjects were brought in for them to work on. Finally, one night they called me for interrogation, but instead of asking questions, they announced that in the morning I'd be released.

Fifteen minutes after they let me go, I was in the railroad station waiting for a train to Lvov. I felt completely free. All my worries about the Germans were in the past. Only a few minutes ago I was in prison, and already it was as if it never happened. I felt as light as air. The train came soon, as if the schedule had been arranged for my convenience. It didn't even matter that we stopped at every crossroads between Przemsyl and Lvov.

I hadn't seen Wusia in four months, yet I felt as if she had kept me alive. Through all that waiting and loneliness, she had been my one real companion. In the woods, waiting to go into battle. In the hospital. In prison. She had been my reason not to lose hope. There was no mail, but I needed no letters. Thinking about her filled my days. I dreamed of her at night, dreams I often couldn't remember, but which left an aura of happiness and well being. I wasn't worried about her. With the Russians in Lvov I was sure she was safe. I couldn't imagine what she was thinking about me, although I fantasized about it. Some part of her, I knew, must believe that I was still alive, even though she had no reason to think so. I had disappeared, like so many dead or missing Polish soldiers, like the prisoners of war whom nobody knew anything about. I had a permanent impression in my mind of the Poles in Kutno and Przemsyl looking at me, searching my face and touching my uniform. Maybe they wondered for a split second if I was the one they were looking for, grasping for some bit of information that might tell them something about a brother or father or fiancée who had not returned.

It was already getting dark when I arrived in Lvov. The trip had taken practically all day. But the Wiener Banhof was only a few minutes away from Sheptytsky. I told the horse cab driver that I didn't have any money, but he took me anyway. In front of Wusia's apartment house I climbed down, balancing on my left foot while I extricated the crutches from the wagon. Getting up to the second floor was hard. I hadn't had much practice at stairs and the straining and maneuvering took all my strength. I had fantasized about this moment for months, but now I didn't have a thought in my head. I leaned forward and knocked. The door opened so quickly I thought for a moment that Wusia might have been waiting for me. But it was her mother, who stared at me, then started to sway a little as if she were about to faint. "Wusia," she called, "come quick!" I saw Wusia come out of the living room. Then she was running into my arms, with the crutches caught half way between us and her mother still staring and her father's voice coming from the living room now asking what in the world was going on.

9

BREAKING THE GLASS

Summer – Fall 1940

In my house a pat on the head was an event. My parents loved each other and their children, but they didn't generally show it with physical affection. Wusia's family was originally from Russia, and Russian Jews are typically warmer than Polish Jews. But they weren't given to public displays of affection either. So I can't imagine what her parents must have thought when they saw the two of us in a death grip. I think that until that moment they didn't really know how serious Wusia and I were. It must have been a double shock to them. First they open the door to find me standing there, an apparition back from the grave. Then an instant later their daughter unexpectedly bares her heart to them.

Holding Wusia, enfolding her, feeling her pressing against me, I was suddenly free, liberated, as if someone had magically cut loose the worries and fears that had wrapped themselves around me for so long. All the tension disappeared, the frustration and anxiety of the war, the hospital and the Russian prison, it all dissolved like a bad dream. With her in my arms, pressing against me, her cheek warm against mine, the past four months vanished in a heartbeat.

Later Wusia's brother Sunio came home. While we ate dinner I was forced to talk for what seemed like hours. The whole family was so glad to see me, they wanted to know every detail of what had happened. But the evening was a blur. All I wanted was for them to go to bed so Wusia and I could be alone. I couldn't tell if they saw the glances we exchanged, even though we were doing our best to keep our eyes off each other. At one point I excused myself to call home. There was only one telephone in Krasne, at the police station. So I called there and the police went to get my brother Max who lived just down the street. Max was so overjoyed to hear I was alive he almost collapsed. I just had time to tell him that I was planning to take the train the next day to Grzymalov before he dropped the phone to tell Mother that I was safe. I didn't have a chance to mention that I couldn't walk.

When her parents and Sunio finally went to bed, Wusia and I sat on the sofa together. In a way it was as though I had never left, as if we were simply picking up from our last evening together in the Jesuit Garden. We felt so comfortable in each other's arms, so at home. And when she kissed me the tenderness of it was almost unbearable.

"I needed to hear your voice," she whispered. "I wanted to hear you tell me you were alive. I wanted you to say that you hadn't forgotten me." My skin was hot where her fingertips brushed my eyelids and ran over my cheeks.

"Wilo, I was so miserable when we said good-bye on Grodecka Street. I wanted to tell you things, but I didn't have the courage to say them. While you were gone I never let myself believe you were dead. The worst was thinking that you might have been," she rested her head in the hollow of my shoulder, "and that I had never told you that I love you."

How strange, hearing her say it, how remarkable, after imagining the sound of those words a thousand times. How unbelievable to be here in this place with her instead of lying in a strange bed conjuring up her image in my mind. "You did tell me," I said. "I heard you telling me the whole time. I talked with you every day and every night when I couldn't sleep. I heard you. I know you heard me. "

"Did you remember what I said about our initials?" Wusia asked. She had found herself writing them out again and again. She knew it was silly, childish, like a young girl with a crush. She was afraid her mother would find the papers.

"This is a dream," I said. "This is the dream I've lived every night. In a moment I'll wake up and find out that I'm really in a hospital or a train station. Maybe on the floor of my cell. I know I can't be here." She kissed my mouth shut.

For the first time we talked seriously about the future. For the present, there was no way for me to stay in Lvov. I had no place to live, and with my injured leg, I couldn't go back to teaching at the Korkis School, even if they'd take me. I'd never be able to get up and down the stairs. The thing to do, as I saw it, would be to go back home to Krasne and recuperate there with my family. Dr. Mieses, our family doctor from Grzymalov, was an excellent physician. He could treat my leg as well as anyone. I'd come back just as soon as I could walk again, which hopefully wouldn't be very long. Then Wusia and I could decide what we wanted to do.

Wusia thought that was fine. As long as I was alive everything was all right. I should stay in Krasne as long as it took to heal myself. Meanwhile, she had a new job in Lvov. The Soviets had hired her as manager of a group of apartment buildings on Nabielacka Street. They liked the fact that she was young and that she had never been political, which made them think she might be trustworthy. It also seemed to Wusia that they trusted Jews more than Poles or Ukrainians. In any case, it was a good job. The only thing I had to think about was getting better.

That night I slept on the sofa, and early the next morning I was on the train to Grzymalov. As usual, the ride was excruciatingly slow, but I had plenty to think about. I was so glad to be alive, and that Wusia had the same feelings for me as I did for her, despite my condition. She didn't seem that concerned. The crutches hadn't upset her. She thought that Dr. Mieses could help and that I'd come back to Lvov walking as well as ever.

I wasn't so sure. The fact was that the ankle hadn't gotten any better since they took the cast off. Until now I had never paid any attention to invalids. I mostly ignored them. Now I realized that there were quite a few in Krasne and the nearby villages. A lot of men had come back crippled after fighting in the Great War. A man in Touste had been blinded and our neighbor, Taras Haidemak, had to get around on one leg. Others just stayed at home. You rarely saw them or knew exactly what was wrong with them, except that they had been hurt in the war and their families took care of them. People would say that so and so was on an invalid's pension.

This was a whole new field to let my mind wander over. Some weren't hurt in the war but had had accidents on the farm, and a broken leg or arm could make you a cripple for life. I was lucky. Some cripples didn't even have crutches. Some sat on wooden planks with casters pushing themselves, or even just shoving along on the bare ground. One thing seemed clear. If you were an invalid, you stayed an invalid the rest of your life. The world didn't come to an end because there were a few invalids.

These thoughts absorbed me as the train inched toward Tarnopol, then turned southeast to Grzymalov. I was in a world where most people walked unaided and running wasn't a problem. But with a little effort I seemed to be able to remember every cripple I had ever seen. The question was, would I now be one of them?

In the past going from Lvov to Krasne had always been a happy journey. The train ride meant I was on my way to vacation. I had always liked being in Lvov, first for school, then when I went to work. But more than anything, I loved going home. It wasn't only that my family was there, I loved it because of the simplicity and naturalness of the place. In Krasne there were no streetcars, no locked doors where if you got home after ten you'd have to pay the superintendent to let you in, and if it was after midnight you had to pay him more. Krasne had no grocery stores. People ate the produce from their gardens, their potato fields, their orchards. The cow in the stable gave you milk, the chickens gave eggs. On weekdays there was the smell of bread baking, and challah on Friday. The air was sweeter, purer. Big city innovations like electricity were unnecessary. Kerosene lamps and candles did at least as well. In the winter the tiled ovens in each room radiated warmth. I was happy in Lvov, but in my heart I always missed the village. Coming home had always been one of my greatest pleasures.

But now everything had changed. When I was last in Krasne it had been part of Poland, now it was Russia. When I left I was in good health and good spirits, now I was returning on crutches, my head crammed with doubts.

Max met me with the sled at the Grzymalov train station. As I climbed down from the car and he saw the crutches his big smile turned to concern, if only for a moment. In the sled, he had a long fur coat for me and heavy fur blankets to put over our legs and feet. This was the only way you could travel there in the winter; without them you'd literally freeze.

Two hours later we were home. When my mother saw me she kissed and hugged me not once, but over and over, as if she had to keep touching me to reassure herself that I was real. She was still tall and graceful, but her beautiful face had aged after my father's death and even more now with all the money problems and worries about the family. For Mama, just seeing me alive was overwhelming, with crutches or without crutches, to her it didn't matter.

She fixed glasses of tea for us and when we sat down she told me about a strange dream she had had many years earlier about my brother Zalman, who had left for America before I was born. In her dream she had seen Zalman walking on crutches. We knew that in 1917 Zalman had fought with the American Expeditionary Force in France. He had written to us about that, but we had never heard anything about him having been wounded. Mama thought that maybe the dream was just an expression of her fears, but now, she said, several weeks ago, she had a dream where she saw me on crutches. Now here I was, the dream had materialized.

This made her worry even more about Zalman. Maybe he had really been hurt too.

Over the next few days all our friends and neighbors came to visit, and for each of them I had to describe my heroic battle against the Germans. Being knocked off a wagon, then run over might not have sounded like the height of heroism to most people, but the story seemed to strike our friends in Krasne, especially the Jewish ones, as an extraordinary example of courage under fire. I was a sort of unusual phenomenon for them anyway. How many people from Krasne ever went to Lvov even once in their lives? I not only lived there, but I was a teacher there. And now all of a sudden I had unexpectedly come back alive from the war against the Germans, into whose clutches I had actually fallen. For them the whole thing was like a work of fiction.

Every time I told the story my family sat around to listen, my mother, still touching me whenever she passed by, my sisters Esther and Dvorah, Dvorah's children and her husband David. Max was often there with his wife and five children—he had married Henia, the daughter of David Hirsh Zeftel our local cantor, and Zeftel too came over frequently. I had truly returned to the bosom of the family, all of whom were elated by my miraculous survival and wanted to hear about it as often as possible.

With Dvorah, David, and their three children living with us, the house was noisy and crowded, but the basic

The three brothers are reunited! Left to right: me, Herman and Zalman, 1962

My Family—Max's wife, Henya; their daughter, Manya; my brother, Max; Aunt Gusta; my mother; my sister, Dvorah, holding baby Michael; Dvorah's husband, David; and my sister, Esther (top row, left to right). Max's children: Jonah, Ceil, Leon (kneeling); and Dvorah's children: Herman and Henia (sitting, left to right), 1939

rhythm of life went on as it always had. Almost everything that happened in the house set off sharp memories from my childhood. While my mother cooked she sang softly to herself, Yiddish melodies that had been in my head as long as I could remember. *Oyfn Pripetshik brent a fayerl, Un in shtub is heys, Un der rebe lernt kleyne kinderlekh, Dem aleph-bays.* In the tiny grate burns a flickering flame, And the room is warm, And the rebbe teaches little children, The ABC.

Closing my eyes I was six years old again lying on the bench on our front porch with my head in her lap, listening to her sing while the village life passed in front of us. She baked the weekday bread on Mondays, on Fridays challah, in preparation for the Sabbath. In the attic dried fall apples were stored under a deep blanket of straw. They froze up there and when she brought them down to thaw the house smelled like an orchard. The prune butter evoked pictures of the bushels of ripe plums we used to empty into our big vat and cook for hours until we had enough to put up for the winter. Mama still had bottles of cherry brandy, brewed from dark sweet cherries, and jars of preserves she had made from the strawberries and raspberries that grew in the garden and wild blueberries she gathered every summer from the forest.

The big shelved closet in the hallway still held the library we collected when my teacher Gedaliah Gottfried lived with us back in the twenties. I hadn't looked at the books in years, but I had read them all, Sienkewicz and Prus and Adam Mickievicz, the Polish writers; Mendel Mocher Sephorim, Dovid Frishman, Sholom Aleichem and the other great Yiddishists. Pushkin and Tolstoy too, Turgenev, Victor Hugo and Emile Zola, Sinclair Lewis and Guy DeMaupassant. I took down my old copies of Tczernichowsky and Chaim Nachman Bialik, whose poems I used to memorize out in the forest on summer afternoons with the sunrays streaming through the trees. Some of these poems I still remembered. I'd practice saying the lines to myself until I memorized them. Sometimes I'd shout them while I rode the trees, climbing to the top of young birches or aspens, then riding them down as they bent under my weight. I was what they called in Hebrew *ha yeled sha'ashua*, the child of my parent's love, the last one, the free one. The beloved one.

Just to sit in the kitchen with my bad leg on a stool, reminiscing with Mama and Esther and Dvorah over a cup of tea from the samovar, or just meditating on the past was the most wonderful medicine. It made me feel I was being restored spiritually. Unfortunately, at the same time, my ankle wasn't getting any better. I rested and ate well, but I still couldn't put the slightest weight on it. When I tried I'd feel a sharp pain, exactly the same pain I felt in the Kutno hospital when I had broken the ankle for the second time.

I had talked to Wusia about Dr. Mieses, but the truth was I didn't believe he'd be able to do anything. The doctors in Gostynin and Kutno had already set the bones twice, and it hadn't helped. Dr. Mieses was a good family physician, but what would he be able to do that they hadn't. My hope was that time and rest would make a difference, but as the weeks passed it was becoming obvious that I just wasn't going to get better.

I knew that if the ankle didn't heal, my life would change dramatically for the worse. I'd be faced with a new set of questions, the first of which would be how to make a living. What kind of life could Wusia and I have if I were a cripple? Somehow I had to overcome this, but I couldn't see how. I wasn't desperate about it, but I was heading in that direction when suddenly it occurred to me that maybe I should visit Franka.

I had never met Franka, even though she lived in Touste, the neighboring village. A Ukrainian peasant woman whose hands supposedly had mysterious healing powers, Franka was known throughout the area as a magical bonesetter. People said that in her younger days she had started by treating animals that had broken their legs. She would manipulate their fractured limbs and soon after they would begin to walk again. Before long she became so famous as an animal chiropractor that people began coming to her with their own injuries. At one point her reputation for healing attracted the attention of the government medical authorities and they began to persecute her. That stopped when the Polish administrator of Kopycynce fell and fractured his back. According to the story, he was brought to her lying on the flatbed of a wagon, but when she had finished manipulating him he was able to get up and walk away. That was the story, and there were only a few who didn't believe it. Franka was a legend.

The sled ride to Touste took only fifteen or twenty minutes. We pulled up to a primitive, one-room peasant cottage, with a single-stall stable behind it for Franka's cow. Franka herself came to the door to meet me, heavyset and short, but with a broad smile and radiant blue eyes. She had me sit down and helped take off my high winter boots. Then she began feeling my ankles, tracing the bones with her fingers, all the while smiling beatifically at me. "Your ankle is not put together properly," she said, and she began manipulating it very gently. "I have to put things back in their proper places." As she worked I felt strange things happening, not painful at all, just odd. She'd knead something and there would be a slight movement, just a discernible dislocation or realignment, almost like you feel if a joint cracks, or you crack your knuckles. Her eyes were mesmerizing, she never took her gaze away from mine. In fact that look of hers engaged me much more than what she was doing to my foot. I wasn't sure how much time went by, but it seemed only a few minutes before she was satisfied that she had done what was necessary. "Now," she said, "don't expect your ankle to be normal. It will never be the same as it was, but don't worry, after a while you will be able to walk on it again."

I thanked Franka and paid her, then I put my boots on and walked out of her cottage using my crutches, exactly as I had walked in. It was an interesting experience, but I didn't have much confidence that she had accomplished any good. All she had done was run her hands over my ankle for a few minutes. Nothing dramatic had happened, certainly nothing like the story of the official with the broken back. I tried gingerly to put some weight on it, but I was rewarded with the same sharp pain as always.

A few weeks later, though, I thought I noticed that the pain was slightly less. At first it was hard to judge. I wondered if maybe I was just getting used to it so it didn't seem as bad. After a while I was able to put a little pressure on that leg, so I knew that something was changing. As time passed the pain turned into a kind of discomfort, then even that began to disappear. Finally I found I could get rid of the crutches. I had no idea what Franka had done, but whatever it was it had obviously worked. I was walking again. My gait wasn't normal; I still favored that ankle and had to limp a little. I couldn't run at all. But I was definitely able to walk.

In the early spring I wrote to the Korkis School, telling them I had recovered and asking if my position was still open and could I have it back. Horatzy Horowitz answered, the former chief engineer who had apparently taken Badian's place as director, saying that I was welcome to return again for the September semester. Meanwhile Wusia and I had been writing, although in the Soviet concept of mail, private correspondence didn't count for much, so only a few of our letters got through. I understood that Wusia and her family were well, but that life in Lvov was becoming more difficult. Food was being rationed, she wrote, and shortages were common.

By June I was ready to go back. Although I couldn't wait to see Wusia, it was hard to wrench myself away from my mother and the rest of the family. We had celebrated a difficult Passover. The feast of liberation and new beginnings contrasted with a dark mood that had been settling down over the family. There was still food in the larder, but income from the tavern and our little store was dwindling. David, Dvorah's husband, still hadn't been able to find work, which meant there was less and less income to feed the seven people who made up the household. I was the eighth. However it was no consolation to anyone that my departure would mean one less mouth to feed.

What made it worse was that David's plan had been to bring Dvorah and the children to Argentina, then to send for my mother, my sister Esther, and me. But David had decided to return before the war. Not moving the family to Argentina had only been a disappointment then. Now it was beginning to seem like a potential tragedy. Over everything a sense of forboding hovered. Life under the Soviets was more precarious than it had been before and the Nazis were only a day's trainride away. The news that was seeping out of their half of Poland was ominous.

Leaving them was bitter. Our neighbor Dziuda brought a wagon to take me to Grzymalov and they all stood in front of the house to say goodbye, Dvorah's family, Max's family, David Hirsh Zeftel and his family. Mama sobbed as she hugged me. Everyone standing behind her on the porch and the street was in tears. An unpredictable, frightening future lay ahead and to all of us this leave-taking was sorrowful in a way no other departure had been. It felt like we were being torn apart, and no one could say when we might see each other again. "Got zohl dir hieten," Mama said through her tears, "un Got zohl dir benshen." "May God take care of you, Wilo. May He bless you."

Dziuda, the wagon driver, was a friendly, gregarious man. He loved to talk, especially about the years he had spent in New York working and saving enough to come back to the village and raise his living standards. In New York they hadn't been able to pronounce "Dziuda." so they just called him "Jew," which Dziuda, a Pole, found humorous. But I wasn't in the mood to talk. I felt almost desperate about leaving my mother, but also elated at the prospect of being reunited with Wusia. Throughout the entire trip to Grzymalov, and then on the train to Lvov, I was lost in conflicting emotions.

I showed up at Wusia's door with two suitcases. One held my clothing, the other was bursting with dry foods and smoked meats that I had been hoarding ever since I had heard about the food shortages. For a couple of days I slept on the living room sofa. Then she arranged for me to rent a room in one of the buildings she managed on Nabielacka Street in a beautiful tree-shaded quarter that had been one of Lvov's most exclusive residential neighborhoods. On Nabielacka Street, elegant four and five story apartment buildings with wrought iron balconies overlooked flower beds and ornamental shrubbery in what I imagined was a facsimile of the best neighborhoods in Paris or London.

The area was so attractive that when the Soviets took over they evicted the former wealthy residents and sent them to Siberia. Then they moved their own high officials and NKVD families into the vacated apartments. The room Wusia arranged for me was in a large apartment formerly belonging to an elderly aristocratic lady. Because of her age the Russians had permitted her to stay, along with the almost equally aged woman who took care of her and was her companion. The two of them were now living in one of their three bedrooms. An accountant and his pregnant wife occupied the other bedroom, and I would live in the third. The building superintendent was a Ukrainian woman, Kataryna Wowkowa, a simple, friendly person, with a ready smile, who lived in a basement room. We'd say hello whenever we saw each other, but there was nothing at all about her that would suggest the extraordinary courage that she would display later on.

Meanwhile, Wusia's parents made arrangements for me to see a famous orthopedic surgeon whom they had heard about from a doctor friend. Professor Gruca was not only a great specialist; he had a lot of experience treating war injuries. When the Soviets came in they had taken him to Leningrad to treat the wounded returning from their disastrous invasion of Finland.

His opinion was the same as Franka's—the bones had been improperly set in Gostynin and Kutno and now the foot wasn't aligned correctly. But Professor Gruca's preferred course of treatment was different from hers. "If you want to walk normally," he said, "I'll have to break the ankle again and reset it properly."

I agreed instantly, although the thought of breaking the ankle for a third time was sickening. Still, this was an opportunity to recover completely and I couldn't turn it down. On July 13, my friend Chaim Rosen took me into Dr. Gruca's office, where he had a small operating room next to his examination room. The only other thing I remember is Dr. Gruca fitting the ether mask and telling me to breathe in and count to three. Supposedly by three you would be fast asleep. At twenty I was still counting. I seem to recall Dr. Gruca looking at me with a funny expression. When I awoke I had a cast on my right ankle.

Two weeks later Dr. Gruca removed the cast. He examined my foot and measured it. "Good," he said. "Now have a shoemaker raise your sole an eighth of an inch and your heel a quarter of an inch. Then you'll be all set." And that was that. Between Franka, the bonesetter of Touste, and the great Professor Gruca, my invalid days were over.

In September school started. The Soviets had made some changes, the most obvious one was that they had sent Badian and his family to Siberia and had elevated Horaztzy Horowitz. Apparently a Korkis staff member, nobody knew exactly who it was, had denounced Badian as a reactionary. The fact that he had been a Czarist officer sealed his fate. I felt very badly about Badian and his wife Maria, who had been so kind to me. But given what happened later, it turned out that the Russians did them a great favor. The whole family survived Siberia, which would have been unlikely had they remained in Lvov.

Although the Russians changed directors, they didn't change the make-up of Korkis' students. The school had always been for Jewish students and it stayed that way, but they eliminated the Jewish part of the curriculum. They probably would have arrested Rabbi Bartfield, who taught those subjects, but he was widely admired and somehow Horowitz and the others managed to hide him in an administrative job.

Another Soviet change was that the school now had a *politruk*, a political officer. Every day started off with an assembly of the students and teachers at which the *politruk* would give us a political lecture. This usually consisted of a recap of the news and its meaning from a Communist perspective, at the end of which the whole school would intone "Long live Father Stalin." Every other function or gathering at the school was also concluded by a chorus of "Long Live Father Stalin", and each classroom was now furnished with a large smiling picture of the "Father of the Peoples."

The Soviets brought their own way of doing things to Lvov. They had a powerful dislike of religion and wealth, and they were ruthless. They simply got rid of rich people or those they considered reactionary, either by sending them into exile or making them disappear into the dreaded Brygidki prison. If you fell into either of those categories, the NKVD made you very afraid.

But if you didn't, life under the Soviets had some definite advantages—for Jews especially. Suddenly people became very respectful. The Soviets made anti-Semitism a crime, and in Russia the crime rate was very low. The NKVD didn't believe in different levels of criminal activity. They didn't divide offenses into misdemeanors and felonies of different degrees. They just sent you to Siberia, and that was the end of you. The result was that all crimes became extremely rare, including insults to Jews. Besides that, you

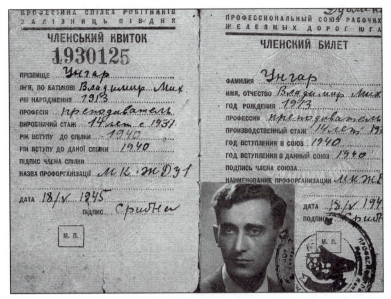

Identification as a teacher at the Technical High School in Lvov, under Soviet occupation, 1940

began to see Jews in high positions, which would have been unthinkable before. There were Jewish army officers, Jewish party members, and Jewish city officials. The atmosphere had changed entirely.

Ever since I had come back to Lvov, Wusia and I spent every minute we could together. I had some hesitation about proposing to Wusia until after my ankle had healed and I saw how it was going to work out with my job. But soon after the school year started I decided it was time. That night on a bench in Jura Park I proposed. It wasn't a matter of getting down on one knee. Each of us knew what was in the other's mind and neither had any doubt about our love. I'm sure Wusia was just waiting until I felt confident enough to bring the subject up. It was an emotional moment when I told her I loved her and that I thought we should finally be united once and forever. Her eyes shone with happiness. "You know that's what I want, Wilo," she said. We remained on the bench till late that night, making plans, so excited by the idea that it was finally going to happen that we didn't want to leave. It was another soft, starry night, like that night a year ago in the Jesuit Garden when Wusia had told me "I hope God brings us together soon." Such incredible things had happened, but here we were again. We felt blessed, as if we really were a pair made in heaven.

The next Sunday we ate at Wusia's house, along with her brother Sunio and his fiancée. By this time her mother and father were prepared for what we had in mind. It was no surprise when I told them that Wusia and I wanted to get married and that we were asking for their blessing. They seemed delighted. They had always liked me, and now that I was healthy again and had a good job whatever nervousness they might have had was gone. October 7 seemed like a good day for the wedding. It was the Soviets' national day, and to celebrate the Revolution they gave everyone a short vacation. Getting married on the seventh would allow us to have a few days honeymoon.

I don't know exactly what Wusia was thinking during the four weeks between our dinner that night and our wedding. I was living in another world completely. Somehow I did all the things I had to. I got up in the morning and dressed. I found my way to school. I taught. But these activities had nothing to do with my inner world, which was filled with expectation and longing. I felt on the verge of a new life, as if I was watching myself being changed into something I had never been. I didn't understand it. This wasn't some sudden, falling headfirst in love with someone you have just met. I had known Wusia since she was sixteen. We had come to know each other gradually. We had fallen in love by degrees. But only now, with the consummation of our love so near, was I beginning to understand what she meant in my life. Perhaps it was something about being one with the one you truly love—this is how it seemed to me—there was something transforming about that, something that changed you, that made you come alive in a new way. When you put one together with one you get something greater than two, something that liberates you from your old way of being. You put off your old clothes and put on your new. I was full of an electrifying tension at the prospect of our union. I was beset by my need for her.

We were married on the seventh, by Rabbi Freund, in the Zamarstynov Street synagogue. Sunio was my best man and his fiancée was Wusia's maid of honor. Wusia wore a light blue dress with a matching hat and a short veil. From under the wedding canopy I watched her come down the aisle, so graceful, so beautiful, her mother and father on either side. Halfway up they both kissed her cheeks and I came down to escort her the rest of the way. Under the wedding canopy the rabbi recited the traditional seven blessings, then made the blessing over wine and offered us a sip from the cup. We should not, he said, be discouraged by the obstacles we would inevitably find in our path, but should always love each other according to the holy commitment we were now making. In the sanctity of our marriage, with God's blessing, we would live in the hope of a future filled with happiness. I put the wedding ring on Wusia's finger—a seamless circle the rabbi said, symbolizing the eternity of marriage and love. We were now, he said, husband and wife. I lifted Wusia's veil. Still standing under the wedding canopy, we kissed. I broke the wine glass, symbol of the destroyed Temple, a reminder that even in the midst of happiness sorrow lurks, that grief touches joy. I kissed her again, listening to the shouts of *mazel tov* from our family and friends.

The reception was at a small hall we had rented. Chaim Rosen was there and other colleagues from the Korkis school, Wusia's family and friends as well as a few companions from my old days in the Zionist youth movement. But from Krasne there was only Dvorah, sent by my mother to represent the family. There was little money for tickets, and the Russians wouldn't give permits for what they considered unimportant travel. One per family was enough for a wedding. I knew how my mother would have loved to be there, what a joy it would have been in her life. It hurt badly that she had been denied the chance. Sorrow in happiness, I thought. Suffering in joy.

A dream fulfilled.
Wusia under the wedding canopy, October 7, 1940

We went home from the reception, to the room at Nabielacka 12. I didn't carry Wusia across the threshold. It was only after we were inside and I closed the door that I picked her up and lifted her onto the bed. I can still to this minute feel her clasping her hands behind my neck. I think the feel of her lips when she kissed me made a permanent impression in the memory center of my brain, the place that records our history. For many years I remembered that single kiss almost daily. I am still reminded, after decades. Does each marriage have moments of such permanent clarity, or is it only those that burn like brief but incandescent candles, extinguished before the years accumulate their rollcall of other joys and sorrows? We lay on our marriage bed and embraced an embrace without end. "Your eyes are like pools in Heshbon." The words from the Song of Songs of King Solomon came into my head though I hadn't read them for years. "Your eyes are like pools in Heshbon, your breath like the fragrance of apples. Your mouth like choicest wine. Let it flow my beloved, as new wine glides over the sleepers' lips." How many times had we looked into each other's faces that still we could not look enough? "Do you remember your story from the Talmud?" Wusia said when at last I turned off the light. Later I felt her finger tracing a pattern on my back, something familiar. It was the W that I recognized first, then the U.

When I opened my eyes late the next afternoon, an angel's smile was on Wusia's lips. I awakened her with a kiss to our first day of togetherness.

10

SILKEN GLOVES

October 1940 – July 1941

The next few evenings we spent with Wusia's parents, otherwise we rarely went out. We lay together in bed and talked. We decided to take our summer vacation in Krasne where Wusia would meet my mother and the rest of my family and I'd be able to show her the places of my childhood. I'd take her to the pond where I skipped stones and the apple orchard where I loved to lie in the shade and read poetry or memorize verses from the Prophets. We'd explore the forest, which I knew so well, and we'd walk the path to Sadzawki where I went so often to meet friends.

I told her the secrets of my youth. I hadn't always been the polite, quiet boy she knew I said, and I boldly related the story of Blima Zeftel and the frog that I found one day in the Zeftel's backyard. I told her how I caught the frog and put it in a can, then put the can upside down on Blima's head. How Blima didn't know what was jumping in her hair and how her yells and screams had been so satisfying. I told her how I had broken the painting of the Polish kings during a game of indoor catch when the teacher wasn't there, how they expelled me from school, and how once I had set fire to the back door of our house when my older brother Herman locked me out. I even told her the story of my brother Max's baby girl Manya, which I had never told to anybody before.

It had happened when I was about ten or eleven years old and Manya was maybe fifteen months. Max and his wife Henia wanted to go to the yearly fair in Skalat and they asked if I would baby-sit. I said sure. At first everything was fine. I played with Manya and she seemed to be having a good time. Then, for no apparent reason she started crying. I did everything I could think of to distract her, but nothing worked. Finally I held her upside down and shook her. But that didn't do any good either. If anything it seemed to make her cry even harder, so I put her down. By then she was practically hysterical. She was still at it hours later when Max and Henia came home.

Even then Manya didn't stop, until finally Max and Henia became concerned. In Krasne whenever a child suffered from some mysterious affliction, the custom was to consult the old Ukrainian woman who specialized in incantations. In the Jewish *shtetls* a Jewish person served this function, an *ubshprecherin* they called this person, a spellbinder. But Krasne's Jewish community wasn't big enough to have our own spellbinder, so the Jews went to the Ukrainian woman instead.

When Max and Henia explained the problem, the old woman made her divinations, which she did with the help of a chicken egg. When the egg had finished its business she told them that the baby was crying because she was afraid of a young boy. Fortunately for me, the egg didn't reveal the young boy's identity, and Max and Henia never imagined that I might be the culprit. I had escaped judgment. Eventually Manya stopped crying and no one knew any better.

My brother, Max; his wife, Henia (sitting); and my sister, Dvorah (standing), 1920

Wusia laughed at my stories, but there were few secrets from her own childhood that I didn't know already, so it was hard for her to reciprocate. We had a lot in common, both of us the youngest children of parents who doted on us and loved each other. But whereas I had grown up running free in the forest, Wusia was the only daughter, always the most sheltered and protected of children. She tried to answer my stories, but all she could think of was one boy who had liked her in junior high school and expressed his affection by developing stomach aches through which he hoped to win her attention. When she told me about that we both laughed, not so much at the boy and his unrequited love as at the innocence of Wusia's life.

In those days the Soviets had shut down most of Lvov's social activities. They had gotten rid of the rich, who had supported the theater and opera, and they had closed the ethnic and religious social organizations and their cultural programs. The Jewish community center was now gone and the Zionist groups outlawed. But we didn't care that there was little to do; we were lost in each other. During the day we went to our jobs. In the evening I was now taking engineering courses at the Polytechnic (previously it had been almost impossible for Jews to get in, but the Soviets had opened its courses to everyone who was qualified), but I was always back by 8:30 or nine. After I got home we'd spend the time in each other's arms, talking, planning, and remembering that, after everything, all the dreams we had dreamed in the Jesuit Garden were coming true. We loved our marriage. We loved our lives. We were sure that the universe was good and that we had found the secret of its meaning.

A month or so later Wusia went to her family doctor for a regular checkup. I can't remember that I even knew she had an appointment. That night when I got back from the Polytechnic and we had settled down with each other as usual she said she had news. The doctor had told her she was pregnant.

Wusia was as surprised as I was. Neither of us expected it. We hadn't planned on having a child so soon, but once we started talking about it we realized that now that it had happened we were both extremely glad. Giving life to a new baby would be the extension of our being together, the most natural and wonderful result of our love.

I had thought that nothing could make me happier, but the anticipation of this child did. Wusia was exuberant. People say that women become more beautiful in pregnancy because of the physiological changes. For Wusia I think it was the inner happiness this baby in her womb brought her. I could see her changing. Her skin began to acquire a soft luminescence; her hair became more luxuriant and lustrous. Her ordinarily happy nature now seemed to me like a radiant aura. We didn't choose names. Nor did we buy any baby paraphernalia—there were Jewish customs about such things that we adhered to without thinking. Until a baby is born, you don't prepare anything in advance, so as not to attract the evil eye. We talked endlessly about how our lives would be different when the baby arrived and about the joyous future the three of us would have together. Expecting the baby and looking forward to this new life brought us even closer. We imagined what the baby would be like and talked about how we would rear our child.

———————

June 1941

The room at Nabielacka 12 was our world. Whatever might have been going on outside, we had each other, and we had this wonderful new being who would soon be joining us. In fact *Pravda* and *Izvestia*, which were now the city's only two papers, didn't carry much news about the war that was still going on between England and Germany. The previous June we heard that France had surrendered, but after that the news became even sketchier. Dunkirk wasn't a name anyone in the Soviet Union knew. We heard nothing about Goering's *Luftwaffe* bombing Britain or the British airforce responding over Germany.

With 30,000 Jewish refugees in Lvov from western Poland, there was a lot of talk about German atrocities there, but here too, the Soviets did their best to suppress information. The fact was that by the summer and fall of 1940, a year after the war, some of the refugees even started going back. Most had left family behind and they had no good way of weighing the risks. The Russians even made a big announcement in the newspapers that conditions were tolerable in the German area and people should register to return. Thousands did, although it turned out to be a horrible Soviet trick. Once people registered, the Russians arrested them as untrustworthy elements and sent them off to Siberia.

Whatever might or might not be happening on the German side, it was pretty clear that Russia and Germany had reached some kind of *modus vivendi*. Now that the issue of Poland was settled, the Soviets wanted only peace and goodwill. Everyone could see that. From where we sat it seemed that Germany wanted the same.

Wrapped in the cocoon of our love, Wusia and I had little interest in the subject, especially as the months went by and her delivery time drew closer. One day in early June at the Korkis School morning assembly the *politruk* made an odd remark. During the usual rundown of current events he mentioned, "our friendly neighbors," with what seemed to be a sarcastic edge. Then, a few days later he said in passing that "our western neighbors with their silken gloves are not perhaps to be fully trusted."

His phrasing stuck in my mind, the "silken gloves" part. Before he had never said a single derogatory word about the Germans. Strange, I thought. Was there something going on between Russia and Germany? I didn't spend much time pondering it. We were well into June already and our baby was due in July. There was a lot to think about. With only a month or so to go Wusia's belly suddenly seemed much bigger. While our one room on Nabielacka was perfect for the two of us, we were beginning to think that maybe we should start looking for something a little more spacious.

On June 22 I went to school as usual. The school year was almost over and as I walked from Nabielacka to St. Teresa I was thinking about the summer. With Wusia's time so near we weren't going to be able to go to Krasne as we had originally planned. Instead we'd stay home and enjoy our baby. Having this child in the middle of the summer would actually be perfect. With school on vacation I'd have all the time in the world to be at home. True, I didn't have any idea what it meant to take care of a baby, but I knew Wusia would be a wonderful mother, and I wanted to do everything I could to help her. Of course her mother would be there too, so it seemed to me we had everything arranged.

I got to Korkis as usual that morning at about eight, before the students arrived. As I walked past the office Chaim Rosen came out of the teacher's room looking pale. "Did you hear the radio?" he asked.

"No. Why?"

"We just heard it. The Germans attacked this morning at Przemsyl."

"What?" I couldn't believe it. "Why did they attack?" My first thought was that something must have happened at the border that had flared into a fight, some incident.

I thought about the bridge over the River San and the two checkpoints. Had the Germans attacked the Russian border guards at the bridge?

"Nobody knows why," said Chaim. "But it's not just Przemsyl. It's the whole border. The Germans are attacking everywhere."

Other teachers were milling around in the hallway now as the students started to come in.

"Listen," said Chaim. "Where's the *politruk?* He'll know what's going on." But nobody had seen the *politruk,* and none of the other Russian administrators seemed to be in school either.

"What are we going to do?" asked another teacher. "Are we supposed to run?"

"What do you mean run?" said Chaim. "Where would we run? Besides, the students are coming in. We have to have assembly."

We had assembly. The *politruk* never showed up, so there was nobody to give the news and commentary and nobody to lead us in thanking Father Stalin. After a few minutes we just dismissed the students to their classes. In my math class I even tried to put on a show of teaching for a few minutes. But it was a charade. Instead we started talking about what was happening, but they didn't know anything at all. Before long we just decided to let the students go home.

After that the Jewish teachers, which were most of us, stayed and talked. What should we do if the Germans come? Chaim suggested to me that maybe the two of us and our families should climb up into the attic in his building and pull the ladder after us so that the Germans couldn't get up there. It was a joke, but an uncomfortable one.

The fact was that nobody was prepared for this. People feared the Nazis, but who could have believed that Germany would attack the Soviet Union. Even now nobody was screaming that we should get out any way we could, even if that thought might have been in the back of people's minds. Maybe the Russians would drive them back, and anyway, where could we go? Besides, with Wusia nine months pregnant running was unthinkable. Where would money come from? How would we live? How would we get there? We had no car, nothing.

Wusia's reaction when I got home was like mine. She was worried, but not panicked. We didn't have a radio, but we heard things from neighbors. The Fascists were attacking all over. The radio was making appeals to patriotism, calling on people to fight for the fatherland. Outside there were no signs of war yet, no bombing or artillery, but Russian military units were moving through the streets and lines had started forming at the state run grocery stores.

That night Wusia and I were tense. We talked about what to do, but the only real course was to hope for the best.

It didn't seem impossible that things might still come out well; after all, the Red Army was tremendously powerful. That's what we had been hearing for the last year and a half. We had even learned the patriotic and military songs, and listening to those deep Russian basses sing gave you such an impression of strength and resilience. The great Red Army might be a little chaotic, but it didn't seem likely that such a massive force could be anything but invincible in the end. Russia was a gigantic, vigorous country. How likely was it that Germany could defeat her?

Over the next few days Wusia went to work each morning and I went to school. We had dismissed the students; it was just about the end of the semester anyway. But getting together gave the teachers the chance to share the news and give each other moral support. By now it was obvious the Russians were clearing out. All their movement was toward the east, a bad sign. For everybody the conviction was that we could expect hard times. We knew that soon we would be facing what the Jews in western Poland had experienced during the past year—armbands, mistreatment, labor camps, food shortages. We knew the Germans were beginning to segregate Jews and restrict them in various ways. We had heard about atrocities, shootings, disappearances, but these were mainly rumors. One could at least hope that they were exaggerated, or maybe even untrue.

It was obviously going to be a bad situation, but people had no real fear for their lives yet. A bad situation, all right, but how bad could it be we asked ourselves. People began talking about the German occupation twenty some years ago during the World War. For the most part they had been decent, one could even say civilized, especially compared to the Russians. After all, German culture was the world's highest—Goethe, Schiller, Heine, Beethoven, Brahms, Mendelssohn. Heine had even been a Jew, as was Mendelssohn. Anything could happen in war, of course. But Jews were always prepared for bad times, and it wasn't so great under the Polish anti-Semites either. Among the Korkis teachers, among all Lvov's Jews I think, a thousand rationalizations flowered into psychological escape routes, each promising the hope of security. Nobody had yet heard the word extermination. Despite pogroms, even despite the memories of Khmelnytsky, I think that until then no one truly believed in the actual existence of pure Evil.

July 1941

On the morning of July 1 a rumor circulated that the German army would march into Lvov. For several days we had seen no Russians; the last of their units had moved out and people were saying that German paratroops were cutting off their retreat to the east of the city. Supposedly the victors were planning to hold a parade down Leona Sapiehy Street, three blocks from Nabielacka.

I decided to go and see what the German soldiers looked like. I had been bombed and strafed and I had been lying in their hospitals, but except for a few border guards in Przemsyl I had never actually seen German soldiers. Jews were going to stay as far as possible from this parade, but I could blend in easily enough. I didn't expect any danger.

The crowds were already thick on Leona Sapiehy Street when I got there. They seemed to be almost all Ukrainian, clapping and cheering and shouting enthusiastic 'Heil Hitlers,' even though nobody was in sight yet. They were really worked up. They couldn't wait for the Germans to arrive to hand over the keys to a free western Ukraine.

I pushed to a place near the front where I could get a good look. While I was making my way forward the crowd suddenly began roaring; it sounded as if they were going into some kind of frenzy. A minute later the first Germans came down the street. As they began to pass by my spot I could only think of one thing—Roman Legions. It was like looking at the triumphal march of the Roman Legions, with all the regalia and symbols of the conquering armies of Augustus Caesar. The only thing missing was a triumphal arch. First the generals rolled by in huge open cars. Then came other high officers riding magnificent stallions. Red and black Nazi flags and swastikas waved past, carried by ramrod straight bearers. With a rumble that made the ground vibrate came the tanks—tank after tank after tank. I had seen a few Russian tanks in Lvov, but never up close. These German tanks I watched from feet away—huge, frightening, steel monsters that growled like giant engines of death. Finally the infantry came by, goose-stepping. I thought of my artillery regiment's poor excuse for a parade before we left for the front. All show with no substance, artillery soldiers wearing cavalry boots—and not much show either compared to this. Rank after rank goose-stepped by with perfect precision. You could smell their arrogance. We had been right out of the 19th century. The Russian troops who occupied Lvov after Poland's defeat were slovenly and careless. These Germans were precision marchers, and precision, disciplined killers. It was no wonder they had destroyed the Poles so easily and run the Russians off with hardly a fight.

The parade went on and on, it took the infantry almost three hours to march by. The Germans had obviously organized this to make the biggest impression they could. I stood there, mesmerized, caught between the inhuman strength of the goose-stepping Germans and the fanatic enthusiasm of the crowd which through all that time never stopped screaming "Heil Hitler" and throwing out stiff-armed Nazi salutes.

11

ANOTHER
WARM SUNDAY

Summer 1941 – Summer 1942

Back home I told Wusia not to go outside under any circumstances. I described what I had seen, the wild crowds and the endless ranks of goose-stepping Nazis. Whatever the Germans wanted to do, would be done. If they decided to stir up the Ukrainians into action against the Jews, who knew what the consequences might be? We could find ourselves in the midst of a bloodbath. I thought neither of us should go out, at least for a day or two until we could see how the situation developed. The last thing I wanted was to expose Wusia to danger, or myself either.

For the next week we stayed inside, though now and then I ventured out. A Ukrainian militia was on the streets hunting for Jews. I wondered where they came from—nobody had ever heard of a Ukrainian militia. People said that Ukrainian officials had arrived with the Germans, members of Stepan Bandera's nationalist movement which had been working alongside the Nazis even in Berlin. Supposedly these

"Banderists" had organized the local Ukrainians. I saw militiamen arrest a few Jews near our house and I heard they were carrying out large-scale pogroms and roundups in the Jewish quarter. I didn't investigate. It was best to stay away from trouble, I thought. Not many Jews lived in our neighborhood. It wasn't likely the Ukrainians would come marching down Nabielacka Street in force.

I knew that as long as we stayed out of the way we would be relatively safe. But even in our room it was hard to suppress a feeling of being hunted. Rumors circulated. Our neighbors talked about the murders, shootings and beatings. People were being abducted. We heard the Germans were sending large numbers of Jews into the Brydigki prison, which until a week ago had been the NKVD's headquarters. Now it was the Gestapo's. Someone said that Rabbi Yehezkiel Lewin, one of Lvov's leading rabbis, had been killed under mysterious circumstances. Something strange and terrible was going on inside the Brydigki, but what it was we couldn't learn.

Wusia and I were afraid. I made little excursions outside to get some news and buy food, but I never went far. Depending mostly on rumor and some of our neighbors' first hand observations, we had the impression that death was loose in the streets. The Germans had set the Ukrainians off into a bloodthirsty frenzy. Jews were being herded into Gestapo prisons on Lecki Street and Zamarstynowska as well as into the Brydigki. It was said that nobody who went into these places came out again.

About a week and a half after the Germans arrived posters went up on walls and lampposts, written in Polish and Ukrainian. The posters announced that from now on all Jews over 12 years were to wear a white armband with a blue Star of David on it. Those caught without one would be liable to the severest penalties. Jews over 14 were ordered to register for work, at their previous place of employment if they had one. Only people with working papers would be eligible for bread coupons.

It seemed as if the Germans were pulling in the reins. First they gave the streets to the Ukrainians, but after a week and a half of mayhem it was time to bring things back under German control. They had made the point that they could unleash terror whenever they wanted. Now it was time to impose order so they could proceed more efficiently. Not that we saw it that way at the time. The German method only became comprehensible after you were exposed to it for a while. To understand it you had to grasp the enormity of what they had in mind, which almost no one had the imagination to do. There were a hundred and sixty thousand or so Jews in Lvov. You couldn't just start slaughtering that many people without causing uprisings and flight and other inconvenient reactions. With so many people, the only way to proceed efficiently was step by step. And to go step by step you needed order.

But we didn't see it. That first week and a half taught us that you could be terrorized and hopeful at the same time. The Germans had introduced us all to the art of denial, whose guiding principle is: Just because it's happening to others doesn't mean it's going to happen to me. When I reported to the Korkis School to register for work, I began the second and most deadly stage of my education according to this principle, which eventually led me straight to disaster.

The Germans who took over Korkis weren't anything like the robots I had watched on Leona Sapiehy Street. The new director was a heavyset Prussian named Hildebrand, whom we just glimpsed the first day and who stayed in his office after that, emerging only on rare occasions to inspect the school. He did this by marching ramrod straight through the hallways, looking neither right nor left, until he had completed a circuit of the entire building. The man who really ran things was Herr Luftig, a friendly individual who showed no animosity toward Jews. Luftig announced to us that Korkis had been reorganized. The school was now going to become a technical training center to prepare Aryans for work in German military industries. From this point on the training center and all its employees belonged to the *Luftwaffe*, the German air force. All of the staff would be retained and each of us would receive a special *Luftwaffe* identity card. We would be working under German administrators, but the faculty would still be in charge of the educational side of the school.

The announcements instantly put me and the fifteen or twenty other Jewish teachers at ease. An ID document gave its owner a degree of security. An ID card announced that you were an officially recognized person, with certain rights—the right to work, to buy food, to go from place to place. It said you were legal. And ours were going to be *Luftwaffe* cards, which had to be the best available. After all, what could be safer than being an essential worker for the *Luftwaffe*? You could practically hear the sighs of relief.

We didn't feel quite so relieved though after the announcements and registration were through and we all had a chance to talk and find out what everyone else knew. Wusia and I had heard about the roundups at the Brydigki prison. But some of my colleagues knew more. Apparently the Germans had decided that the Brydigki would make good propaganda. The Soviet secret police had used the place for interrogations, and it was common knowledge that they had executed people there. Somehow the Germans learned that many of these unfortunates had been buried in the prison courtyard and they decided to make the Jews exhume the corpses as a public spectacle that would forever associate the Jews with the Bolshevik murderers in the minds of Lvov's citizenry. Every day large numbers of Jews were commandeered and put to work in front of crowds of jeering Ukrainians and Poles, breaking through the courtyard stones and dragging decomposed bodies out of their graves. Afterwards many of the diggers were taken into the prison and shot. The same kind of exercise also went on at the Lecki and Zamarstakowa Street prisons, which had also been NKVD execution sites.

It seemed that almost everyone knew about Rabbi Yehezkiel Lewin, who had indeed been murdered. When the Ukrainian mobs went on their killing rampage the day after the Germans marched in, Rabbi Lewin had gone to see Metropolitan Andrei Sheptytsky in his palace on Jura Mountain. There, Sheptytsky had told Lewin he would do what he could to stop the killing, and he had promised to immediately write a pastoral letter on the subject. Then he asked the Rabbi to stay with him in the palace, at least until the streets were safe. Lewin refused, saying his place was with his people. One of Sheptytsky's priests was sent to accompany Lewin home. But somewhere along the way Lewin had told the priest to go back. Shortly after that the Rabbi was abducted by the Ukrainian militia and shot, either by them or by the Germans, nobody knew for sure. Word did get out later about his burial site, an unmarked grave in the Holosko woods outside the city.

That first day of school was the beginning of a strangely schizophrenic life. With the Gestapo and Ukrainian militia roaming the city, no Jew was safe from beatings, roundups, murders or disappearances. At the same time I was possessed by a strange and illogical, but nevertheless powerful sense that I myself would not be touched. Not wearing the Jewish armband was a death offense, but I didn't wear one. Each morning I walked from Nabielacka to the school strutting along like any Ukrainian or Pole. Nor did we have to wear one in the school building itself. Herrs Luftig and Hildebrand didn't care about it; they acted as if armbands weren't any of their business.

The German school administrators weren't SS, they were educators who had to make sure they got their job done, and as such they had to be disciplinarians, not toward us, but toward the students. At the former Korkis School German order was now observed, which meant that students always showed the utmost respect for teachers—even if those teachers happened to be Jews—who, when outside, were allowed to be kicked and beaten at will. They lined up at attention for roll call, called me "sir" and stood whenever I entered the room. I'd tell my classes "Good morning," and they'd answer back "Good morning, sir professor," in unison, exactly as if the etiquette of the Empire were still in place.

At home, Wusia and I pushed our anxieties into the background. We were more and more consumed by the approaching birth. In some inexplicable way, expecting the baby made it impossible to be too morose about the grim prospects that had arrived with the Germans. Whatever the present was like, we both took it for granted that the future would be bright. How could it be otherwise? We spent hours visualizing our baby and talking about how we would bring it up. With my ear pressed to Wusia's belly I listened to the interior noises. I felt the baby's movements, the kicking and twisting and stretching. Toward the end of July it didn't seem that she could get any bigger.

On July 21 I came home from school to find a note from Wusia's parents—they had taken her to the hospital. I didn't go there. In Poland it was not the custom for the husband to be there to provide moral support for his wife in labor, so men weren't particularly welcome at maternity hospitals. Instead I spent a sleepless night at home, wondering how things were going and trying to picture how our baby would look.

The next day after classes I walked to her parents' home on Sheptytsky Street. Her father answered the door and clasped both my hands in his. Wusia had given birth to a beautiful, healthy, baby boy. Wusia's mother was still at the hospital, but all three were expected home in a day or two. The plans were already made. For a while she'd be staying at their house where there was more room and Wusia's mother would be there to help.

Two days later Wusia returned home. I walked in after school and there she was in bed, the baby in her arms. I was instantly entranced. I had never seen anything so perfect. Wusia showed him to me, though I was afraid to hold him. As the youngest at home I had never been exposed to the care and feeding of babies. They were a mystery to me, even this one that I had helped create. A miracle, yes, but how does one hold a miracle without dropping it? Wusia showed me the perfection of his fingers and toes, his delicate ears, his eyes, which were her eyes, his fine blond hair, like mine. We looked at each other and couldn't believe that there was this new being who all of a sudden belonged to us and was part of us, but there he was.

At eight days the baby was circumcised. Even under German occupation, the idea of not circumcising him never entered my head. Trying to look back at that time, not with hindsight, but through the eyes of those days, the truth was that even with Jewish blood being spilled daily, Wusia and I saw the future not as death and destruction, but survival. I hadn't the slightest doubt that this child of ours would flourish and that we would be there to nurture him. As the *mohel* began the circumcision I recited the blessing, "Blessed art Thou O Lord our God, King of the universe, who has sanctified us with Thy commandments and commanded us to enter our sons into the covenant of our father Abraham." Then I gave him my father's name—Michael.

And so my son took his place among his people. Outside, at the very moment of his circumcision, a whirlwind of death was sweeping through Jewish neighborhoods. The Petlyura Days had started, a Ukrainian pogrom organized to commemorate the assassination of their hetman Simon Petlyura at the hands of a Jew in retaliation for Petlyura's massacres as he marched through Galicia in 1921. Ordinarily, circumcision is a joyful affair when a child is welcomed into the covenant. But Michael's rite of passage meant something additional, which I think everyone in the room felt keenly. Here was hope in the midst of fury, a new Jewish life announcing itself in the face of the destruction of Jewish lives.

Thirty days after Michael's birth we celebrated the redemption of the firstborn son. As this ceremony has to be performed by a *Kohen*, someone from the priestly class, we invited my friend David Kahane, a fellow teacher from the school. Some relatives, friends and neighbors attended, and everyone commented on the serene child who was already beginning to give little smiles to anyone who looked in his direction. Among Wusia's parents' closest friends were the Orlinskys, a childless Polish couple who lived in the same building. From the way they cooed at Michael and looked at him so lovingly, even I could tell how they longed for a child of their own. They told us how beautiful he was, and how sweet tempered. Mrs. Orlinsky held him for a few minutes, and it seemed almost painful for her to give him up. Only much later did it occur to me that, had we only asked, they would have taken Michael as their own in an instant.

It was a terrible summer, a summer of wrath. After the Petlyura days the Germans burned down all of Lvov's synagogues. They rounded up people for forced labor and often those they took away were never seen again. But on Nabielacka Street we remained safe and out of the way.

Wusia and I came to think of our room as a haven from the storms engulfing so many others. At school, I also felt secure, teaching Aryans who were badly needed by the German war industry, with the *Luftwaffe* imprimatur stamped on my identity card. We also had Michael, who kept us so enchanted with his remarkable development that it was easy to forget the outside world.

I had long ago gotten over my nervousness about holding him. When Wusia finished nursing I would carry him around feeling his face against my shoulder, another of those unforgettable sensations. Michael was an easily satisfied baby who soon began to sleep through the nights nestled between us in our bed. When he was awake he treated us to concerts of low-keyed baby sounds, as if he were talking to us. He stared at Wusia while he suckled, as if he was searching her face for something. What kind of associations must he be making, I thought. I was in awe watching her care for him. She never tired of holding, soothing, playing with him, seeing to his least need as if nothing else existed in the universe. I thought about the transition this had been for us, about the passion of our love being transmuted by the presence of this child into something deeper and richer. We tried to discover signs of the kind of person he would become someday. We wondered if his essential personality and character were already there, if we could only know how to see it.

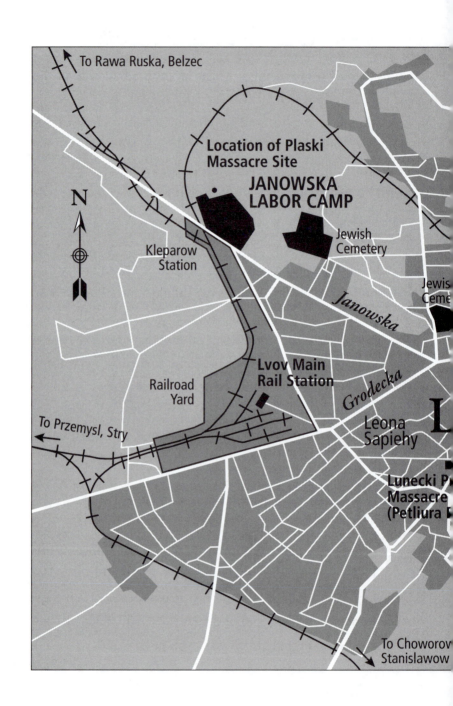

To Rawa Ruska, Belzec

N

Location of Plaski
Massacre Site

**JANOWSKA
LABOR CAMP**

Kleparow
Station

Jewish
Cemetery

Janowska

Jewis
Ceme

Grodecka

Lvov Main
Rail Station

Railroad
Yard

To Przemysl, Stry

L

Leona
Sapiehy

Lunecki P
Massacre
(Petliura

To Choworov
Stanislawow

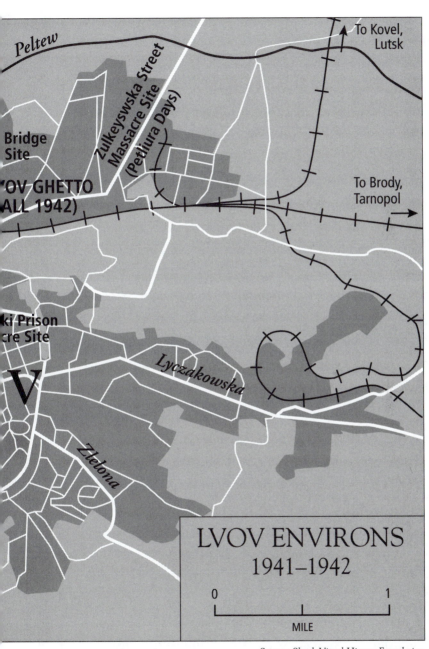

Peltew

Bridge
Site

Zulkeyswska Street
Massacre Site
(Petliura Days)

'OV GHETTO
ALL 1942)

To Kovel,
Lutsk

To Brody,
Tarnopol

ki Prison
cre Site

V

Lyczakowska

Zielona

LVOV ENVIRONS
1941–1942

0   1
MILE

Source: Shoah Visual History Foundation

Fall and Winter, 1941/1942

At the end of September our lives suddenly changed. Notices appeared in the streets announcing the division of the city into three sections, one for Germans, one for Poles and Ukrainians, one for Jews. From now on Nabielacka Street would be reserved exclusively for Germans. Almost immediately a swarm of Nazi officials and Gestapo arrived at our building to claim the best apartments for themselves. At the same time the notices sent many Jewish families into a frenzied search for new quarters in the rundown streets of the Jewish section. Lvov's hundred sixty thousand Jews had to find a way to crowd themselves into neighborhoods that hardly had enough space for those who already lived there. Frantic people hunted for friends, relatives, building janitors, anybody who might know of a spare room or an apartment someone was willing to share.

We were luckier than most. Wusia's grandmother and two aunts still lived at Berka Joselewicza 3, in the apartment where I had once rented a room. The three of us, along with Wusia's parents moved into that apartment. We took very few belongings; there was barely room for the people. The five of us squeezed into the larger of the apartment's two bedrooms. But it wasn't the crowded conditions that bothered me. It was that we had suddenly become vulnerable. The safety of Nabielacka Street was gone. If the Germans wanted to round up Jews, they were now all in one place, Wusia, Michael and I—all Jews. After curfew all Jews would be at home, ripe for snatching. I still believed in my heart that my *Luftwaffe* ID would protect us, but being exposed like this raised new fears.

Another German innovation was the *Judenrat*, a Jewish governing body purportedly serving the Jewish population but whose true function was helping the Germans implement their plans more efficiently by doing much of their work for them. The first president the Germans appointed, Dr. Josef Parnas, disappointed them. Faced with a demand for five hundred Jewish workers, Parnas refused to have them rounded up and turned over. He understood that once these "workers" were taken they would not be seen again. It was reported that he told the Germans the Judenrat wouldn't deliver other Jews to death. This act of great courage cost Parnas his life. The day after his refusal he was arrested and shot. His successor, Dr. Rotfeld, complied with the German demand.

The roundups were led by the Jewish auxiliary police, or militia, whose job was to make sure Jews followed whatever orders the Germans gave. Most of these people volunteered because they thought that being a policeman would help them and their families survive. Some did their best to treat other Jews as well as they could under the circumstances, even on some occasions warning and helping them. But many acted more like devoted servants in the hope of ingratiating themselves with the Gestapo. Others were just callous, brutal people, untouched by any of the nobler sentiments when it came to hunting down their fellows.

That was how the Germans turned Jew against Jew. Often long after curfew the militia was sent out to round up a quota of people for disposal. It might be only 20 or 50, but that was enough to make the whole community afraid of going to sleep. No one knew if the knock on the door might come that night and whether all their loved ones would still be together in the morning. Even though my *Luftwaffe* ID gave me a sense of security, we all knew that anything could happen. Mistakes could be made, and once you were grabbed the chances for rectification were slim.

And so it happened. One night in late fall I was awakened by an incessant banging on our door. I opened it to find two Jewish policemen, an older man and a young tough looking one. I was told harshly that they had orders to take me to the police station.

"Wait a minute," I said. I knew that once I gave myself over to these two I'd be in trouble. I quickly got my ID card and showed it to them.

"You see this? You're making a mistake. You must be looking for someone else."

The young tough one glanced at it. "This doesn't mean anything," he said, tapping his club against his leg. "Just get moving."

"Why? Do you see this or don't you?" I held the card up and pointed to where it said *Luftwaffe*. "I'm an employee, you understand that? You can't take someone who works for these people." Like all the Jewish police, these two carried clubs, like the batons French police use, but no guns.

"Goddammit, when I say move I want you to move," the younger one said, jutting his face into mine. Behind him the older one was hanging back, edging away from us. The young tough gripped my arm. "You son of a bitch," he growled, "Let's go. Now!"

The next instant I stepped on his left foot with my right, grabbed his shirt front with both hands and started shaking him, getting him so off balance he would have toppled if I hadn't been holding him up. "Go with you," I yelled. "Why would I go with you? What are you going to do, beat me?" He jerked away and scuttled back out of range, surprised and snarling with anger, "We'll see who beats who, you bastard. We'll be back to teach you a lesson you won't forget." He turned and disappeared down the steps, his companion tagging after him.

The commotion had awakened the family, but I told them to go back to sleep, everything was all right. When I got into bed Wusia was nursing Michael. "What happened, Wilo?" she said softly. "Is it really all right?"

"Yes," I put my arm over her and the baby. "It was two Jewish policemen, but it's okay now. They went somewhere else." The strange fact is that I was so sure of that ID and so lulled by the warmth of the bed and the little gurgling sounds Michael was making that I dropped back to sleep myself.

Sometime later an even louder banging dragged me out of a dead sleep. When I opened the door this time I looked up into the eyes of a giant standing there with the other two policemen. "Herzl Tismenitzer!" I said, startled. "Wilo Ungar!" said the giant. "What in the world are you doing here?"

I'm exaggerating when I say that Herzl Tismenitzer was a giant. In fact he couldn't have been more than six foot six or seven, but that made him tower over even tall Ukrainians and Poles, let alone Jews. Herzl was an old friend from Krasne. In fact, he had taken over my brother-in-law David's position as manager of the big Wolica estate after David left for Argentina.

"Ungar," he said. "I never expected you to be this violent revolutionary they're talking about. What did you do to them?"

"Nothing," I said. "I did nothing, Herzl. I just told them I'm not going to any police station, and that I'm working for the German Luftwaffe," I showed him my card—"So why should I have to go anywhere?"

"Well," he said, "you'll have to come with me anyway. But don't worry about it. It'll be fine."

A few minutes later the four of us arrived at the former Jewish Community Center on Bernsteina Street. To my surprise, the place was being used as a courthouse. I had no idea anything like this existed, but there it was, judges, lawyers, clerks, and a jail where prisoners were being brought in and registered. A complete nighttime travesty of justice.

A minute later I was standing in front of a "judge," listening as the younger policeman accused me of resistance and abusing him verbally, as well as striking him. When he was finished with his testimony he and his companion were dismissed, leaving me there with Tismenitzer, who was obviously some kind of superior officer. "From what I've been able to find out," Tismenitzer said to the judge, "this man was actually willing to go with them. He did not resist arrest in any way, but his wife was ill in bed with a 104-degree fever and he was afraid to leave her. I think the other two must have misunderstood. He came along with me without causing any trouble."

"Fine," said the judge. "If that's what happened there's no reason to hold him. Case dismissed."

Outside the courtroom the two policemen were waiting for orders to take me away. When I walked by them a free man, they looked perplexed, as if such a thing had never happened before. I was greatly relieved to get back home, where I was met by exclamations of joy from the whole family, all of whom had been in a high state of agitation since I left. The experience was a sobering one. If it hadn't been for Tismenitzer it might have ended very differently. If they put me in jail, I thought, the thing to do would be to get a message to Herr Luftig, the school's amiable assistant director. With his authority he'd be able to get me out instantly. I even knew where to find him after school. Luftig and his family had moved into Nabielacka 12, our old building, where Kataryna Wowkowa was still the superintendent.

By the winter of 1941/1942 we could feel the screws tightening. In a workshop and industrial compound out on Janowska Street, the Germans had established a labor camp where it was known that people were being tortured and murdered. The camp head, a Gestapo named Gebauer, was reputed to be a ruthless sadist. Not far from the camp the Germans had turned a barren, scrubby area known locally as "the Sands," into an execution site and mass grave. To provide workers and victims for Janowska, roundups became more frequent. This increased the frenetic efforts by Jews to get work in factories or organizations that were thought to be important for the German war effort and so might give employees a measure of safety. Many of those arrested didn't end up in Janowska, but simply disappeared, to other labor camps, it was said, somewhere in "the East." By March or April rumors began circulating that one of these camps was located near Belzec, a village not in the east at all but 50 or 60 miles northwest of Lvov where something mysterious and evil was said to be occurring.

That winter Abe Rosenman, Wusia's father, got sick. We had been worried about him for a long time. With no job, he had become more and more depressed, especially after our move to Berka Joselowicza. He was also suffering from an increasingly painful stomach. No one seemed sure of what was wrong; it didn't seem to be dysentery or typhus—two of the prevalent killer diseases. When his condition worsened we took him to the hospital the Judenrat had set up on Rappaporta Street, but after a few days there he died. His death cast gloom over the household, compounded on my part by the anxieties I had about my mother and the rest of my family, whom I had now learned were no longer living in Krasne.

One of my students was from Grzymalov, which we heard had become a concentration point for Jews from the little villages in the vicinity. The Germans had forced all of Krasne's Jewish families out of their homes and transported them there, a worrisome development. Through my student I was able to exchange a few messages with my mother, but nothing she said alleviated my fears. I considered trying to get to Grzymalov to see them, but the danger would have been immense and I didn't feel I could leave Wusia and Michael alone. Under German regulations, wives and children were considered to be covered by a husband's work card. If he was exempt from arrest and deportation, so were they. Taking myself and the protection of my Luftwaffe card away from them, even for a short time, just wasn't an option.

Looking back, I still am appalled when I try to explain or understand just why I placed such faith in that card. I lay the blame on my naiveté, and on illusions and false hopes that I allowed the Germans to instill in me. This was all compounded by the sense of optimism I was born with. I had great confidence I would always have the ability to get by somehow. Despite everything, it seemed to me that my fate was in good hands.

But this is also true, although it gives me little comfort. As frightening as our circumstances were, almost no one guessed at the truth of the Germans' intentions. Terrible things had happened, and more were evident every day, which we saw with our own eyes. But in a way we Jews have been inoculated by our history. With all the pogroms and massacres of the past our people had survived. After each disaster our communities had reestablished themselves and flourished. In Poland suffering was part of our experience, extermination wasn't. Neither the Crusaders nor Khmelnytsky nor Simon Petlyura had ever considered such a thing as a "final solution". Consequently none of us was prepared to grasp so enormous an idea, even as it began to envelop us.

I should have considered what happened to me one Sunday afternoon at the end of April as another warning. Ordinarily the Germans took Sunday as a day of rest from Jew hunting, and I was strolling along Sloneczna Street less cautiously than I should have been. Suddenly, right in front of me two Gestapo were stopping Jews and demanding ID cards. I was so close there was no way of dodging them or running.

"*Du*," one said, "*Jude. Hier. Kennkarte, schnell!*" Little curt orders, given in a staccato bark. I showed them my "*kennkarte*"—my work card, and my precious ID. "Get on the truck," he said, waving toward a flatbed truck waiting some yards away, already half filled with Jews.

"Sir," I said "would I be permitted to drop a note to my family that I am going with you?"

"Yes," came the answer. "You can even tell them you're going to work at Sknilow for the day."

Gingerly I took my ID card from his hand to use it as backing for a scrap of paper that I could scribble a message on. While I was writing the German turned away to capture more victims. Quickly, I jumped on the truck and slipped the ID into my pocket. My senses felt tuned up, as if I had drunk several cups of strong coffee. For several minutes I stood there, watching what was going on and thinking, "This truck isn't for you, Wilo. We might be going to Sknilow, but do you think we're coming back from Sknilow? You've got to do something." A moment later both Germans turned their backs to the truck to deal with yet more Jews and I jumped down. Neither of them saw me as I sprinted behind the nearest building and huddled there listening for noises of someone coming after me. When it seemed safe, I walked down a side street and circled toward home.

That might have served as a warning, telling me my *Luftwaffe* card wasn't the key to salvation I thought it was.

In fact it had the opposite effect. My escape seemed yet another indication that if I kept my wits about me I would be all right. My destiny was clearly to survive, both me and mine.

Summer, 1942

Sometime toward the end of June on another warm Sunday, Wusia and I were talking about going for a walk with Michael, who was now eleven months old and seemed to be getting ready to take his first steps. At some point we became aware that the usual street noises had stopped and other sounds had taken their place. Something was going on. When I looked out the window I saw German police lined up on both sides of the street, not the regular police, but some special unit whose uniform I hadn't seen often. As I watched I saw that groups of police were going from house to house. Already they were herding people into the street; seemingly emptying entire buildings. I just had time to think how odd this was—normally *Aktions*, as they called these large scale roundups, were directed at certain categories, the elderly, the sick, invalids, children, the unemployed—segments of the population that were useless to them. But these police weren't looking at cards, they weren't being selective, they were taking everybody. I just had time to register this, when the banging started inside our building. A moment later the door flew open and one of these police was yelling "*raus, raus, raus*—out, out, out. Everybody out! Now!"

There was no place to hide. Even if there had been a place there was no time. The next moment we were all on the street, grandmother, aunts, Wusia's mother, me, and Wusia holding Michael. As the houses emptied the number of people in the street grew. Above the hubbub I heard voices pleading and crying. I could feel the hysteria building. But there was nothing to do, no way to escape, no one to talk to about your place of employment or anything else. Before long we were lined up in columns with police on both sides as we began to march.

After fifteen minutes or so we were herded into an open area next to the Jan Sobieski School. And there we stood. An hour passed, two hours. Wusia held Michael until her arms became weary, then I held him, then Wusia again. Thousands of people were in this place, obviously brought from other areas than just Berka Joselowicza. This was a huge *Aktion*, much bigger than anything that had happened before. We waited, getting more fatigued and agitated. People around us were breaking down, women were in tears, children cried. Listening to it was almost unbearable. Then the Germans started taking people into the building, individuals, husbands and wives, entire families. When we got inside the commotion was worse than outside. It made you disoriented, the Germans barking their orders, the wailing, the babies screeching. Some German asked for my documents and I gave him my card. He looked at it a moment, then he pushed me to the right and Wusia and Michael to the left. We had no chance to speak. With the others sent to the right I was being propelled out the door. I turned back toward Wusia and our eyes met for an instant, then I was outside in the schoolyard, standing there alone.

I looked at the school building. There was no way back in. For an endless minute my mind was blank, then a thought came, a name. Luftig. I had to get to Luftig.

12

IF ONLY

Summer 1942

I looked around again frantically. No, there was no way in, no way to get back to them. I began walking toward Berka Joselowicza, panicked, my mind blank except for the name, Luftig. Herr Luftig. I knew of cases where people had been rounded up, then someone from the German establishment, from a business or some Nazi agency, had gone down and retrieved them because they were necessary for the war effort. Luftig could do that, I was sure, inasmuch as he was the deputy director of the *Luftwaffe* school. Why not? Wasn't I an essential worker? Wasn't my family covered by my *kennkarte*? A terrible mistake had been made, but one that Luftig could rectify. What I had to do now was get to him and ask.

It was Sunday. Luftig would likely be at home in his apartment at Nabielacka 12. My thoughts were racing. What would I say to him? I didn't know where they were planning to take Wusia and Michael. To a labor camp? To Janowska? Somewhere else? I didn't even want to think where that somewhere else might be; perhaps resettlement in the East, and who knew what that meant? They had taken thousands of people in this *Aktion*; it must have been something special. Luftig could find out. All I needed to do was go and explain it.

I was thinking this as I walked not toward Nabielacka, but toward Berka Joselowicza. Telling myself what I had to do, but inside sick with fear that maybe Luftig wouldn't do it, wouldn't put himself out for some teacher's wife and child, whom he didn't even know. I had to compose myself. If I was going to ask him something like this I couldn't seem hysterical. I had to be able to explain it all coolly and rationally, make him understand that this was a tragic error and that he could put things back in their proper order.

At our apartment I paced around, trying to control myself and rehearsing what I might say to him, what would be the best way to approach him, the best way to phrase my request. This was the most important thing I ever had to do. All my hopes were on this, I had to gather every ounce of my courage. Finally I just closed down the wild thoughts and disconnected sentences that were jumbling in my head. I took off my armband, went out the door, and headed for Nabielacka.

A moment after I knocked, Frau Luftig opened the door. For a second I couldn't find my voice and just stood there. From her expression I could see that she knew she wasn't dealing with somebody normal, even though I was trying hard to keep my composure. What could she think, someone in panic speaking to her in bad German, wanting to see her husband? She knew it must be a Jew, on Nabielacka yet, and on a Sunday. She was polite. Might I speak with Herr Luftig? Yes I might. He was in the study. She would get him.

When Luftig came out we had a short conversation in the hallway. I told him what had happened. "I don't know why they took them, Herr Luftig. They examined my *kennkarte*, then they pushed me in one direction and my wife and child in the other. They made a terrible mistake. I'm sure with all the noise and crowds they were in a hurry and got confused. Would it be possible, perhaps, for you to intervene so that they wouldn't be sent away?"

"Ungar," he said. It was obvious from the way he listened that he was sympathetic, even concerned. "Ungar, I can't give you an answer right now. I'll have to look into it and find out what happened. I don't know what I might be able to do, but let me think about it and make some inquiries. I'll let you know in school tomorrow whether I can help you in some way."

When I got back to the apartment it was late afternoon. Just a few hours earlier the rooms had been crowded with family. Now they were silent and empty. I lay down in our big bed, pictures and thoughts racing through my head of what might be happening to Wusia and Michael, where they were now, where the Germans might be taking them. My fear for them was making me nauseous. But I had hope too.

Luftig hadn't exactly been reassuring, but he hadn't been negative either. He was going to make inquiries. He'd help if he could, and why couldn't he? He could even go to Hildebrand the director, I thought. Hildebrand wasn't an anti-Semite either.

I was still lying on my side of the bed as it got dark. I could almost feel Wusia and the baby, who always slept between us. I fell asleep for a few hours, dreaming of them, but I was awake again before dawn, praying that in a few hours Luftig would have good news for me. "I will cast a faintness into their hearts"—for the first time I truly understood the Biblical verse. When I tried to get out of bed my legs trembled. I felt as if Luftig was going to pronounce a verdict of life or death for me.

I was at school before eight, a little earlier than usual. I can't say I was either optimistic or pessimistic as I waited for Luftig to show up. But the day seemed to have a thin, edgy quality that frayed the nerves. A few minutes after the hour I saw Luftig come out of his office. He looked around, probably for me. His face seemed set, non-committal. I walked up to him from where I had been waiting. "Ah, Ungar," he said. "Yes, well, you see, I can't do anything for you. I'm sorry. In this particular case I'm powerless."

About the next few days, I can't recall much. A haze enveloped me, making me numb. I worked on at school somehow, although I have no memory of it. I hardly heard or saw anything, except at night when I had the most vivid dreams in which Wusia and I would be lying in bed carrying on a normal conversation, with Michael nestled between us. We'd try to hug him or make faces at him, to see how he would respond. But there was something wrong, some flicker or ripple of fear would be lapping at my brain, getting stronger and more disturbing until I'd wake up in a sweat and find that I was alone. For a moment after I opened my eyes the world seemed all right, then the horror of what had happened would wash over me and the spasms of anguish would start. When I would finally get myself under control I'd lie awake, thinking of the things I might have done to save us from this.

The truth was that once we moved from Nabielacka to Berka Joselowicza nothing could have saved us. In the Jewish section we were like rats in a trap; they could have come for us at any time. But before then, while we were still living on Nabielacka, I could have made arrangements. Wusia looked as Polish as I did. Her Polish accent was as good as mine, without a trace of Yiddish. Nothing about her would have given away her Jewishness. We could have left Michael with the Orlinskys, her parents' childless friends who would have been overjoyed to care for a baby. I could have gotten us forged papers and scouted around for a safe place. We could have gone somewhere where we weren't known and set ourselves up as a Polish couple. With Wusia's bookkeeping skills and my technical experience we would have found a way to get by.

But I had been fooled. Had I known it then, lying there in my own sweat, I was still being fooled. Even then I didn't suspect the Germans' plans for total annihilation. Eventually this would pass, I thought, things would change for the better. Most of us believed that, which was why there was no uprising, no resistance to their atrocities. The Nazis moved with such methodical precision. This wasn't something done by garden variety murderers. It wasn't the Russians holding a pogrom in Kishinev, where one day they get drunk, break the windows, kill some people, and that was the end. The German plans were laid by intellectuals, professionals, experts in maintaining the illusion of hope. "If only," was the name of their deception. If only you had the right identity card, if only you worked for the right organization, if only you were strong and healthy.

True, there were roundups, but they came at intervals. The *Einsatzgruppen* surrounded an area, picked up certain categories of people, and took them away. But after each *Aktion* the situation would calm down, and they'd tell the *Judenrat* not to worry anymore. "We'll issue new *kennkartes* and you'll be safe, there's nothing more to be concerned about." Then would come a period of relative quiet and renewed hope. Human nature responding. People *wanted* to believe them. After all, *you* have been given the right to live. Who then would take a reckless chance to run or fight and choose almost certain death? And so you live. Until the next roundup.

In my imagination it began to seem more and more evident that Wusia and Michael must be alive. True, they had disappeared, but who knew what was really happening. The Germans had talked about resettlement. Sometimes families of those who were rounded up received a postcard, with messages that they were well and working hard. Of course, rumors were also spreading that deportees were being killed and the postcards were fakes, but the facts were not known. I wasn't sure, how could I be? And the doubt fed my dreams.

Maybe, I thought, just maybe, no matter how slight the hope, they would survive. And if not Michael, then at least Wusia. She was young and strong, it would make sense for them to put her to work somewhere. I would see her in my mind, hoeing a field or cutting wheat with a sickle. With any luck she could survive that and eventually we'd be back together. The war would end, maybe soon, and she would come back to me. Which meant that I had to do everything I could to survive, to keep myself alive for that blessed day.

That's why I started thinking of escape the minute we were told that when school ended in a few short weeks, the Jewish teachers would be dismissed and sent to the labor camp on Pierackego Street, near Janowska. I wasn't alone. The announcement sent all of us into a frenzied search for a place to hide. We all believed that this could be the beginning of the end. I was thinking frantically about where I might go when one day after classes my assistant, Edward Wawer, approached me with an unexpected offer.

The Germans had organized the school so that every Jewish teacher had an assistant, usually one of the better students. The idea was that these Aryan assistants would take over as instructors once the regular Jewish faculty was disposed of. They could do that because the Germans had no interest in teaching anybody theory or anything else at a high level. Theory meant nothing; the only thing the Germans cared about was preparing the students to work on machines—the lathes, milling machines, drills, presses, and so on—so that they could be sent off to work in the German war factories.

Edward Wawer, a lanky, blond, blue eyed Pole with a pleasant disposition, was my assistant. Edward was several years older than most of the students, not much younger than I. Over the course of the year we had become friendly, to the point where he invited me a number of times to his sister's house, where he was living. She and I had also become friends. She knew I was Jewish, but like Edward she was an easygoing person with an open, relaxed way of treating people.

After math class one day Edward stayed, as if he wanted to ask me some questions about the material. Instead, he said quietly, "Everyone knows that Jews are looking for places to hide. I don't have anyplace to offer you, but I can do something that might be as good."

"Wawer, what are you saying?"

"*Panie* Ungar, listen to me. I feel I owe you a lot. You've taught me enough so that they aren't going to send me to Germany. They're keeping me here to teach. I'd like you to have my papers. I can give you all my documents. The only thing I ask is that you don't stay in Lvov. It could be dangerous having two Edward Wawers around."

"Edward, you're talking about *giving* me your documents?

"Yes, I owe you. I want you to take them."

It wasn't unheard of for Jews to acquire Aryan documents, but there was always a high price involved. Wawer was offering these out of the goodness of his heart. We had never spoken a word about what the Germans were doing to Jews. He had never given a single indication of what he thought. And now, out of the blue, he was offering me this chance to survive.

The next day during the mid-day break Wawer and I met in the school's machine shop, away from prying eyes. "I've got five documents here," he said, handing me an envelope. "My birth certificate, my seventh grade graduation diploma, my apprenticeship papers, my quota fulfillment certificate, and my certificate of good behavior by the local authorities. But you'll still need a German ID. Can you get one of those?"

"Yes, they're available. Listen, I don't know how I can compensate you for these." I didn't know what to say. "What can I do for you?"

"Don't worry about it. As far as I'm concerned you've already paid me. We can talk more after the war, when life will be better for both of us."

The only thing I needed now to give me a complete Polish identity was an official ID card, which could be gotten without too much trouble. Many Jews worked in German offices. Someone who spoke German, for example, might be employed as a clerk or cleaner or in some other low-level capacity. Because many of the companies issued ID cards, they had blank forms, some of which might easily go missing without ever being noticed. All you had to do was have your picture taken and find a forger who would create what looked like a legitimate card in whatever name you wanted.

In a few days I had a card. Under my picture I scrawled the name "Edward Wawer," doing my best to imitate the real Wawer's signature. I had practiced it dozens of times from his apprenticeship papers. It didn't come out badly. These papers weren't foolproof. I knew I'd never be able to stand up to an interrogation, for instance. I didn't know any of the details of Wawer's family life. And other than the "Our Father" I didn't know a single Catholic prayer. Any Gestapo inquisitor worth his salt would see through me in a minute. But for a cursory inspection these would work perfectly. These documents made me as Polish as my looks did.

I *had* to save my life, for the day when Wusia and Michael and I would all be reunited. I also *wanted* to save my life. With one part of me I knew that my hopes for their survival were illusionary, that my desires were at war with reason. But with my heart I believed. It wasn't possible that they were just gone, that one moment we were together and the next they had simply been swept away forever. How could there be a universe where such things happened? Somewhere, then, they must be alive. The conviction fixed itself in my head—they *were* alive and we *would* be together again.

Was my mind making excuses for my will? Over the years I've asked myself that often. Was I finding justification for my own determination to survive, even though they might be dead and gone? It could be. For the first time since my father died I felt fragile, battered. I knew my inner life was coming apart. I was shaking all the time. But my instinct to survive pushed me to safety.

Wawer's documents gave me the ability to masquerade as a Pole, but I still didn't have anywhere to live. Even before Wawer gave me his papers, though, my friend Chaim Rosen and I had decided to try to find a hiding place together, for the two of us plus his niece and her boyfriend. I came up with something first.

Someone had recommended that I see a Polish woman, who owned a little farm on the outskirts of Lvov, out on Janowska Road. She was a trustworthy person, I was told, in need of money. When I went to see her we came to terms quickly. She had a barn with a big hayloft that would make a perfect hiding place. Her young daughter and she were the only people in the house; her husband had died earlier. Nobody visited her. The only person we'd have to look out for was her helper, a man who came to the barn early each morning to take the horses out to the fields. In the evening he brought the horses back, fed the animals, and locked the barn. "He won't be a problem," she told me. "Just keep yourselves still when he's around."

As the end of the school year approached I sold the furniture in our apartment to the superintendent. He was a rough, unpleasant character with a permanently bad disposition from having had the bad luck to superintend a building located in the Jewish district. Like all the other superintendents in Lvov, he supplemented his salary by charging a small fee to open the outer door at night after 10 p.m. For tenants who returned home after midnight, the fee was a little larger. Those had been the rules in normal times. Now all his tenants were Jews without money, Jews who had been stripped of everything, moreover, Jews who weren't even allowed out after curfew, which meant that his additional income had dried up completely.

The bright side for him was the money he could make from Jews who were rounded up. When the Gestapo or *Einsatzgruppen* made an Aktion, they took people but left their furniture, which turned janitors into furniture dealers. Peasants from Lvov's suburbs knew where the Jews were

My Aryan identification card bearing the name of Edward Wawer, 1942

concentrated and seemed able to learn instantly where roundups were taking place. Hardly had the Germans disappeared with their captives when the peasants would arrive with their horses and wagons. Paying off the superintendents, they'd ransack the newly vacated apartments, like vultures feasting on the leftovers from a lion's kill. You'd see them loading furniture and other possessions and driving through town, their wagons piled high with the belongings of condemned Jews.

So I told the superintendent to get his friends or other buyers in because I was leaving. Later that day the peasants came. I watched as the superintendent sold off all the movable things from our apartment, the furniture, clothes, utensils, all of it. I had to leave everything, Wusia's belongings as well as the baby's. I felt like I was losing part of me. But I had no choice. Then I walked away from Berka Joselowicza with my briefcase, inside of which were my pajamas and my razor. This is what was left of my life. I was happy to get the money, though. With that maybe I could find a way to get by.

13

WOWKOWA

Summer 1942

The farm wasn't far, a two or three mile walk out Janowska road, but by the time I got out there night was already falling. In the shadow of the barn I waited for a half-hour or so until Chaim, his niece Chaya, and her boyfriend showed up, right on schedule. The farm lady had told me what to do, and the four of us climbed the ladder that led to the big trap door into the hayloft. The place was even better than I had imagined, a big breezy rectangular area with straw stored on one side and hay on the other, with plenty of room to spread out.

Early the next morning we heard the helper come in to take care of the animals, just as the farm lady had said. Then he left for the fields. An hour or so later the lady herself climbed up with a jar of milk, a pot of soup and bread, our food for the day. The arrangement seemed perfect; this was going to be an ideal place to hide in for a few months, after which things were bound to change. We didn't worry about next year or the year after. It didn't seem possible the war would take that long. The basic idea was to live one more day, then the next, and the next. People in distress will believe in miracles, and we were absolutely convinced that the Germans would be defeated. It was only a matter of time.

Of course, up in the hayloft, we had no way of telling what was happening in the outside world. Even when we lived in Lvov no one had more than rumors to go on. There were no newspapers except for some German propaganda sheets, no radio, nothing. People lived by their hopes. They created the news by themselves. Rumors would come from someone's verboten crystal radio or by reading between the lines of the German newspapers—but there was no way to verify anything. Now, in the loft, we were even more isolated. At night we would hear gunshots. Then we'd see flashes of light from the Jewish area and we'd know some Aktion was taking place. Still we believed that before long the Germans would be defeated. We sat there and waited for it to happen.

Chaim and I spent most of the time talking, growing even closer than we had been before. He was one of those people you wanted to be with, someone you would think of to take to a desert island if you could only have one person to keep you company. He too was a congenital optimist, but much more outgoing than I. A humorist and story teller, an athlete, and very attractive to girls, with his blond hair and easy ways. Like me, Chaim had done his army service in the mid-30's, and afterwards he had been hired as an instructor by Badian. During the pedagogical course in Warsaw we had shared a room, and we had been best friends ever since.

Coming from a well-to-do family, Chaim used to squirm and make noises under his breath during our morning assemblies under the Russian *politruk*. The NKVD had transported Chaim's parents to some rural area for being capitalists and he found it hard to listen to the *politruk's* glowing accounts of the glories of life under communism. When it came time to chant "Long Live Father Stalin," if you were sitting close enough to Chaim you could hear him mumbling sentiments of a different sort.

If he was concerned about his family then, now his anxieties were on another level altogether. His father had since died, and one brother was off somewhere fighting with the Red Army. But his mother, uncle, and another brother were trapped in Lvov's Jewish section. Chaim worried about them incessantly, talking about how if they were careful they could survive, and how happy they would be to be finally reunited after all this was over.

Like Chaim, my own anxieties were at a fevered pitch, not just for Wusia and Michael, but for my mother and the others who had been deported from Krasne to Grzymalov. I considered trying to go there to see them. With my Polish papers I'd be able to travel. But once again I decided against it. I was known in Grzymalov, and I thought I'd probably never come back. It would have been a suicide trip.

Chaim and I talked often about Wusia and the baby. I still held tight to my hopes, but I could hear the desperation in my own voice. I began more and more to consider the likelihood that this was not going to end happily. During the daytime I thought about them constantly. I was obsessed by fantasies about where they might be and what might be happening to them.

Without being invited, death intruded into my reveries. One night trying to get to sleep I had a flash of memory in which I saw my mother lying in bed with her eyes closed looking as if she were dead. My father and I were in the room with her, and my father was sobbing. It seemed sad that my mother was so ill, but I was more deeply disturbed by my father's weeping, a thing I had never seen before—nor after. I was a little boy, no more than four or five years old, which would have made it about 1918, the year of the great flu epidemic. I remembered being told that my mother had almost died then. How terrible it was to see him grieving for her. I thought of my father's deep affection, how loving he always was toward my mother, how attached he was to her.

The unexpected memory of my mother's near passing and my father's tears made me think inevitably of his own death when I was seventeen, and her wild mourning then. It had happened in the middle of July, almost exactly ten years earlier. I was home on vacation from my first year as a student at Korkis when he got sick. He went first to Dr. Mieses in Grzymalov who told him he had to go to the hospital in Tarnopol. Tarnopol was a long way off, six or seven hours by train, and I was chosen to accompany my father. "Wolci," my mother said as we left, "Take care of your father, and come back soon."

On the porch steps they embraced, unusual for them. Mama looked distraught. I wasn't particularly worried, though. Father had been complaining of pains somewhere, but he looked healthy enough to me. We'll go to the hospital, I thought, and after a few days they'll cure him. Then we'll come home.

My first sight of the Tarnopol hospital gave me such a lifetime aversion to sickness that even thinking about hospitals made me ill, which is probably why the effects of my war injuries had put me into such a state of shock. The hospital looked fine from the outside, a large, imposing building. But the instant we stepped inside I was blasted by the smell of infection. This was before antibiotics, even sulfa, and I don't know if every hospital in the world reeked of pus in those days, but this one did. The smell almost knocked me off my feet.

After the doctors examined father they told me he had a gall bladder inflammation that would require an operation. I still didn't know the seriousness of it; a gall bladder operation didn't sound that bad. Besides, the doctor who told me didn't seem worried, and doctors then were next to God. No matter what they said, people accepted it. I accepted it.

That night I stayed at the home of Margulis, the brother-in-law of David Hirsh Zeftel (my brother Max's father-in-law from Krasne). The next day I was sitting in my father's hospital room when they wheeled him in, still unconscious from the operation. He looked terrible. He lay there, slowly coming out of the anesthesia while the three other patients in the room complained loudly and endlessly about their own suffering. The pungent aroma of pus permeated my nasal passages and worked its way up into my brain. As the anesthesia wore off father awoke into a world of pain. That was when I started to worry.

The next day he was still in agony. From time to time nurses came in to give him something and the pains subsided. His appearance was different, his skin seemed waxy and pallid. The doctor came and stuck a big needle into his arm, an injection I thought, and then I saw blood seeping into the glass syringe. I had never seen blood drawn before and I didn't know what was happening. I felt dizzy. I wanted to leave. Instead I gritted my teeth and stayed, holding his hand.

After the doctor had gotten his syringeful of blood he left, without saying a word to me. I sat there and watched my father suffer. An hour passed, and another. It seemed to me that his eyes were becoming glazed. Then, soon after I noticed his eyes, he gave a deep sigh and stopped breathing. I got up and leaned over him, but his chest wasn't moving. In a panic, I ran out into the hall yelling for the doctor. They all came, the doctor, several nurses. The doctor looked at him carefully, and then he took his pulse. "Unfortunately," he said, "your father has expired. He's dead." Then he walked out.

Dazed, I left him in the room and went back to Margulis. While Margulis made arrangements I telephoned the police station in Krasne and they went to get Max. "You should come with mother," I said. "But don't tell her yet. It might be too hard for her to take." "Yes," said Max, "you're right. Meanwhile, why don't you call Uncle Nissen? He's closest to mother. He'll know what to do."

Uncle Nissen was mother's dearest brother, an unusually good-natured person. He was helpful to every member of the family who might need him in some way. Nissen was an egg dealer, a big middleman. He bought eggs from local merchants throughout the region, packed them, and exported them to Germany and other neighboring countries. When he came to our area on his buying trips, he stayed with my grandmother in Postulufka. I knew him well from the many times we visited grandma while he was there. I'd see him too, when he arrived in Krasne visiting the shopkeepers in our villages.

When I called Nissen he said he would come immediately, and in fact he arrived in Margulis's house at almost the same moment mother and Max did. While mother was with Mrs. Margulis, Nissen and Max discussed what to do. I heard most of it, overheard it really, listening to their talk from the next room. "It might overwhelm her," said Nissen. "You know how she adored your father. He meant everything to her. I'm afraid she might suffer some very bad consequences herself. It could really endanger her health."

"You might be right," said Max. "What do you think we should do?"

"I'd like to get her back home," Nissen said. "It will be better to tell her while she's at home with Esther and Dvorah around, not in this strange place where she hardly knows anybody."

So they decided that Uncle Nissen should persuade my mother to go home. "Feige," he told her, "the hospital has restrictions on visitors. You'll probably have to wait a day or two before you can see Mechel. What's the point of staying here and being uncomfortable? Wouldn't it be better if you went home? Esther's there by herself. Go back to her. Take a day or two, and then you'll enjoy seeing him, instead of suffering here. We'll bring him home. I don't know why it was necessary for you to come in the first place. I don't know why Max brought you. He made a mistake. Max and I will find a place to stay overnight, but you should go home."

Mother trusted Nissen. She had never had any reason not to. Of course, she wasn't expecting anything bad. If there was good news, fine. She'd go back to Krasne for a day or two and her husband would come home. It never entered her mind that Nissen was deceiving her. So she left.

We buried him later that day. Margulis came and some people from the local burial society. Max, Nissen, and I walked behind the wagon that carried his coffin. We watched as they positioned the coffin at the grave and slid the bottom board out, letting father's shroud-wrapped body tip into the hole. Max put two or three shovelfuls of earth on him, then a *chazzan* we didn't know led us in Kaddish and some other prayers. I was numb. It wasn't something I could comprehend or react to, that father's existence on earth had come to this sudden end.

Afterwards Uncle Nissen left for his home in Kopyczynce and Max and I took the train to Grzymalov, wondering how we were going to break the news to mother. It was a terrible dilemma. Under any circumstances father's death would be the greatest imaginable trauma for her, but this was even worse. The closest people had lied to her. Moreover, she was expecting father to come back to her.

I left it to Max to tell her even though I was standing there next to him when he did. "Mama," Max said. Esther was there too. "Mama, unfortunately father didn't get better. He got worse. Unfortunately, Mama, he passed away. We buried him yesterday."

I thought she was going to collapse. All the color drained from her face. Then she and Esther were crying uncontrollably and she started after Max.

"Why did you send me back home? Why didn't you give me a chance to see him a last time? Why didn't you let me go with him to the cemetery?"

"Look, Mama, Uncle Nissen thought it would be too much for you. He thought it would be best if you could go home to be with Esther. Mama, don't cry so, Mama." But she didn't stop. She cried constantly. Her grief seemed bottomless, enormous. She abandoned herself to it. She never forgave Nissen for depriving her from seeing her husband for the last time.

Father had been taken from her, snatched unexpectedly, with no mitigation, no preparation, no good-byes as he was dying or farewells when they buried him. Like me, I thought, up there in the hayloft, just like me. A quick glance of eyes meeting, then…nothing. Absence.

Early one morning a couple of weeks after we arrived at our loft hiding place the helper came as usual to take out the horses. As always when he was in the barn, we lay silent and still, Chaim and I together, Chaya and her boyfriend a little distance from us. Then I noticed that the boyfriend had gotten up and was walking toward the far end of the loft, where we sometimes went if we had to relieve ourselves. Stupid, I thought, you can't wait a few minutes until the farm hand leaves? But of course I couldn't call or run to stop him. He went to the far end and urinated. And something happened. The urine trickled down through the floorboards and the helper happened to be working just below and saw it.

He went to investigate. We didn't even hear him climbing the ladder. All we saw was that suddenly the trap door pushed up, his head appeared, and there he was, staring at us.

We were scared to death, but he was very calm. He understood instantly who we were and what we were doing there. For him it was like finding money. He was very matter of fact even, very blunt. "Okay," he said, "now you pay me. If you don't, I'm reporting you to the Germans."

"Wait a minute," I said. "We're just here temporarily. We're not doing you any harm, so what do you care that we are here? If you report us you'll kill your employer too. You want to do that? Don't worry, we'll pay you. We don't have much, but we'll pay you. Just keep quiet."

I had money, from the things I had sold. Chaim did too, and so did Chaya and the stupid boyfriend. But that money was lifeblood for us. After some back and forth I convinced him that we could only give him a certain amount, a lot less than he wanted. And he agreed. Afterwards he went off to the field with the horses as usual, but we knew we were no longer safe.

The farm lady knew it too. She came in later in the afternoon, distressed and afraid for her life. "I'm sorry," she said, "but you can't stay here any longer. It's just too dangerous." We felt the helper probably wouldn't betray the woman he owed his livelihood to, but she wasn't ready to risk her life on it. And we weren't going to endanger ours either.

The woman let us stay one more night while we tried to find some other place. She also gave me the name and address of a friend of hers in Zimna Woda, a summer resort area just outside Lvov. This friend lived in a remote area, the lady told me, and she was trustworthy. She might agree to take us in.

The next day, I remember it was a Sunday, I left Chaim and the others and walked the four or five miles to Zimna Woda. It was a beautiful day for a walk, warm and sunny, and after I turned off the main road onto a dirt path I was in the midst of a deep forest that reminded me of Krasne. I felt at home. I thought, if this lady is as good-natured as her friend, this could be even a better place to hide.

Eventually I came to the house, but before I knocked on the door I heard voices and music coming from the backyard. I snuck around for a look. Out back there was a kind of party going on, with several girls and German soldiers. I ducked back to the front of the house, my heart suddenly pounding. Then I thought I better say hello to the woman. If I didn't and anybody had seen me, it might look suspicious. This obviously wasn't a place where we could hide. The soldiers must have been from some nearby German army camp.

When I knocked on the door the lady answered, extremely friendly. I told her that I had just stopped by with regards from her friend. We had a nice conversation about the weather and the general conditions after which I left, without a mention of what I had come for.

When I got back I told Chaim and the others the bad news. We had no place to hide, and we couldn't stay in the barn any longer, which meant we had to separate. I was very unhappy to be losing Chaim, but there wasn't any alternative. It was just as disappointing for him, but he wasn't someone who lost hope easily. He thought he'd probably report himself in to the labor camp on Pierackego where the Germans had been planning to send all the Korkis teachers. He was a highly skilled machinist and technician, young and in good condition. He thought he'd probably be all right there.

We parted, Chaim to Pierackego, Chaya and her boyfriend to somewhere they were thinking of, and I back toward Lvov. I didn't intend to stay in the city. If I was going to be Edward Wawer, it would be best to do so in another place, where there wouldn't be two of us. What I needed right now was somewhere to spend the coming night, some place where I'd be safe and could think things over.

The only likely possibility that occurred to me while I was walking was Nabielacka 12, our old apartment building where Herr Luftig now lived. The building was full of Nazi officials and Gestapo families, but with any luck I'd be able to avoid them. The person I was thinking of was Kataryna Wowkowa, the superintendent. Katy was a simple, warmhearted soul who had been Wusia's employee during the time when Wusia was building manager for the Russians. She had always been friendly to both of us, during both the German and Russian occupations of Lvov. Katy had a tiny basement apartment in the building. She might be too afraid to let me stay a night, but I felt sure that no matter what her answer, she wouldn't turn me in. I still had my keys to the building. Coal storage stalls for the various apartments took up most of the basement. If worse came to worst, I might be able to hide in one of those.

I got to Nabielacka at nine or so that night—after dark. I had walked through Lvov like a Pole, as if the city really belonged to me even if the Germans happened to be occupying it at the time. I didn't attract a single glance. As I got near the building I kept alert to who might be around. I didn't want someone to suspect that I was loitering. I especially wanted to stay out of Herr and Frau Luftig's way.

Luckily, no one was on the street. When I got to Number 12, I quickly peeked in at the ground level window of Katy's one room apartment. The light was on, and there she was, alone with her baby. As long as I had known her I had never met her husband. All I knew of him was that he had been drafted into the Red Army early in the occupation. So it was just Katy and the infant. The Nazis were all in their apartments; the building was quiet. I found my keys and let myself in.

I knocked softly on Katy's door, hoping she wouldn't make any noise when she saw who it was. She didn't. She was surprised to see me, but didn't seem shocked or terrified. "Panie Ungar," she said, "what are you doing here?" Then she let me in and closed the door.

"Pani Wowkowa," I said. I need a place to stay tonight. Just for one night. Would you mind if I stayed here with you? Maybe you'd let me sleep on the sofa. If not, the floor would be fine too."

"Panie Ungar, of course you can stay. Please, the sofa is yours. There's no problem at all."

It struck me then that Katy might not have been too aware of what was happening to the Jews in the city. She didn't go out, she didn't read. As the superintendent, she had her hands full taking care of the building. What she knew was that the Germans weren't friends with the Jews, but what was unusual about that? Neither were the Ukrainians, her own people, though personally she had nothing against Jews. And of course the Poles were anti-Semites. She had heard that some Jews were being killed, a pogrom. It wasn't her business. She wasn't involved. She had her baby, she had the building, and it was enough work just to haul the ashes out from eight apartments.

That night I stayed in her room, on the little sofa. While I was lying awake an idea formed in my head. The next day I would take a train to Warsaw. My friend Gromb was there, at least when I had last heard from him. I'd try to connect with him. Gromb was a strong, resourceful character. Between the two of us maybe we could work out a plan.

14

NOVY DWOR

Summer 1942 – Winter 1943

I had received a postcard from Gromb while Wusia and I were still living on Nabielacka. He had written from a Warsaw suburb called Legionowo, and I had kept the address. Of course that was more than a year ago and who knew what might have happened since then. I didn't have any idea what the situation was in Warsaw. But what I did know was that Gromb was steady as a rock. There was at least a chance he was still there.

I had met Gromb, as I had Chaim, at school in Warsaw where we had become friends. Then, after the German invasion, he had showed up in Lvov as a refugee. Through the almost two years of Russian occupation we had gotten to know each other well. But once the Germans took over in Lvov there was no reason for him to stay, so he went back to Warsaw and moved to the Legionowo neighborhood.

Going off to look for Gromb was an act of desperation. God only knew what the Germans were doing to people in

Warsaw. I hadn't heard anything, but it wouldn't have surprised me to learn that they had ghettoized the Jews there (they had). Or that they were deporting or killing them (they were). Gromb himself could be dead; I could be searching for a deceased person. But I had to get out of Lvov and I didn't have a lot of options. Even with all the uncertainty, Gromb still seemed like the best chance.

The next morning I said good-bye to Katy Wowkowa and left. I didn't want to go to the Wiener Banhof, I thought it was probably being watched. There was another station out in Zimna Woda, the suburb where I had gone to look for a new hiding place the previous day. The trains stopped there because so many people from Lvov used to spend their summers in the area. Nowadays there weren't any, so I thought the train station would probably be quiet.

I also knew someone in Zimna Woda, a Polish teacher who had been on the staff at Korkis School, a friendly, older man by the name of Chris. We hadn't known each other that well, but he was an amiable colleague, not at all the kind of person who might turn me in for no reason, I was pretty sure of that. I thought I'd surprise him. With any luck he'd invite me to dinner and offer to let me stay until I could catch a train.

I wasn't wrong about Chris. When I arrived after the long hike from Lvov he seemed glad to see me, as friendly as he had always been. His wife, whom I hadn't met, turned out to be equally gracious. The idea of having a Jew in the house, obviously on the run, didn't seem to bother them at all. I'm sure they assumed I was carrying Aryan documents, without them they knew I wouldn't have dared to travel so openly. Our evening was as normal as could be. We had dinner and a pleasant after dinner talk exactly as we might have had under other circumstances. Beneath the surface, though, my anxieties were building. I was about to enter the unknown. Lvov had become a lethal place, but at least it was a place I knew. Warsaw was terra incognita. Maybe I could find safety there, but it might turn out to be even more dangerous than where I was.

That night in Chris' guestroom I had difficulty sleeping. But when I did fall off I had the most wonderfully vivid dream of my father. He was alive and well, dressed as always in his black suit, black hat and white shirt. Seeing him again, I was overcome by happiness. He knew I was about to leave on a perilous journey, he said, which was why he had come to see me. He wanted me to know that I shouldn't worry. I would be all right. "Be well," he told me, God would surely be with me.

I woke up refreshed, his words still in my head. After breakfast I said my good-byes to Chris and his wife and left for the station to catch an early train, buoyed by an optimism I hadn't felt in a long while.

Zimna Woda was a typical little country railroad station, with a small wooden station house from the last century and a single platform. I had expected to find myself more or less alone, but when I arrived quite a few people were already waiting for the train. A group of teenagers, students obviously, were bantering and playing around noisily while several older people gave them annoyed looks. Off to one side I noticed a slender, dark haired girl who immediately caught my eye as someone who might easily be Jewish. I knew I should keep to myself, but I felt drawn to her. I also think my guard was down a little, partly from the strange sense of well being I had been given by my father's appearance in my dream, and maybe also from my relaxed evening at Chris' which had seemed so utterly normal. More to the point, I knew the big train stations were watched, but I didn't expect to find police in an out of the way place like Zimna Woda. The upshot of it was that after glancing around quickly for any suspicious looking people, I moved along the platform until I was standing next to the girl. When I struck up a conversation, I saw fear in her eyes. No question, I thought, she's as Jewish as I am.

What I didn't notice was the Polish policeman who materialized just as the train pulled up and we were boarding. He got on behind the students—that was when I saw him out of the corner of my eye. Instantly my heart started to race and a shiver went down my back, but only for a moment. Instinctively I wrapped my Polish identity around me, which by now had become almost second nature. Wolf Ungar disappeared. I was Edward Wawer. Born in Koryczany. Graduated from seventh grade in 1933, served as a blacksmith's apprentice. In the minute it took for the policeman to make his way through the students, I had put myself into a one hundred percent Polish frame of mind.

"Your papers!" he said, to the girl and me. The tone was gruff, even angry. I took mine out of my brown leather billfold and handed them over. She gave him hers. Without a word the policeman put both sets in his pocket and walked off through the car. As he moved away, my fear returned. I had to squash it, show no disquiet whatsoever. I was an innocent Pole trying to get to Warsaw. Young enough even to take up with this rambunctious bunch of students, I thought. I turned to them. "What's going on boys? A little outing? Where are you headed?" By the time the policeman came back I was deeply involved in schoolboy talk, standing so I could keep half an eye on what he was doing. I saw him watching me, and then he too came over to join the conversation, positioning himself right next to me, the pocket of his jacket almost rubbing up against the pocket of mine. Could this be a coincidence? I thought. With my right hand I fished around in my wallet for some bills. Discreetly, I slipped them into the beckoning open pocket of the policeman's uniform.

A minute later, as we all stood there talking, his own hand slipped into the pocket and felt what was there. By this time the students were telling jokes and stories. As they laughed I felt movement in my own jacket pocket and when I put my hand in to check, I felt papers. I fingered them surreptitiously, counting them. All six of my Wawer documents were back in my possession; a silent exchange, done without even a look. The girl wasn't so lucky. At the next station the policeman got off, taking her along. As they stepped out of the car she looked at me desperately, pleading silently for me to do something. But I was frozen to the spot. I watched them walk off down the platform, haunted by her black eyes and that anguished last look, so like Wusia's that for a moment I felt faint.

The train stopped at every possible station between Zimna Woda and Warsaw, 600 miles away, taking on and letting off crowds of peasants, most of whom seemed to be carrying fat, heavy sacks of food, doubtlessly bound for the black market. With the girl's arrest, my sense of elation dissolved as if it had never been, leaving me disheartened and increasingly aggravated at our tedious pace. Through the window the countryside passed, then disappeared as day turned into night. It wasn't until the next morning that we finally pulled into the Warsaw station.

Though I had never been to Legionowo, I knew it was north of the city. I hired a horse-drawn cab with a driver who obviously knew his way around. When I said "To Legionowo," he looked at me, sizing me up. As I understood later, the one look told him all he needed to know, namely that I was a smuggler, one of those who specialized in doing business with Jews. That was the only possible reason a Pole with a briefcase would want to go to Legionowo. He was familiar with the type, having driven a number of such businessmen to the suburb which, as I soon discovered, had been transformed by the Germans from an ordinary neighborhood into an annex of the Warsaw ghetto. "This is it," said the driver after twenty or thirty minutes of silence. "They're cramming Jews in here like sardines. I'll drop you off at a place where you can get in without any trouble." I kept my mouth shut, just beginning to understand what he was talking about. Later I realized that he hadn't brought me to the main gate, but to an out of the way spot on the perimeter where there were no guards. He knew that businessmen like myself needed to slip in and out without any unnecessary encounters.

Inside Legionowo I asked around and eventually found my way to the address on Gromb's postcard. By now I felt virtually certain that I had come all this way for nothing. But when the door opened to my knock, there was Gromb standing behind it. We both stood there a moment in amazement. I don't know which of us was more surprised. Then we were shaking hands and hugging. I was so relieved to see him I could hardly talk. While in the cab, and then trying to find his address, I had been wondering what I would do if he wasn't there. I knew no one and was completely ignorant of the conditions in this place. Now I felt I had a chance.

Gromb and I spent the next couple of days bringing each other up to date and trying to work out a plan of action.

Warsaw was a disaster, he told me. All the Jews of the city had been sealed inside a ghetto for more than a year and a half. Conditions were inhuman, unbelievable. The Germans had so restricted food supplies that people were starving to death in the streets. Typhoid, dysentery, and other epidemics had killed thousands, maybe tens of thousands. Almost from the beginning the SS had been shooting people at random or taking them away for forced labor, often never to return. Even more ominous occurrences had started recently. Word had seeped out of the ghetto that the Germans were now rounding up large groups of people, thousands at a time. They were herding them into boxcars and shipping them out in long freight trains, nobody knew where. The community was deeply fearful about the fate of those taken.

A lot of this sounded all too familiar. The only difference was that when I left Lvov there was a Jewish section, but the Germans hadn't set up a formal walled-in ghetto as they had in Warsaw. Listening to Gromb I couldn't believe I had come here looking for safety. So far, he said, they had mostly left Legionowo alone, but it was obviously not going to remain that way. The best thing to do would be to get out now, while we had time.

But where to go? Gromb knew as I did that there were partisans living in the forests in eastern Poland. But neither of us knew anyone who had gone there or had any idea how to find them. And even if we could find them, we both thought the chances were pretty good that a Polish partisan group would be as likely to kill Jews as not. Gromb had some contacts in other places who might offer possibilities. But the more we talked the more it seemed that the best idea would be to get back to his family in his home town, Novy Dwor, only forty or fifty miles west of Warsaw. Gromb's mother, brother, and sister lived there, along with other family members—uncles, aunts, and cousins. He had heard that Novy Dwor's Jews were restricted to one area, but that they weren't suffering too badly.

There was one big negative about Novy Dwor, though—it was located in the region the Germans had annexed to the *Reich*. The town was now an official part of Germany. Our first thought was that if Polish Jews were suffering, it would probably be worse for German Jews, if not now, then very soon. Going to Novy Dwor might be like jumping from the frying pan into the fire. Then we began to think that maybe the opposite was true. Maybe inside Germany would be safer—the calm at the center of the storm. Maybe in their own country the Germans wouldn't be as ferocious as they were in Poland and Russia or other places where the population was hostile. But one fact was clear, Legionowo would soon go the way of the rest of the Warsaw ghetto. We had to get out. The *Reich* might be our best possibility.

Gromb's girlfriend was going to come with us. Neither of them had papers, but that wasn't so important because we were going to have to smuggle ourselves into Novy Dwor anyway. From Warsaw to Novy Dwor were deep forests, which would be perfect for us. We'd keep off the roads, travel by night, and hide during the day. The Germans had put a bounty on escaped Jews. We'd have to keep away from Poles as well as German patrols. Our advantage was that Gromb knew the forests between Warsaw and Novy Dwor as well as I knew those between Krasne and Sadzawky.

Getting out of Legionowo wasn't hard. The ghetto was lightly guarded and Gromb knew the best places to slip through. We left on a black, overcast night sometime at the end of August or beginning of September. By now I was beginning to lose track of exact dates. We moved furtively along an alley that led out of the ghetto, then through darkened empty streets. It wasn't long before the houses became less frequent and giant trees loomed all around. Gromb never hesitated. He led us into the woods, deeper and deeper. In the blackness I couldn't see a thing, but I had complete confidence. Gromb reminded me of myself in the woods around Krasne where nighttime altered nothing, where I knew each tree almost instinctively.

We walked all night, until dawn began to lighten the sky behind us. Then we found a deserted spot behind some bushes and fell asleep, exhausted. For the next two or three days we walked at night and slept during the day. We picked wild strawberries, blueberries, and lingonberries. A few times we stumbled across patches of golden chanterelles which we passed by only with great reluctance, but we knew we couldn't take the chance of making a fire to cook them.

Early on the fourth night we found ourselves on the outskirts of Novy Dwor. Gromb hadn't been there since the German invasion, almost three years ago. To avoid stumbling into a dangerous situation, Gromb first contacted a peasant friend he thought he could trust. His friend took a message to Gromb's brother-in-law, whom Gromb had heard was president of the local Jukenrat. Then we waited in a field, keeping watch for Germans or peasants. No one came by, and about an hour later a wagon showed up to take us into town.

When we arrived at Gromb's mother's house, the family broke out into a welter of excitement. Gromb's mother grabbed him and wouldn't let him go, then, when the uncles and aunts finally claimed him, she turned her attention to his girlfriend and me. People came into the house, greeting him like a long lost child. From what I had seen, Novy Dwor was a well-to-do old wooden town, more civilized than towns in the east, with architectural embellishments on buildings and red tile roofs. The main streets were flanked by sidewalks, an innovation that had never made its way to Krasne.

Gromb's information about Novy Dwor had been correct. The Germans had imposed restrictions of various sorts, but people were still working and nothing drastic had yet happened. There was still an almost relaxed, prosperous air about the place. We settled down into the Gromb family's large, well-furnished home, joining his widowed mother, a sister, and his younger brother.

Life in Novy Dwor quickly settled into a routine. Except for the fact that the three of us stayed off the streets during the day, we could have been living a normal middle class existence, a kind of enforced vacation with pleasant company and plenty of books. But a current of tension ran through everything. Rumors abounded. At some point we heard that the Germans had now sealed the border, although on our trek through the forest we hadn't noticed any demarcation between Poland and Germany. We also began hearing more and more about the existence of secret death factories, places where Jews were taken to be destroyed like cattle. Most couldn't believe that was possible. But the rumors persisted. It was said that the information came from people who had seen these places first hand, eyewitnesses who had escaped. I didn't know what to believe. Wusia and Michael had been taken months ago, and I still thought about them continuously. I had the gravest fears for my mother too, though I tried to convince myself that she and the others were as safe in Grzymalov as we seemed to be here in Novy Dwor.

We stayed with Gromb's mother through the winter of 1942/1943. But in March the word began to circulate that the Novy Dwor ghetto would soon be closed and all its inhabitants removed to a larger ghetto somewhere.

When Gromb's brother-in-law, the Judenrat president, confirmed that this was probably true, we knew once again that the time had come to make other plans.

By now we had plenty of time to think about alternatives. It had become generally known, for example, that Jews in Hungary were not being persecuted. One possible idea would be to return to Lvov to see what the situation was there. Then, if that didn't look good we would find a way across the border into Hungary. With my Aryan papers I could travel, at least once we made our way back into Poland. And in Warsaw, Gromb thought he might be able to arrange documents for himself and his girlfriend through one of the forgery mills.

The first step would be to get back to Warsaw, which would be more difficult now that the Germans had actually established a border with barbed wire and guards. But when we started investigating possibilities, we found that there was an active trade in food smuggling from Germany into Poland. In Poland black market prices were so high that well-organized teams were routinely transporting large quantities of food across the border. The chief smugglers had developed safe routes, ways of avoiding border patrols and getting through the wire. For the right price, we heard, we could find someone willing to take us along.

Gromb made the arrangements. In a few days he had concluded a deal with a smuggler chief and had set up a night rendezvous for us. The smuggler would spirit us across the border and make arrangements for us to get to Warsaw. From there we'd have to find our own way to Lvov.

We were set to go—Gromb, his girlfriend, myself, and a fourth person, a friend and neighbor of Gromb's from Novy Dwor who had pleaded to join us. I kept my mouth shut, but from the first time I met his friend I was leery about the idea of traveling with him. He looked intensely Jewish, his hair, his features, everything about him shouted it out. More disturbing, he seemed completely naive about what it would mean to travel through half of Nazi-ruled Poland where Jews were being relentlessly hunted. He had had no experience, no exposure to danger. He seemed to think that if Gromb was doing it, then he could as well. It never occurred to him that he would be putting all our lives at risk. I didn't feel it was my place to say anything, especially since Gromb himself didn't seem too concerned. But this person made me feel extremely nervous.

The afternoon before our nighttime rendezvous with the smuggler, another hitch arose. Nobody but the four of us knew what we were planning, and when Gromb finally told his mother she became hysterical. She was crying, "How can you leave me? How can you leave me? What son would do this to his mother?" She made such a scene that Gromb changed his mind about going. True, there was another brother and sister at home to take care of her, but Gromb had deep feelings for his family. Since his father's death he had been the head of the family, in a manner of speaking—even though he had never stayed around his hometown much. He wasn't the type. His mother knew that Gromb had an adventurous personality and was likely to take off just for the sake of taking off. In her opinion that wasn't a good enough reason to leave her alone at a time like this. And since neither he nor she suspected that staying in Novy Dwor would mean death, she collapsed tearfully until he gave in to her pleas. So Gromb and his girlfriend decided to stay, which meant that my sole companion would be Gromb's dangerous neighbor.

15

LUBLIN STATION

Spring, 1943

Gromb was a person of great self-confidence. He understood how risky it was for Novy Dwor's Jews to be moved to another ghetto. But with his big, broad shoulders, he was a man of enormous physical strength coupled with an agile mind. He had never been in a situation that he couldn't overcome one way or another. As perilous as deportation might be, it didn't bring him visions of death. Of course he didn't know about the German machinery of annihilation, so under the circumstances, his mother's tears were too much for him to take.

We said good-bye very unhappily. He wanted to go and I was doing my best to suppress my anxiety about having his friend rather than him as my companion. As we left the house he gave me two items to take along— a small diamond ring and an American twenty-dollar bill. I put the ring in my pocket. I folded the bill small enough to hide in the bottom of a little matchbox I had.

Possessing foreign currency was a capital crime, even for a bona fide Aryan Pole.

Gromb had previously shown me the way to the smuggler's house, a half an hour walk outside town. Now his friend and I made our way through the fields in the dark, without saying a word. When we arrived, the smuggler was waiting alone, although Gromb had said we would be part of a large group. The smuggler, a squat peasant with glinting black eyes and a cunning look, asked for the money Gromb had agreed to. I gave it to him, a little unsure about what was going on. Then we were told to climb up into the hayloft of the barn, close the trap door, and not move until we heard the signal.

In that dark hayloft it was easy to think that I might have just walked into a trap. We had paid the money. What was to stop the smuggler from turning us in and collecting the bounty too? Time passed, hours it seemed, without a sound from down below. Had he gone off to get the Germans? Maybe we still had time to get out and run back to Gromb's house. I considered it, but decided to stay put. If the smuggler had betrayed us, running to Gromb's house wasn't going to save us, and it would mean the end of Gromb and his family too.

It must have been close to midnight when we began to hear muffled noises. I put my ear to the trap door, trying to find out what was happening. Slowly the noises grew louder, until there seemed to be a commotion of many people.

Then we heard a whistle, two shrill notes, the smuggler's signal. When we opened the door and looked down, the barn was crowded with people. Some had sacks rigged on their backs, others were carrying bags and boxes of various descriptions. More baggage was scattered around the floor. We climbed down into what looked like a scene of barely controlled chaos.

The noise stopped dead the moment the smuggler opened the barn door. At a word the group of twenty-five or thirty people shouldered the sacks and packs and arranged themselves in single file. In addition to the people, a cow joined the line near the middle. I noticed that some of the sacks seemed to be writhing furiously, as though whatever was inside didn't want to be there. The smuggler, I now saw, wasn't the only chief of this operation. He had a partner, a pale, bony character with a scraggly blond mustache. After conferring with this person for a moment, our guide took his place at the head of the file while his partner went to the end. The whole caravan started moving silently, under a sky bright with stars.

My companion and I were walking just behind the leader as we headed off on a narrow path through the fields. The only sounds were the footfalls of the carriers and the occasional shifting of somebody's load. There was no talking, nobody hummed any marching songs. These people obviously were experienced. The loads were heavy, but there were no complaints or groans. They had all done this before, I was sure. We walked in silence under the immense sky, heading east toward a dark line of trees that marked the beginning of the great forest.

Suddenly a high-pitched, terrified, squalling pierced the night. For a second my heart stopped. I whirled toward the sound and saw that part of the line in the rear had broken up and people were scrambling through the stubble that bordered the dirt track as if they had become suddenly insane. It took a minute before I realized that they were chasing something—a screeching, screaming piglet running this way and that and making noises that didn't seem possible. The volume was ear-shattering, and the more frantic the chase became the louder it got. Then the cow started mooing. The cacophony was enough to wake the dead. If there was a German patrol within miles they would already be running in our direction at full speed.

Finally someone caught the piglet and jammed it into a sack, which muffled most of the squeals. We started moving again, but I'm sure everyone else's blood pressure was as high as mine. It wasn't until fifteen or twenty minutes had passed and no patrols had appeared that I began breathing normally again.

Not too long after calm returned, we noticed a flickering light in the distance, up against the darkness of the tree line. The leader stopped and the second smuggler, the blond mustached one, came up to discuss it.

"It's a flashlight," he said, as we strained to make it out better. "Could be a patrol. I think we had better change the route."

"No," the first one said, "there shouldn't be any patrols over in that direction. It's probably just someone passing by out there. I don't think it's anything we have to worry about. Changing routes will be a big pain. I don't want to do it."

The discussion started out normally, but it turned angry fast. Although they kept their voices low, I was standing at the front and heard everything. When the squat one wouldn't change his mind, the younger one finally said, "Goddammit, if you think I'm going to walk into a German trap, you're crazy. I'm going the other way, and my people are coming with me. Understand?"

"You can do whatever the hell you want to do," the squat one growled. "Take them and get out of here."

"Fine," said the younger one, "I'm going. Just hand over my share of the Jews' money." He motioned to us.

"Like hell I will," said the squat one. "What business is that of yours? The Jews never made any deals with you, only with me. You didn't have anything to do with it."

They glared at each other, their eyes shining with anger. If one of them pulls a knife, I thought, we're going to have real trouble. Then the younger one said, "You son of a bitch.

I'm going, but I'm going to teach you a lesson you'll never forget." With that he gathered his people, about half the group, and headed toward the north. The cow stayed with us.

We kept walking toward the tree line, everyone tense and alert, even though the flickering light had disappeared. If it was a German patrol, as the other smuggler had said, they could be lying in wait for us. The dirt track took us to the forest, where the smuggler immediately found a path that went into the woods. There was no sign of anything unusual. For the next two hours we walked in silence until we came to a halt before a barbed wire fence that stretched out into the trees in both directions: the border. From his pack the smuggler drew out shears and cut the wire on two sides, making a hole big enough for the cow to walk through. Quickly we crossed into Poland.

After another mile or two we came to a small river where a fisherman's house perched on the bank. In the yard the carriers put down their loads—this apparently was the drop off point. For the first time there was some muted talk as they waited for the smuggler's order to head back. From what I could understand, a second group would be arriving soon to take the contraband and deliver it to the distributor, whose own network would sell it. There were large numbers of people involved, a whole organization that managed to gather the food, transport it, distribute it, sell it, and keep the financial arrangements straight. I wondered how they got their information about German patrols, and if they had any way to protect themselves.

We waited as the chief smuggler talked to the fisherman. When he finished he came over to me and said, "You shouldn't stay here. It's not safe. I'm afraid my friend who left us back there could be up to some mischief. You'd better leave immediately. This man here,"—gesturing toward the fisherman—"can take you to the other side. There's a railroad station not too far off. You can get a train there for Warsaw."

"Okay," I said, "that's what we'll do. We want to thank you for your help."

"One more thing," he said. "Take this." He gave me a piece of paper. "It's the address of a priest in Warsaw who can help you get train tickets. You might not be able to do it yourselves."

The fisherman had a rowboat tied to a little pier that jutted into the river. We climbed in and two minutes later we were on the other shore. There the fisherman led us to a path. "Follow this a mile or so," he said, "and it'll take you right to the railroad station."

The sky brightened in front of us as we walked. At the station the ticket window was already opened and I bought two tickets for Warsaw while my friend hung in the background keeping out of the ticketmaster's view. We didn't have to wait more than ten or fifteen minutes before the train arrived, packed with laborers going to Warsaw for the day's work. We got on and stood in the crowd as the train swayed and clacked toward the capital.

The train felt safe—there was a kind of anonymity among all the grim, silent workers. Then I heard a voice in my ear. The man standing just in front of me was whispering. "Look there," he said, flicking his head toward my companion. "You see what's standing behind you? It's a Jew." I glanced at my friend. "Who knows?" I said to the informant. "Who the hell knows who he is?"

In Warsaw we found our way to the priest's address the smuggler had given us. My impression was that this priest was probably working for the Polish underground. He didn't ask a single question, he just did what he could to help. He gave us food, then went out and bought us train tickets to Lvov. With hindsight, I guessed he was part of the organization that was working with the Jewish underground, helping Jews acquire arms, or escape, or putting children into monasteries and other safe places. There were networks that did such things, as I learned later on, and more than a few Catholic priests were involved.

It was already March 1943. I had been in Novy Dwor for about seven months and momentous things had occurred outside my closed world, about which I knew absolutely nothing. A little over a month earlier, the Germans had suffered their great defeat at Stalingrad. In the north the

Russians had pushed them back from Moscow. Even the siege of Leningrad was over. Nor did I know that in Warsaw the Jews had begun to fight back. In January a fighting group had repulsed a German patrol and killed some of them. When my companion and I had been in Warsaw, the Jewish fighting organization had been making plans to defend the ghetto. The Uprising itself was only a month or so off.

When the priest came back with the tickets he told us the best way to get to the main station. We planned our walk so that we would arrive there shortly before the train was to leave. Of course the Warsaw station would be full of watchers, hunting for Jews. The incident with the worker on the train was a warning. We were just lucky nothing further had come of it. By now my traveling companion was acutely aware of the dangers. But instead of making him more careful, it had turned him into a nervous wreck. He was terrified, and everything about him showed it.

We got to the station without any problems and entered the waiting train. One hurdle gone, I thought. Sitting in a compartment instead of loitering in the station cut our chances of being spotted. The next danger would be from the conductor or from the police who sometimes checked the trains. But Lublin, where we were going to have to change trains, really scared me. Lublin was a major city with a busy station, and we would have to wait there several hours. Alone, that wouldn't have been a problem, but with this person along, it was a different matter. I didn't have a clear idea what to do about it, but I was feeling extremely apprehensive.

Four hours later we arrived in Lublin. The conductor had taken our tickets and his eyes lingered on my companion, but then he had moved on without saying anything. Luckily there didn't seem to be any police on the train. But the Lublin station was another story. We walked from the platform into a large waiting room crowded with people, some sitting on benches, others buying tickets or just waiting for their trains. I saw two or three uniformed Polish police talking to each other near the ticket booth. There were no German uniforms in sight, but I could sense that agents and informers were in the crowd. I scanned the room, trying to spot anybody suspicious but not wanting to draw attention to myself. "You sit over there," I told my companion, pointing out a bench with some open seats. "It's too dangerous for us to sit together. I'm going to sit right here where you can see me. I want you to watch me and do exactly what I'm doing. Okay?"

He nodded his agreement. But when I went to a nearby bench to sit down, instead of going where I had indicated he followed me. When I sat, he sat next to me. His hands were shaking. Sweat beaded his forehead. I couldn't raise my voice. I wanted to talk to him as little as possible. "Don't be close," I whispered under my breath. "Don't stay next to me. It's too dangerous." He didn't give any sign that he understood.

I waited a few minutes, doing my best to keep the anxiety off my face. Then I whispered, "Don't come," and got up to change my seat.

To my horror, he stood up and followed me to a bench a few rows over. I thought quickly about sitting between two Poles, where there would be no room for him to squeeze in. But I thought he would probably just stand hovering over me. It was obvious his fright had overwhelmed him. He had stopped thinking rationally and was hanging on to me as if I was some kind of island of safety. We sat down together again. I concentrated on being my Polish self, trying mentally to distance myself from the man at my side.

It was another two nerve wracking hours before they announced the train to Lvov. My gut told me we must have been spotted, though nobody had made any moves yet. If we can just make it onto the train, I thought, we'll have a chance. We joined the line of passengers showing their tickets in order to get onto the platform. As I came up to the attendant I held mine out for him to see. But before he opened the door to let me out, two uniformed men materialized at my side. My heart stopped. They were wearing the black hats of the Gestapo. "Komm mit mir," said one. I saw they had my friend too. They herded us toward a door I hadn't noticed before at the side of the waiting room.

We walked through the door into the station office of the Gestapo. My knees felt a little weak, but in my head

I was transforming myself into Edward Wawer, putting him on like a familiar suit of clothes. I had told myself a hundred times that there was no way the identity would stand up to a real interrogation, but now that I was facing one, I couldn't think of that. I was Polish, nothing else. A Pole from the village of Koryczany.

Inside the station office my companion and I were immediately separated. He was led off down the hall and I was taken into a small room. Behind the desk sat a Gestapo officer; a second one was off to the side. The second one was holding a whip in one hand, smacking the handle lightly into his other palm. "Everything out of your pockets," the one behind the desk said, *"Leer dein taschen aus."* I took out my billfold, a few coins, and my incriminating box of matches. But I left Gromb's little diamond ring. *"Name!"* he demanded. "Your name!" *"Was machst du hier? Wo gehst du hin?"* "What are you doing here? Where are you going?"

"My name is Edward Wawer," I said. I took the documents out of my billfold. "I'm traveling to Lvov."

Suddenly my head was on fire with a pain so sharp my vision started to darken. The second Gestapo had cracked me with the whip, which must have had a lead weight at the tip. "Jesus Christ!" I screamed. "Why are you hitting me?" My eyes cleared slowly. I put my hand to my ear. It came away smeared with blood. *"Sancta Maria,"* I mumbled. "Don't hit me."

The one behind the desk stood up. "*Runter mit dem hosen,*" "Put your pants down," he barked. He mimed undoing his belt and dropping his pants. Now my time is really up, I thought. This is the end of the game. They were trained to do this, it was obvious. Smack them when they're not ready and see if the say "Oy vey," or maybe "Shema Yisrael." If they do, you know you've got a Jew. If not, make them drop their pants.

I pulled my pants down. He gestured again. I slipped my underpants to my knees. The two Germans stared at me. Just then there was a knock at the door and a third policeman walked in, this one in a Polish uniform.

"*Ist er Jude?*" "Is he a Jew?", asked the one behind the desk. The Pole looked.

"*Jahwol,*" he said. "*Er ist.*" "Yes, He is."

"*Nein, dummkopf!*" said the Gestapo. "*Er ist nicht Jude.*" "You're a fool, idiot. He is not a Jew."

Then to me, "Pull up your pants. Now pick up your things and get the hell out of here. I'm telling you, if we ever catch you transporting Jews again, we'll shoot you like a dog."

16

THE TRACKS

Spring/Summer, 1943

Out in the waiting room I managed to walk casually to an empty bench. The instant I sat down, an immense weariness came over me. The hall was full of people and noise, but I hardly heard anything. The only distinct sound was the pounding of my own heart. I slumped in the seat, too tired to move my eyes to see if anyone was watching.

I was trying to understand what had happened back there, but my head seemed filled with cobwebs. All I wanted to do was sleep, waft away somewhere in a soft bed where I could collapse and sleep the sleep of the dead. The one thought that emerged through the cobwebs was that I had come back from death. In some miraculous, incomprehensible way, I had been saved. Death had ejected me from its maw and flung me back into the world of the living.

Slowly the sounds of the station began to grow louder, as if someone had turned up the volume on a radio. What really had happened? I tried to imagine the Germans being trained in Jew hunting. "All Jews are circumcised. Make them pull down their pants and see if they're Yids or not." But nobody had told them what a circumcision is. They stare at me, but they don't know what they're supposed to be looking for. Then a Pole comes in, who does know. But to them he's just a dumb Pole, an inferior sub-human himself. What *ubermensch* in his right mind would pay attention to anything some idiot Pole might think? And so here I am, sitting among the living while my poor friend is on his way to death.

It was nearly midnight before the next train to Lvov arrived in Lublin. In all those hours I don't think I moved, but now I got up and walked out to the train, only a little shaky. In the compartment I sat down and almost instantly felt myself slipping off to sleep. Before I lost consciousness I had time to think for a moment about Hungary, where Gromb and I had planned to escape. Not such a good idea now, I told myself. No Gromb, no partner. Also, my ankle still had some weakness. On the all-night hike with the smugglers, it had felt sore and fragile. Nothing serious, I hoped. But it probably wouldn't be such a great idea to test it out trying to escape on foot through the Carpathians. I had a brief, half-asleep image of myself in the mountains during hikes a decade ago with my young Zionist group, then I slept.

I was awakened out of a dreamless sleep by a premonition that something was wrong. The gray light of an overcast dawn filtered into the compartment; five, maybe six hours had gone by since we left Lublin. The first thing I noticed was that I was no longer alone. Two travelers had joined me while I was sleeping. They were both sprawled in their seats, their legs stretched out, snoring softly. The train moved deliberately, almost lethargically. I looked out the window, still troubled by a sense of foreboding. Then I saw, scattered along the sides of the railroad bed, drab patches of clothing, rags really, dingy remnants of dresses and suits, pants and shirts, black, white, no real colors, strewn on the bare gravel and mud off the right of way. I shook my head to clear the sleep from my eyes, and suddenly I knew what I was looking at. The train was chugging slowly not through strange heaps of discarded rags, but through a jumbled trail of corpses that had been tossed haphazardly alongside the train tracks.

For a moment I stared. Then, as if by reflex, I jumped up and went into the corridor to look out the other side. Here too they lay, the same litter of dead people. Men, many of them, but women too. And children, flung here and there in the slack, disjointed postures of death. The train had slowed, as if specifically to give me time to absorb the details of tiny hands and bare legs and a face or two gazing skyward in innocence.

Jews, from some transport. It couldn't be anything else. I felt my body trembling and at the same instant I realized I had been searching those forms for a woman I would recognize, one with a baby in her arms. In a few seconds they were gone, the last heaps receded, then disappeared. I stood frozen in the corridor, unable to think, yet flooded with all the knowledge I needed. The rumors, the wild speculation about these transports, trains filled with Jews bound for unknown destinations, vanishing from the earth. The meaning was revealed to me as if a veil had suddenly been lifted.

I re-entered my compartment and carefully sat down. My companions were still snoring away, oblivious. The dead, gray landscape had turned strangely turgid, viscous. The train seemed to be laboring through a thickened, nameless gelidity that drained muscles and nerves of their vital force. The texture of the air itself was transformed; it congealed and cloyed. I had the distinct impression of struggling for breath. I knew something I hadn't known before, but though I tried I couldn't identify it. It wasn't till later that I realized that what I saw along those tracks was the personification of Evil itself. With all I had witnessed and lived through, I had resisted in every way I could, consciously and unconsciously, the single great, soul-destroying revelation of Evil enthroned on earth. And now I knew. I knew, but I did not then have the capacity to understand, nor do I even now, so many years and decades after that vision. And so I didn't dwell on it. Instead, as the train covered the final miles to Lvov, my mind mercifully filled itself with vivid, living pictures of Wusia and Michael.

By the time the train arrived at Lvov's Wiener Banhof I had decided my next move. Seven months ago, after we had been forced to abandon the barn, Chaim Rosen had planned to report himself for work at the labor camp on Pierockiego, the one they called the HKP. The other Jewish teachers from Korkis had already been sent there at the end of the 1942 school year. The labor camp was an annex of the Janowska concentration camp, which was a hellhole. But we had heard that conditions at the HKP were much better. The camp's main function was to repair German military equipment and that required skilled personnel who had to be kept in at least minimally decent health. Most of the workers were Jewish prisoners, but free Aryans also worked there. The only real difference was that the Ukrainians and Poles went home at night. I could apply for a job there as Edward Wawer. All I'd need after that would be a place to sleep in Lvov.

What I needed first, though, was somewhere I could go to catch my breath. I was suddenly ravenous. My last meal had been with the priest in Warsaw, twenty-four hours ago, an eternity. It was now the middle of the morning. At this hour I didn't dare go to Nabielacka, where there was a good chance the Gestapo families would be up and around. Chris was a possibility, my old colleague, but he was way out in Zimna Woda and I didn't feel up to the walk. The only other Christian person I was friendly with in town was Edward Wawer. Edward and his sister Helena lived on Kaspra Boczkowskiego, not too far away. Edward wouldn't be home at this hour, but Helena would. I needed a meal and a bed for the night. She had welcomed me to her home in the past. I felt sure she would again.

To my surprise, Edward and Helena were both at home. Neither of them expected such a guest at their door, but they welcomed me warmly and quickly invited me in. I was pretty sure that Helena didn't know I had Edward's documents, though she must have assumed I was carrying some kind of Aryan papers. I wouldn't be out in daylight otherwise. Edward would not have mentioned giving his identity to a Jew to anybody, even his sister. It would be too dangerous. Helena couldn't suspect that she now had two Edward Wawers under her roof. When I asked if I could stay the night, she agreed without hesitating. I wasn't happy about imposing on them, especially since Edward had originally asked me not to stay in Lvov with his papers. Now there didn't seem to be any choice and Edward with his usual good humor didn't bring the subject up, even after Helena had gone to sleep.

The next morning I thanked Edward and Helena and left for the HKP. Pierockiego Street was off only a short distance from the Janowska concentration camp, of which the HKP was technically a part. On one side of the street were the labor camp kitchen and barracks, where the Jews were kept at night. On the other side were yards and workshops where damaged weapons and vehicles were repaired, then shipped back to re-equip the Wehrmacht. In the office I registered as

Edward Wawer and listed myself as an experienced technician, competent with machinery of various kinds. They signed me up without a second glance. I had exactly the skills they needed. The clerk gave me an HKP identity card, and then someone walked me across the street into the enclosed yards and pointed out the workshop I was assigned to. "Report to the foreman," he said, then turned around and went back.

The first person I came to was leaning over the engine of a small truck where I could only see his back. But the back looked strangely familiar. When I said hello, he turned around and it was Chaim Rosen, looking no different from the time we said good-bye more than half a year ago. A huge smile spread over Chaim's face, and the next instant we were hugging each other and practically jumping up and down for joy. When we calmed down, Chaim said, "Wait, I have to show you who else is here." He called out as we walked toward the back of the shop, and in a minute Horowitz, Probst, and Shiff were standing around me pumping my hand, "There are more too," said Chaim, "in the other workshops. A lot of the old crew is still working here. The place is full of our instructors and engineers."

A few minutes later I was bent over the fender of the truck next to Chaim, but we were talking more than working. "It's not bad," he was telling me. "The food's terrible, and there isn't much, but at least they feed us. The head of the camp is Hartmann, an Austrian. It sounds crazy, but he's a really good guy, a *mensch*. He tries not to hurt people. But the Gestapo show up pretty often, so you've got to watch yourself. They come from Janowska to check up. Sometimes they just want a little fun. The sadistic bastards will shoot people for nothing. I'll show you the ones to look out for."

"Chaim," I said. I wanted to hear everything, but the images of death along the railroad tracks were pressing on me. I hadn't been able to get them out of my mind. I had to find out what Chaim might know. As matter of factly as I could, I told him what I had seen. I steeled myself to keep a grip on my emotions. "There were bodies," I said, "all along the tracks on both sides—men, women, and children. What happened there, Chaim? Please, do you know?"

"Where was this?" he asked.

"Outside Lvov, sixty, maybe eighty kilometers."

"Near Belzec?"

"I guess. Not far."

"Wilo, people are being shipped to Belzec, from the ghetto. It's been going on for at least six, eight months, maybe more. They've systematically emptied the sector. I don't know how many they've taken already."

"Your mother and your brother?"

"They're still here, thank God, though I haven't seen them in a year. I've talked to my uncle, though. He's in a labor gang they brought here to work a couple of times.

Something is happening in that forest, Wilo. Nobody who goes to Belzec comes back. Nobody escapes. No one gets messages out. Those people you saw, the bodies? We heard that a trainload left for there two days ago. They must have pried open a boxcar and jumped. I'm sure that's what it was. Everyone takes prying tools now. The Germans must have machine gunned them."

I listened carefully. What Chaim was saying about Belzec was the same kind of thing I had heard in Novy Dwor, that the Germans had set up killing places where they were gassing people to death or electrocuting them. But the fact was that he didn't know. The idea was still incomprehensible. Mysterious, terrible things were happening, that wasn't in dispute. But killing factories? I knew that whatever was going on, Wusia's chances for survival were slim, Michael's even slimmer. But I clung to the hope with all my might. Miracles happened in this life. Somehow Chaim's report set my determination in steel. No matter what it took, I was going to stay alive. Imagine, I told myself, that when this war is over and Wusia and Michael come back from some hard labor camp, and you are not there to meet them because you're dead. Because you allowed these bastards to kill you. I couldn't even entertain the thought.

That night after a meager dinner of watery soup and bread the Jews were locked up and the Aryans (including me) walked out onto Pierockiego Street. They went home.

I was on my way to Nabielacka 12 where I planned to talk to Katy Wowkowa about staying in the basement. That would be the perfect arrangement. If she'd let me, I could stay nights in the coal storage stall of her apartment. I still had my key to the building so I could slip in there after dark, then leave for the HKP early in the morning, before the Nazis were awake.

"*Panie* Ungar!" Katy said when she opened her door. I had let myself in the front. She didn't even seem that surprised. I had showed up unexpectedly seven months ago, and now I had done it again. Katy didn't have an emotional temperament; she tended to accept things as they were without getting too excited. To my everlasting fortune, she was also the kindest of people. She wouldn't hurt a fly, and if she had a chance to do a kindness, she would. I asked her. She knew the risks, but she didn't hesitate for a second. We went into the coal storage area and looked into her stall, a bin about twelve feet long and eight feet wide, with a narrow bench along one wall and a bare, low watt bulb above the door. The stall was half filled with coal, leaving enough room so that I could lie down on the bench. She gave me a thin blanket to spread on the boards. The toilet she used was in a closet off the basement hallway next to her room. I could use it too. As long as I was careful, everything should be fine, she said. I could stay as long as I wanted.

And so I started my life as a commuter. Six days a week I worked at the HKP repairing guns of all sorts, machine guns to artillery pieces, also trucks, cars, tanks, every military item you might imagine that had been wrecked in battle but was still salvageable. I wasn't an expert in such things. My specialty at Korkis had been the construction of industrial machines: lathes, punch presses, shapers, and drill presses. But I was well enough versed to figure out almost any kind of mechanism, and the workshops had all the equipment and tools one might need. We were glad to be together—Chaim, the others and I. We worked in teams, went to the cafeteria for watery soup and bread for lunch, then had dinner—more soup and bread—before quitting time. It was a skilled, capable group. We thought we were in exactly the right place, and that our chances for survival were decent. Who could the Germans possibly need more than they needed us?

Of course all the Jews knew who I was, and why I was disappearing at night. But nobody cared that I was successfully passing myself off as an Aryan. The only exception, I thought, might be Tenenbaum, the so-called *oberjude*, the Jew placed in charge by the Germans. Tenenbaum was the chief of the Jewish workers, but like them he too was a prisoner. We didn't really have anything to do with each other, but from the way I saw him look at me, I thought he might be harboring resentments. What business did I have being free when he wasn't? It was possible I was just imagining things, and after all he wasn't my boss anyway. But I made a mental note to be watchful.

One day while we were eating lunch Chaim said, "Wilo, I'm so worried about my mother. I've been thinking of asking you," he hesitated, then went on, "but I don't know if I have the right."

"Ask what? You can ask me anything."

"I've been thinking of asking if maybe you could get into the ghetto to see her for me. To find out how she is. Maybe with your papers you might be able to do it."

"Chaim, I would be ready to try this instant, but how could I get in there, and if I could, how would I get out?"

"I think my uncle Nemed could arrange it. He's been working at a big clothing factory on Zulkiewska Street. He goes there from the ghetto every morning with his labor gang, then at night they go back. A Jewish policeman takes them in and out, but I'm sure Nemed could deal with him."

The next night after work, instead of going to the kitchen for my meager meal, I left the camp and walked to Zulkiewska Street. With luck I arrived outside the factory just as the Jewish workers were coming out of the building. Slaves would be a better description. They looked much worse than the HKP inmates did. Their clothes were rags. They looked starved and beaten down, decrepit. Still, I recognized Nemed immediately; I had met him many times before the Germans came. I took him aside and told him what Chaim wanted. Then I waited while he exchanged a few words with their Jewish policeman guard. "It's okay," he told me. "Just pretend you're part of the group. There shouldn't be any problem."

The thirty or forty workers shuffled through the streets toward the ghetto without a word, too exhausted to talk. At the ghetto gate the policeman waved toward a Gestapo standing outside the guard booth, then we shuffled through without even a count. Inside, Nemed took me along a maze of streets I hardly recognized. There were few lights. Dark night and a kind of haze or fog obscured dilapidated buildings. People passed by like wraiths, drawn into themselves, silent. A heavy sadness weighed over everything.

We went into one of the buildings and entered an apartment. Inside, with eight or nine other people, were Chaim's mother and brother. I thought for a moment, is this his mother or his grandmother? I tried to remember if his grandmother was still alive, I couldn't recall ever having met her. Then I realized there wasn't any grandmother, it was his mother. She had aged thirty years since I saw her last.

I could feel the fear among the people in the apartment. It seemed as if they had given up hopes of surviving, but that didn't stop them from being terrified by the idea of dying. When I left Lvov, eight months before, there had only been a Jewish district. Not long after that, the Germans had established a closed ghetto, with barbed wire strung around it and guards to keep people in. Since then they had been emptying the ghetto out trainload by trainload, rounding people up and herding them into long lines of boxcars. By now most of the "useless" Jews, the ones too young or too old or too sick to work, had been deported. Those left were now awaiting their own turn.

Chaim's mother talked slowly, in a voice so low I had to strain to hear her. She told me that the ghetto kept shrinking. The more people they took away, the more they contracted the area, the more crowded the conditions became. They had ten people living in two small rooms. There was barely enough air to breathe. Food rations were shrinking too. The Germans seemed determined to kill everyone, if not one way then another. Was there any possibility that Chaim could get them out of here, she wanted to know. I should go back and tell him how bad things were so that he could try to do something. No one knew who would be alive tomorrow. The day after might be too late.

Later that evening a couple of my old friends came by to talk, they had heard I was in the ghetto. Abe Szpach had been a teacher at Korkis, and Pninah Klein was an old comrade from the days when I lived in the "Kvutzah Barzel" Zionist collective. All of this was before I went into the army for my basic training. Both of them had more spirit than Chaim's mother and her friends. But the story they told was the same. Atrocities, shootings, SS and Einsatzgruppen roundups. A steady stream of people disappearing.

That night I slept on the floor, jammed between other seemingly anonymous bodies. Early next morning I said good-bye, then left to join Nemed's group so I could get out of the ghetto and back to the relative normality of the labor camp. In the area before the gate we lined up haphazardly, then we began to move. The Jewish policeman was talking to the Gestapo, giving him some kind of report. Then, as we started to shuffle forward, to my horror everyone took off his cap so he would pass the Gestapo bareheaded. I took off mine too, but unlike me, all the prisoners had had their heads shorn. Some were bald, others had a short stubbly growth. My blond hair stood out like a full moon.

I looked at the Gestapo, who was still talking to the Jewish policeman but throwing glances at the group as we went through the gate. In front of me toward the right I noticed a couple of taller prisoners and moved up awkwardly to get between them, watching to see if the Gestapo's eyes were turning in my direction. My heart palpitated as we passed through the gate. The Gestapo couldn't have been more than fifteen feet away. I tried to scrunch down a little as I walked, keeping the fellow to my left between me and the Gestapo and expecting at any moment a loud shout in German. If it came, I could run. But could I escape, and if I did, where would I go? At last we were outside the gate, plodding reluctantly when what I wanted to do was to run like the wind. My heart was still racing when, to my unutterable relief, everyone began putting his cap back on his head.

17

ESCAPE FROM JANOWSKA

Spring/Summer, 1943

One Saturday evening not too long after my visit to the ghetto I was sitting with Chaim eating, or rather slurping, our usual watery soup dinner, and congratulating myself that I had just found a small, gnarled potato in the bottom of my canteen. Maybe it was a good omen. Goldschlag, the always polite, elderly food server had scooped it up from the soup caldron along with a few bits of greenery. He often did that for me. We were acquaintances rather than friends, but we commonly exchanged amiable hellos and a few words of conversation. Goldschlag had been a prominent attorney in Brzezany. Now he was a soup ladler, but his changed circumstances never seemed to affect his good humor.

I was weighing whether to eat the potato in one bite or nibble it a piece at a time when Tenenbaum, the *oberjude*, walked up to the table. "Ungar!" His voice was loud, hard-edged. People looked around to see what was happening. "When you're through I want you at the barracks. You're on cleaning crew tonight. So don't waste too much time eating, just finish up and get over there."

If the usual cleaners had needed help and Tenenbaum had asked me politely, I might possibly have gone to clean the barracks, even though I didn't live there. Instead, I got angry. The barracks had nothing to do with me, nor I with them. He was jealous, I thought. It was Saturday night and he was furious that I was going into town (I was going off to sleep in a coal bin) and he was locked in. This was his idea of getting even. He was showing me and everyone else that he was the big man here.

Well, I thought, to hell with you, Tenenbaum. What makes you think I'd listen to anything you tell me? I may actually have said those things rather than just thinking them. He got so red in the face I thought he might have a stroke. "I'm the boss around here," he barked. "You might think you're better than everyone else, but you could find things getting unpleasant awfully fast." I didn't pay too much attention, and our little conflict quickly petered out. I didn't go to clean and he didn't push the issue. Under those conditions people often got angry with each other, but almost always tempers died down as fast as they flared up. I have plenty of real things to worry about, I thought; I should worry about him too? I forgot about it, and it seemed he did too. When we saw each other after that we just nodded hello. Whatever bothered him about me, seemed to have been resolved.

One of my worries was money. I still had Gromb's little ring and his twenty-dollar bill tucked into the matchbox. But all the money I had gotten from selling our things from the apartment was gone, which made me nervous. You could never tell what you might need or when you might need it, for bribes, for instance. When you did need it, having money could mean the difference between life and death. One possibility was the black market. I made some inquiries and before long I had found a supplier, the wife of an orthodox priest, who kept chickens and a cow in an enclosure behind her house. From her I obtained some eggs and butter every week, which I sold in the labor camp. I wasn't exactly an egg dealer on Uncle Nissen's scale, but I began to build up a small reserve of cash for emergencies.

The HKP was a chancy place, although a lot safer than the Janowska concentration camp down the street. Janowska was a horror. We heard many stories about what went on there, the torture, the beatings and murders. For many people Janowska was just a storage bin where they were dumped until the Germans could ship them to Belzec. For others it was a place to endure daily brutalization while the Germans starved them to death. According to the stories, the two commandants who ran it, Willhaus and Gebauer, were human beasts who took pleasure in inflicting pain and suffering on helpless people.

The HKP was nothing like that, but if you were unlucky it was a place where you could die quickly, especially when the Gestapo came around. Every few days they would show up, sometimes a couple of them, sometimes as many as four or five, to inspect the camp or just to inspire terror. Occasionally they'd come at night, making surprise visits to the barracks, which I'd hear about the next day. At times, they'd come while we were working. Like all the Jews at the HKP, I learned their names, and knew which ones were the real torturers and sadists.

One day I was getting something from a storage room with a window facing the street. It was lunchtime and most of the workers had already gone to stand on the soup line. Looking outside, I saw three Gestapo marching down Pierackiego, one of them Kolanko, a notorious killer. As I watched they turned into the gate on the other side, where the offices, barracks, and cafeteria were. This could be bad news, I thought, so I stayed where I was and worked through lunchtime. Sometime after the break people started filtering dejectedly back to the workshops. When Chaim returned he told me what had happened. The Gestapo had taken everyone outside and made them line up, all three hundred-plus workers. They announced that someone had escaped from Janowska. Then Kolanko picked three people out of the line at random, and shot them. One was my friend Mr. Goldschlag.

After that, I rarely ate lunch, a bad idea considering our daily caloric intake. But it was more important not to expose myself unnecessarily. I had made up my mind to live, and Mr. Goldschlag's tragic end made a deep impression. The Gestapo could arrive at any time, but it was more likely they'd come while everybody was together, in the cafeteria for instance, rather than taking the trouble to roust people out of the many workshops.

But despite my efforts to stay out of their way, one day they came for me. That morning I was busy repairing a machine gun cooling system, I looked up to see one of the Gestapo walking up to me. "We hear you know how to fix radios," he said. "We have one in the office that's broken. Come look at it." That should have warned me. Before Mr. Badian hired me as an instructor I had worked on radios at Appel's electronics store. That was many years ago, and how did this Gestapo know about it?

But I didn't think of that, so I wasn't completely alert to what was going on until we stepped into the office. A second Gestapo was sitting behind the desk, but I didn't see any radio. Looking at me, he pulled a black Luger pistol out of his holster. He cradled it in his hands for a moment, as if deciding what to do with it. Then he laid it on the desk in front of him. "We're taking you to Janowska," he said. "We hear you like to escape from places. You try anything with us, and this is for you." He patted the Luger. "Now, empty your pockets."

I took out my box of matches and my billfold with the documents, where I also had my egg and butter money.

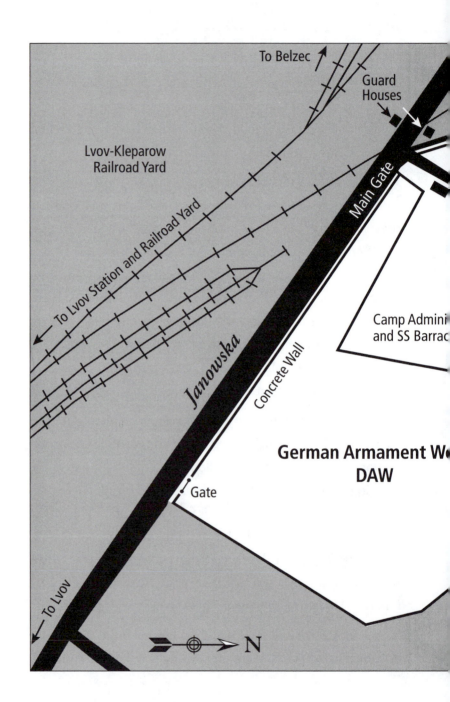

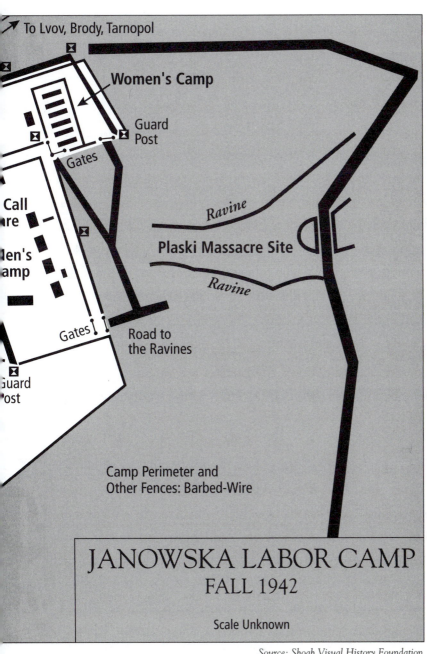

To Lvov, Brody, Tarnopol

Women's Camp

Guard
Post

Gates

Call
re

len's
amp

Ravine

Plaski Massacre Site

Ravine

Gates

Road to
the Ravines

Guard
ost

Camp Perimeter and
Other Fences: Barbed-Wire

JANOWSKA LABOR CAMP
FALL 1942

Scale Unknown

Source: Shoah Visual History Foundation

I managed to slip my watch into my coat pocket, where the ring was. I was taking a chance that they wouldn't search me. But they hadn't done that in the Lublin station. Maybe they wouldn't now.

While I was doing this the Gestapo who had brought me stepped out of the office, leaving me alone with the one behind the desk. When he looked in my billfold, he got excited, not about my papers, which he didn't even look at, but about by my stash of black market money. He took the money out and shoved it into his pocket before the door opened and his colleague came back. Quickly, as if he had just finished examining my effects, he shoved the billfold and matchbox back towards me. Then the first one took my arm and said, "Let's get moving."

A little way down the corridor we passed Tenenbaum, who had his own office in the area. Seeing a Jewish face gave me a sudden twinge of hope, even though we had had problems in the past. "Excuse me," I said to the Gestapo holding my arm. "Might I please be permitted to write a note for Mr. Tenenbaum to give to a friend, just to tell him where I'm going?" To my surprise, he said, "Yes, it's permitted. Go ahead." I found a scrap of paper in my billfold and Tenenbaum fished a pencil out of his jacket. I wrote on the paper, "To Chaim Rosen." With my back to the Gestapo I gave Tenenbaum not just the note, but the whole billfold. "It's got my papers in it," I whispered. "Give them to Chaim."

"Okay," he said, putting them in his pocket. "Good-bye, Mr. Tenenbaum," I said, louder. "Good-bye," he said, and walked off one way while the Gestapo and I went the other.

I walked between the two Gestapo to the corner of Pierackiego, then down Janowska Street toward a sprawling industrial area of factories, sheds, garages, and yards, all behind a high barbed wire fence with machine gun towers at the corners. The Janowska concentration camp. I fought my anxiety. You have to stay alert, I told myself, and this is a place where you'll need to have all your faculties.

The big front gate creaked open to let us in and we walked into the first building, a reception area. There the Gestapo left me in front of a desk where two clerks were sitting, a man and a young woman, whose job was to register new arrivals. It was obvious that they were Jews, and when we started talking it turned out that the man's name was Richter. He was the brother of a boy who had been at the Korkis School, whom I remembered well. The family were Viennese Jews who had fled the Anschluss for the safety of Lvov. "We speak German," he said, "so they made us clerks."

It had never occurred to me that I might be registered by two friendly Jews, who were now filling out forms, as if I was applying for a job. The Germans wanted name, date of birth, family members, education, profession—precise personal details of those they were going to kill.

While they were taking my information, we had a friendly talk. As we finished I gave the young woman my matchbox, watch, and the diamond ring—my only possessions. I had no doubt I was going to be thoroughly searched this time, and I didn't want to be caught with them. "Take these," I said. "Someday if we meet again you can give them back to me."

A minute later a guard came and took me out of the building and through a second gate into the heart of the camp. We went into a big shed filled with tiers of wooden bunks separated by narrow aisles. "You sleep here," he said. He gave me a bunk number. "Take these," he handed me a canteen and a spoon. "Wait here and you'll be told what to do."

I was standing there staring at rows and rows of empty tiers when two barbers appeared, one of them carrying a stool. They were inmates, Jews, but there was nothing friendly about them. "Sit down," one said, "we're shaving your head."

I started to argue. I didn't want my head shaved, the first step in dehumanization. "You can't cut my hair," I said. "I've got chronic migraines and that will make them worse. "What?" said one. "What are you, crazy? Where do you think you are, in some kind of health spa?"

"No," I said. "You really can't do it. I told you, I've got bad migraines."

"Look, friend," the second one said, "don't give us any migraine stories. Just sit down before something worse than a haircut happens to you."

"No. Listen, you know Richter from the registration office? He said the barbers should leave me alone. So leave me alone."

That did it, they heard Richter's name and they left. As long as somebody else was taking the responsibility, it was all right with them.

It was then that I noticed someone at the other end of the barracks. He seemed to be motioning to me, so I walked over to him. As I got closer I realized it was Shiff, one of the Korkis engineers. He had been with us in the HKP, but several weeks earlier they had taken him away. Nobody knew that he had ended up here. Shiff looked awful, hollowed out and spiritless, as if the few weeks here had broken him completely. "I'm sorry to see you here, Ungar." His voice was a rasp. "This is a place of fiends." He barely had enough breath to choke his words out. "You know the Chwila?" The Chwila was a Polish language Jewish newspaper I used to read regularly. "Last week they killed the editor's daughter, the beautiful one. She had made friends with one of the Gestapo. He used to visit her all the time in the women's barracks, bringing her extra food and things. Then last week she heard she was going on a transport to Belzec. She pleaded with him to save her so she wouldn't have to go. He promised her she wouldn't leave Janowska, then he took out his gun and shot her in the head. That's what they're like here."

Shiff went from one story of atrocity to another, as if he could think of nothing else. Finally, with tears streaming down his cheeks, he said, "They killed my son too." They had brought his son to Janowska from the ghetto. Then one morning at roll call they made a selection. The impression I had was that this had happened very recently, maybe a day or two earlier, but I couldn't tell exactly from Shiff's choked description. His son was selected and he and the others were marched into the sand barrens in back of Janowska and murdered.

Even before Shiff started telling me about his son, I was finding it very difficult to listen. I felt as if someone was jabbing me with a hot needle. While he was talking a single thought forced its way into my consciousness: How can I get out of here? Somewhere a bell rang. "Excuse me," I said, "I have to go." I got up and walked away. I don't know where I thought I was going, but I had an overpowering sense that I had to find a way out.

Right outside the bunkroom was a big lavatory where some prisoners were washing out their canteens. They had just eaten, one of them said when I poked my head in. If I was new, I had missed lunch. When I asked where he was working, he told me that his group worked outside the camp in the Jewish cemetery. They broke tombstones into pieces so the Germans could use them as gravel. They had just come back to eat, now they would be going back again.

As I was absorbing this information, a tall Jewish policeman walked into the lavatory. "What do you think you're doing?" he said. "Who gave you permission to talk to these prisoners? Are you up to something?" "No," I said. "I just arrived and I thought maybe I would know somebody. They were telling me I missed lunch. I'm just going." I walked out quickly, feeling his eyes on me.

Down the hall was a second lavatory where another group of prisoners was washing canteens. Like the first group, their heads were shaved and they were wearing striped prison clothes. A guard was with them, but he didn't mind my coming in and striking up a conversation. They too worked at the cemetery, pulling out tombstones and pounding them into pieces with hammers. The stones were used for roadways, they said. Many loads of them had even been brought to Janowska. That's what the gravel walks were made of.

They too were on their way back to the cemetery. When I asked if I could go with them, the guard said, "Look, I don't know anything. I didn't see you. If you want to come, we march out in threes, so walk between two of the tall ones. Maybe they won't notice you."

I went with them. When we lined up I stood between two six footers, then we began moving toward the first gate. Looking back, the whole thing seems crazy. The other prisoners were wearing striped clothes; I had on the same jacket and pants I had been wearing for a year. Their heads were shaved, mine wasn't. But I knew the routine from the time I had gotten out of the ghetto after visiting Chaim's mother. Near the gate I tried to angle myself slightly behind the man on my left so that he'd stay between the Gestapo's line of sight and me. But I needn't have even done that. As our policeman saluted and gave his report the Gestapo was busy talking to some other German. He didn't even look. He just waved his hand without interrupting his conversation and we walked through.

When we got to the main camp entrance my heart was beating like a hammer. I couldn't believe I had gotten through the inner gate—how could I expect a second miracle? Then I saw that there were two Gestapo, not one. Walking forward I mentally intoned a prayer, trying to control my fear. *L'shuatha kiviti Adoshem; Kiviti Adoshem l'shuatha; Adoshem l'shuatha kiviti*—"Upon Thy help I hope, Oh Lord; I hope, Oh Lord, upon Thy help; Oh Lord, upon Thy help I hope." Again the policeman reported while we stood there waiting. I hung my head, like so many of the others, looking down. But out of the corner of my eye I was trying to see what was happening. Astounding as it was, the Gestapo didn't seem too interested. One of them was exchanging a few words with the guard and

I was afraid he might make a head count. But he didn't. The gate swung open and we started to file through onto Janowska Street. In the morning when the two Gestapo had brought me here the sky had been a dingy gray. Now the sun was shining. It was a lovely spring afternoon. I was filled with elation to find myself on the outside.

The Jewish cemetery was only half a mile or so from Janowska. When we got there the prisoners picked up their tools and went to work. Some dug out gravestones and hauled them away from the graves and into a pile. Others used sledgehammers to batter them into big pieces. Off to the side a little group broke these bigger pieces into bits with small hammers. Every so often a truck would arrive and some of the men would shovel it full from a pile of rubble that used to be Jewish gravestones and markers.

While all this was going on no one paid any attention to me. I started out by picking up a hammer pretending to be working, though I couldn't actually bring myself to hammer the stones on which were bits and pieces of Hebrew letters, sometimes even part of a name. The guard seemed to be deliberately not looking in my direction. Slowly I disengaged myself and moved off toward the edge of the cemetery where there were some trees and shrubbery. When I got there I crawled under a bush. Lying on my stomach I scanned the remote areas of the cemetery where other groups were working. I hadn't been noticed.

For the rest of the afternoon I laid there and watched the inmates digging and hammering, wondering how anybody could ever desecrate this cemetery. Did they need the gravel from these particular stones for roadways? This cemetery had existed for centuries. In that time it no doubt had received many who had died in pogroms and massacres, but it had never been profaned. For the Germans it wasn't enough to kill the living. They had to eradicate the dead as well.

As darkness fell the prisoners gathered up their tools to head back to Janowska. I was left alone, feeling more disheartened than I had ever been. I am alive, I thought, with all these dead. Shiff had said people left Janowska only to go to their graves. I had left, and here I was, not one of the dead, just with them. God had taken me out of the camp and put me in this graveyard where I could watch the dead too being dehumanized, the gravestones desecrated and pounded into dust. Wusia and Michael were in my mind, as they almost always were. But in this place I couldn't summon up the living images of them with which I so often comforted myself. I wondered whether I should be envious of the dead. At least they were beyond anguish. For the first time I felt my grip on life loosening. If these dead were all gone, surely my turn would come.

I was startled out of these thoughts when I realized that it was almost suppertime. I wasn't hungry. I hadn't eaten since my sparse breakfast at the HKP, but even the thought of food made me a little sick. But it was mealtime, which meant that soon the HKP prisoners would be filing back from the workshops to the cafeteria. Chaim had my documents. In the dark I could get to the HKP easily enough and with a little luck catch him on his way to eat. At least then I'd have my Aryan identity again.

The labor camp was a ten-minute walk from the cemetery. I used side roads, sticking to the shadows and avoiding the few people I did see. At the camp I circled around and came in through a side area, then carefully made my way to the place where Chaim would have to walk through to get to the cafeteria. Pieces of military equipment were parked here and there, including a big truck that was sitting close to the walkway. Sneaking around to the far side of the truck I climbed into the cab and slouched down in the seat where no one could see me but where I could watch those who passed.

By now it was night. With the blackout, no lights shone. The only illumination was from the stars and moon. But that was enough for me to make out the faces going by. I hoped that Chaim hadn't left work early for some reason. Minutes passed. I was starting to get nervous when out of the darkness I saw him coming, walking alone. As he passed I called his name in a stage whisper. "Chaim. Chaim. Over here Chaim." He looked around, startled. When he saw my face in the window he stared as if he was looking at a ghost. People generally left Janowska either in a boxcar or dead, but there I was in the truck cab. In an instant he hid his surprise, and the next moment he scrambled around the truck and was climbing in the far side door whispering, "Wilo, Wilo, what are you doing here?"

"Chaim," I said. We hugged each other awkwardly. "Chaim, do you have my documents?"

"Documents? What documents? How did you get here?"

"In the morning, when they took me to Janowska, I gave my documents to Tenenbaum to give to you. Do you have them?"

Chaim was silent for a moment. "So," he said, "that's what he was talking about. Wilo, Tenenbaum's been going around boasting that he was the one who had the Gestapo arrest you. He said he taught you a lesson and that he'll teach the same lesson to anyone who thinks he doesn't have to obey his orders. It's about that argument he had with you over cleaning the barracks. Remember? He's obviously been after you ever since. He told us he was waiting in the hallway when they took you, to see if you were going to try to escape. He has the idea you're some kind of escape artist."

That might have been funny, considering I had just escaped, but I didn't see the humor in it. I could feel myself panicking. As soon as Chaim had said, "What documents?" a lump started growing in my throat. Tenenbaum had kept my Wawer papers, which meant I was exposed. Without my Polish identity it would be a thousand times more dangerous. If I was stopped that would be the end of me. Either they'd shoot me or they'd put me in a concentration camp. I'd be finished. I was already desperately searching for some way to get the documents back, but I had no idea.

Fortunately, Chaim was there to calm me down. We started talking, trying to figure out some plan, but there weren't many options. We talked about finding a way to steal them, maybe waylaying Tenenbaum somehow, but nothing made any sense. Finally we decided that the only way would be to persuade a Jewish policeman to demand them. But who might do such a thing for me? Neither of us knew any policemen, besides which, many of them were cruel and unscrupulous. I still couldn't believe my luck that the guard had let me join his work group. The man had put his life on the line for someone he didn't even know, an incredibly selfless thing. From what I knew, most of them would have turned me in without a second thought.

Despite the risks, this plan seemed the only possibility. We didn't know any policemen, so there was no point in looking for anyone in particular. Since that was the case, the sooner we did this the better. Once word got out that I had escaped, it might be too late. Maybe there was a policeman in the camp right now, someone who had escorted a work group to the HKP and hadn't taken them back yet.

As we were talking about this, as if on cue, a policeman emerged from the dark. "Let's try this guy," Chaim whispered. "I'm going to talk to him." And out he went. I couldn't believe my run of luck. If it held, this could be a decent guard.

When Chaim brought the policeman over I thought I must be dreaming. Judging from his expression, so did he. Not only did we know each other, we were almost family. I didn't know his name, but I had met him once or twice at the Rosenman's house. His sister was engaged to Wusia's oldest brother, the one who had gone to Argentina. That sister was often at the Rosenman's. I had met her there various times, and I had met the policeman too. In more normal circumstances, he would have been Wusia's brother-in-law. It wasn't completely impossible that he still might be. Memories flashed back to the night when my old friend Herzl Tismenitzer came to the door of our apartment on Berka Joselewicza to arrest me. Luck wasn't the word for all this. This had to be some kind of fate.

The policeman (whose name I have never been able to recall) was even more stunned when I told him about Tenenbaum, my experience at Janowska, and my escape. He was instantly ready to do what I was asking. "I'll go to this character Tenenbaum right now and see what I can do with him," he said. Then he left.

The next half-hour was excruciating. I told Chaim he shouldn't wait with me, he should go to the barracks. If things turned bad, I didn't want them taking him too. What if Tenenbaum smelled a rat and went to the Gestapo? Or if he just refused to give up the papers, then what? Or if he insisted on a written order for them? Even the slightest investigation would spell the end for Chaim and the policeman. The Germans murdered people all the time out of pure malice. Who needed to give them excuses?

My mind was working out likely scenarios, none of which ended well, when Wusia's would-be brother-in-law materialized with a big smile on his face. He couldn't wait to squeeze into the cab and tell us what had happened.

18

A ROAD NOT TAKEN

Summer/Fall 1943

"Well," he said, hunkering down, "I fulfilled the mission. I told him they needed the documents in Janowska, but the son of a bitch didn't want to give them up. He argued like a crazy person. Then he wanted me to sign a receipt for them, so I did. Here, they're yours. Take them."

The HKP was about a half-hour walk from Nabielacka. With the documents back in my pocket I didn't feel in the least nervous. What I had to do now was to get Katy Wowkowa to agree to my latest plan, which was that I'd become a full time resident of her coal bin. With the Germans searching for me, I couldn't be seen at the HKP, and I didn't have anywhere else to go. Without a doubt, the cellar would be the safest place. The building was full of Gestapo families. No one would ever think to look for a Jew in such a place.

When I got there I checked Katy's window to make sure she was alone. Then I let myself into the building and knocked quietly on her door. We hadn't talked to each since I started staying nights. That was in March and we were now in September, almost six months later. In her room I explained that I had been arrested and had escaped from the concentration camp. Now I had nowhere to go during the daytime. Did she think it would be all right if I stayed in the coal bin full time? I didn't think it would be for long, I told her. The Red Army was already pushing the Germans back through the Ukraine. I was sure they'd be in Lvov pretty soon.

I believed that was basically true, though of course I had no specifics. Katy didn't know anything about the war. What she might have thought about the prospects for liberation was anyone's guess, though few Ukrainians would have called a Russian victory "liberation." From her expression I could see she was taken aback by what I was asking. But she didn't object or even express any reluctance. She didn't say anything like, "I wish I could do this, *Panie* Ungar, but I have a baby. If they catch me, they'll hang the baby too." I know she must have been thinking about that, though. Much later I found out that after she gave me permission to stay she went to her priest and confessed that she was hiding a Jew. The priest, a Ukrainian, one of Sheptytsky's, told her it was God's will that she should save the poor soul in hiding. All I knew then was how relieved and grateful I was when she agreed that I could stay.

The coal bin where I had been sleeping was one of seven identical stalls that took up most of the basement, one for each of the six apartments plus another for the superintendent. Board walls separated the stalls from each other and all of them were kept locked. In the winter Katy would come into the stalls to get coal for the apartments, but now, in early September, no one had any reason to be there. The basement was quiet as a tomb.

Except for a bare light bulb outside the door to Katy's stall, the place was dark. The five or six inches between the top of the door and the frame allowed in enough light for me to read by. Up until now I hadn't paid much attention to reading. With the hard work at the HKP and our scant diet, by the time I got back to Nabielacka at night I was always too exhausted to do anything but fall asleep on my bench. But now I started looking for reading material in the rubbish the Gestapo families threw away, which Katy brought down to the basement before taking it out to the street on pick-up days. From the trash I rescued a German technical manual and a Russian-Polish dictionary, which probably belonged to one of the previous residents. Those were my books, which every week I supplemented with discarded copies of *Der Sturmer*, Julius Streicher's incredibly anti-Semitic Nazi propaganda newspaper.

From the beginning I spent most of the time living inside my head, fantasizing, dreaming my real life.

Before I came to the coal bin to stay, my days had been mostly filled with work and trying to keep out of danger. I was haunted by thoughts of Wusia and Michael, and of my mother and the rest of my family. But these visions came and went. I didn't have the leisure to concentrate on them, even if I had wanted to. And mostly I didn't want to. I was keeping a tight grip on the hope that Wusia and I would be reunited someday. I didn't want to spend too much time thinking about what might have actually happened to her and the baby.

Now, alone in the basement, I couldn't keep my mind off her. It seemed to me that I could recall almost every day of our courtship, and many individual days of our married life. I remembered words we had said to each other. Snatches of conversation came into my head, like a poem you never even knew you had memorized, then suddenly it's on your lips. Worst were the memories I had of how things felt—the sweetness of our kisses in the Jesuit Garden, Wusia running into my arms when I returned from the prisoner of war hospital, snuggling in our big bed. Those were the most painful, the memories in which Wusia seemed to come unbearably alive. At times, with those precious moments running through my head, I thought the pain of missing her might crush the life out of me.

I tried hard to think about other things, not to become completely obsessed. And after a while I found that I could. Of course, the great question was why. Why had any of this happened? There was no reason for it, no logic to why the Germans had come and turned everything to ashes. When I thought about how things had worked out, so much of it seemed like pure chance. My life might so easily have taken some other road. I wondered what Argentina was like, where my brother Herman and brother-in-law David had planned to bring us. I imagined myself in *Eretz Yisrael*, where I had dreamed of going for so many years. My teacher, Gedaliah Gottfried, had managed to get there. He had ended up in Haifa, where he had written me a number of letters before the war, always urging me to learn a trade I could put to good use once I got to Palestine.

Gedaliah had introduced me to Zionism. I had absorbed his words while I was a boy and he had lived in our house. Gedaliah Gottfried was someone who bore a lot of thought. His life was a story itself.

Gedaliah came to Krasne when I was ten years old, not long after they expelled me from the Polish school. That had happened because of an accident I had playing ball, a pastime that totally occupied my classmates and I when we weren't busy with lessons. When it came to playing ball, we didn't care too much about the location, outside or inside. It was only important that the teacher wasn't around.

One day during an enthusiastic game in our classroom a ball I threw hit a picture of the Polish kings and knocked it off the wall, breaking the glass and the frame. At the moment the picture crashed to the floor the door opened and our teacher, Mr. Karpinski, came in. We all stood up instantly and in the silence Mr. Karpinski demanded to know who did it. When I admitted I was the culprit he got very angry. "Go home Ungar," he said, "and take the picture with you. I don't want to see your face until you get it fixed or get a new one. And if you don't, don't expect to get any graduation certificate."

I was scared to tell my father what happened, so I just told Mama. She didn't seem to think it was that important. She just took the picture and put it into the closet, which was the last I saw of it. The result was that I never went back to school. I didn't get my fourth grade graduation certificate either.

When Gedaliah arrived in Krasne he was probably in his mid-twenties, very handsome, with dark black eyes. Even at the age of ten I could tell that the Krasne girls all fell in love with him immediately. The twelve or fourteen Jewish families in Krasne hired Gedaliah to tutor their children. He was most capable, but I doubt they knew exactly what they were getting. They weren't aware that Gedaliah had a dark secret.

Gedaliah's main function was to teach Hebrew, Bible, and other Jewish studies. In these subjects he was deeply versed, having studied until the age of eighteen at the famous Pressburg Yeshiva in Hungary. What very few in Krasne knew—my father may have been the only one, and he kept it to himself—was that Gedaliah had become attracted to

Communism and had quit the Yeshiva for a life as a revolutionary. Not only that, he had joined Bela Kun's Hungarian Communist Party, and when Kun made his revolution Gedaliah was given a post in the government.

Of course, Kun's regime didn't last, and when it collapsed Gedaliah ran for his life, staying one step ahead of the police through several countries. Eventually he came back to Grzymalov, the shtetl where he was born. He had left for the Yeshiva as a young boy, so he thought he would be safe there. Few would be able to recognize him. For extra protection he changed his last name from Landau to Gottfried. Then, when he heard that the Jews of Krasne, an even more remote place, were looking for a teacher, he applied for the job. This was how Gedaliah came to live in our house and be my tutor after Mr. Karpinski expelled me from school.

By the time Gedaliah arrived in Krasne, he had abandoned Communism for Zionism. But he was still an activist, and before long he established a thriving Labor Zionist group. My brother Herman joined the older chapter and I joined the younger, which was made up of boys and girls from Krasne and the four or five surrounding villages. We were part of the youth movement of the Labor Zionists, the party that was establishing kibbutzim in Palestine.

Every Saturday the younger group met in our house, which was big enough and convenient because Gedaliah lived there. We talked about Palestine, politics, labor, socialism, making Aliyah—all the issues that were sweeping through Poland's Jewish communities. Gedaliah made us understand that we weren't just poor Jews living in an isolated backwater of Poland. We weren't just hillbillies. All of us were part of something big and exciting, something historical. We organized a library and kept the books in our big hallway closet. We collected money for the Jewish National Fund, to buy land in Palestine. Later, when we were more organized, we hired musicians and arranged dances, "balls," we called them, which we held in the Polish Catholic hall. The money from these also went to the Jewish National Fund. We even invited speakers from outside to give talks.

Gedaliah had a huge impact on many of us from Krasne, Sadzawki, and the other villages. He straddled the worlds of traditional Jewish learning, European culture, and the militant new world of Zionism, and gave us lessons from all three. He was like a fresh wind blowing into a place that had hardly changed in five hundred years.

Gedaliah was with us for five years. Then he suddenly disappeared. To this day I don't know exactly what he had done when he was with Bela Kun. Whatever it was, it was important enough so the police never stopped looking, and eventually they traced him to Krasne. Fortunately, my father was good friends with our local police chief, who tipped him off. Gedaliah fled with only hours to spare. I was fifteen at the time, and while he was throwing his things together, Gedaliah told me the outlines of his story, which I had never known until that moment. Then he was gone. When I next heard from him it was in a letter from Haifa.

After Gedaliah left, our group kept going and I became one of its leaders. Then when I went off to study I found that Lvov was the center of Zionist activity in Galicia, and after my first year at the Korkis School I threw myself into the movement.

Like the rest of Jewish Poland in the thirties, Galicia was throbbing with Zionist feeling. Every faction had its groups, from the right to the left. I was most attracted to the Buslia, named after Josef Bussel, an early Zionist who was one of the originators of the agricultural collective idea. Bussel had been a member of the first kibbutz at Degania. He believed that Jews had to remake themselves through labor, they had to connect themselves to the land through work. "Back to the soil" was the slogan of all the pioneer groups that sprung up in Poland under his name. I joined one of them that was just starting up, a group we named the *Kvutzah Barzel*, the "Iron Group."

Unlike most of the groups—*kvutzot* in Hebrew— our members had technical skills. Most of the boys were from Korkis, and many of the girls from the Klaftinowa Trade School, our sister school. We dreamed that one day we would form the first technological collective in Palestine. There, we would all live together near a town and put our knowledge to work, building industries in the new land.

Nevertheless, we accepted the Buslia's requirement that to qualify for emigration we had to undergo a period of pioneering training through work on the land. Back to the soil.

Me with Kvutsah Barzel, 1934

That was a major challenge for young people who often had never been near a farm. But the Buslia members weren't half-hearted about their commitments. They hadn't joined in order to have a good time, but to go to Palestine and build the land. This was 1934 and by then I was deeply attached to the vision of *Eretz Yisrael*. There was no one in *Kvutzah Barzel* who wasn't.

To find a place to do our training, I went to my brother-in-law David who managed the Kimmelman estate in Wolice, a few miles from Krasne. David introduced me to

Kimmelman, and he gave us permission to come and work on his land that summer. After the school term ended we went, fifteen or sixteen boys and girls, about half the *Kvutzah Barzel* membership. Coming from a country village, at least I knew how to chop wood, weed a garden, and dig potatoes. None of the others had ever put in a day of physical work.

The train took us to Grzymalov station where a wagon from the estate picked us up. We all piled in joyfully, singing Zionist songs at the top of our lungs as if we were on our way to a socialist festival. All of us were impatient to get a foretaste of ennobling Jewish labor.

In the coal bin, just thinking about these songs was enough to make me start humming. I had to laugh, especially when I remembered the end of that first day so filled with enthusiasm. Sixteen boys and girls stretched out motionless on mattresses in their quarters trying to decide which part of their bodies hurt most. Not one even had the strength to begin an ideological debate, something previously unimaginable in the *Kvutzah Barzel*.

For the next nine or ten weeks we learned how to get up at sunrise, cultivate and harvest, thresh wheat, and make hay. We learned how to wield scythes to cut the tall grass, and sickles, which the Polish peasants used to harvest wheat. We learned how to fall into a deep sleep right after dinner, and also how to endure the jokes and laughter of the estate's peasants, who seemed to find our efforts at farming endlessly entertaining.

By the time we got back to Lvov at the end of the summer we were ready for our next step, learning how to live as a collective. We rented a big house at Szkarpowa 5 and moved in, twenty or twenty five of us, girls in the downstairs bedrooms, boys in the upstairs, six or eight to a room. Then, since most of us had graduated that June, we went out and got jobs. We worked as bookkeepers, designers, seamstresses, technicians—that was when I got my job at Appel's electronics and optical store—where I was still working when I met Wusia. Wherever we worked, our wages went to the collective. The treasurer handled all expenses, including the dispersal of pocket money. If someone had a special situation, maybe needing a sweater or a new pair of shoes, the *Kvutzah* met for a general discussion and vote. As socialists, we felt it was our duty to change the capitalist system. We were determined to create a new way of living and end the exploitation of the proletariat. It's time to do something about it, we said. You can't just preach, you have to change your way of living.

As far as I can recall, in *Kvutzah Barzel* we rarely slept. We worked all day and talked, or argued, all night. And when we were finished arguing we danced, not mazurkas and polkas, but the hora, singing to give ourselves a beat. We had contests, dividing ourselves into Hora A and Hora B and seeing which group could dance longest and hardest. I wondered what our neighbors must have made of all the noise—not at the time, but ten years later thinking about it in the silence of the basement.

I loved the dancing, although I could have done without all the talk. When the *Kvutzah* elected me general secretary I brought in a new rule that all meetings had to be held in Hebrew, which we were studying as part of our preparation for going to Palestine. Having to speak Hebrew had the dual virtue of giving people more language practice while at the same time shortening the debates, which of course didn't mean we slept more, we just had more time to dance. In 1935 I met Ben Gurion, who was speaking to the Buslia's central committee, and someone asked him why he had addressed the last Zionist Congress in Yiddish instead of Hebrew. "Because I wanted the Jewish masses to understand me," he said. Ben Gurion was a round little man with hair sticking up on the sides of an already balding head. But he had charismatic powers. Each word he said seemed to come straight from Sinai.

That year several of our members were able to get British certificates of immigration to Palestine, which were extremely limited in number. Many applied, but the Labor Zionist central office had only a few available and they awarded them carefully. Wasserstein got one, and Shapiro, and Dlugacz. Their names had stuck with me. I wanted so badly to go. I knew that making Aliyah would be the fulfillment of my life's goal. But I hesitated to apply. With my father gone only three years, I knew how much my mother still needed me. So I temporized, and while I did a letter came from the Polish Army, telling me to report to the Field Artillery unit in Kalish for my basic training. I had been drafted.

By the time I got out of the army it was 1936. In Palestine, Arab riots were breaking out all over the country, the beginning of a major revolt. In response England cut Jewish immigration to almost nothing. Before I was drafted it had been extremely difficult to enter Palestine. Now it was next to impossible, although a few people were still managing to smuggle themselves in. At *Kvutzah Barzel* many of my friends had moved on, which made the prospect of going back to the big house at Szkarpowa 5 less attractive. In addition, my mother's situation at the store back in Krasne was getting worse. The job at Appel's was waiting for me, which would make it possible for me to send money back to the family. I could just feel Palestine slipping away.

In the loneliness of my basement ten years later, it seemed to me that I still might have gone. I could have made a superhuman effort. I had technical skills the Jewish community in Palestine needed like lifeblood. I was a trained soldier. I had been on the central committee of the Buslia. I could have persuaded them to smuggle me in. Others had done just that. But I hadn't. Instead I was here in a dark stall covered with coal dust, yearning for my wife and my child, dreaming unfulfilled dreams from a vanished past.

19

My Good Name

Once when Gedaliah was teaching me Torah a friend of my father's walked into the room. Gedaliah, with his many years of yeshiva study, was a learned man. But he had also become an atheist and didn't wear a yarlmuka, which was sacrilegious, especially when studying the sacred books. My father's friend, a Chassidic follower of the Kopyczyncer rebbe, was appalled. After staring at Gedaliah for a long moment he said in disgust, "Why don't you just become a Catholic?" "Look," said Gedaliah, "if I don't believe in God the Almighty, the Omnipotent, the Universal, how am I supposed to believe in Jesus Christ, who was only a human being?" I have no idea what might have brought on Gedaliah's crisis of faith. But here in the cellar I was having my own problems.

I hadn't been an observant Jew since I left my parents' home. But whatever I was in the deepest part of my soul, my Jewishness was inseparable from it. And here in the basement, with nothing to do but explore the world of memory, I found myself silently singing my favorite prayers over and over and over. "I remember Your kindness in my youth, Your devoted love when You went with me in the wilderness where there is no seed and no growth." I had such poignant memories of studying the meanings of the "Remembrance" prayers and others with Gedaliah before the High Holidays, and practicing the music with our cantor David Hirsh Zeftel, who always had me sing the chorus parts for him as he prepared himself for the services. The words carried the faith of the Jewish people, but to me the melodies seemed to express their soul.

And yet now, in Lvov in 1943, how could you not ask yourself, where is God? Where is His mercy? His compassion and loving-kindness? My mind was haunted by images of dead bodies scattered along the tracks near Belzec. Worse were the nightmares that came almost every time I fell asleep, especially the one in which I saw a woman holding a child walking through a forest toward a concentration camp. I'd see them walking and find myself wondering who they might be. Then their faces would come into view—Wusia and Michael—and I'd wake up in a sweat, terrified that I might have been screaming out loud. "I remember Your kindness when You were young, Your devoted love when You went with me in the wilderness." The words went round and round in my head, but what did they mean now? Wise men might have found answers. I didn't.

Two traditional stories of Jewish disaster stuck in my mind. In one the Temple is destroyed and the Hebrew remnants led away into captivity. But the *Shekhinah*, the Divine Presence, stays with the people, saying, "I will dwell among them." The second strikes a different chord. In this one the High Priest, the last guardian, stands amidst the flames of the burning Temple with the great keys in his hand. Turning, he hurls them into the fire. "You have burned it," he shouts to Heaven, "You take the keys." Isaiah, always my favorite among the prophets, kept his faith even after the people were ground to dust by the Babylonians. "What will happen with the night, everything around us is dark?" he asks. And the answer comes, "I have made the night, and I will also make day." But if a new day ever came to Lvov I wondered if I would be alive to see it. Would any of us?

Spring 1944

In the spring of 1944 *Der Sturmer* became more and more agitated. It was obvious that the *Wehrmacht* was being beaten back from large parts of Russia and the Ukraine. I couldn't wait for the Gestapo families to toss away their weekly editions so I could grab them from the trash and read feverishly between the lines. I drank in the news that the German army was "shortening its supply lines" or "straightening out the front," euphemisms for retreat,

retreat, retreat. In my mind's eye I could see the Red Army advancing inexorably across the Ukrainian steppes, thousands upon thousands of tanks and endless legions of brown-coated soldiers.

Then one day during the spring of 1944 sirens began to sound. I was lying half-asleep on my bench when their eerie wail penetrated the basement. For a minute I wondered what the sound was, then I realized that the Russians must be bombing the city. I hardly had time for this momentous thought to sink in when I heard a clatter of feet on the stairs and frightened German voices. A moment later the noise surrounded me as the tenants rushed into the basement to take cover. Doors slammed opened and closed. In the stall next to me a child started crying. Women were talking in excited voices, "*Verdampte Russen. Was denken sie?*" "It's those damned Russians. What do they think they're doing?"

I stared at the door to my stall frozen with fear, expecting it to crash open any instant. But it didn't. The German families all seemed to have gotten into their own stalls, almost as fearful as I was, waiting for the bombs to come whistling down and smash the building. I lay there hardly breathing, afraid to move, a one-quarter inch thick board wall separating me from my fate. An eternity passed. At some point I realized the sirens had stopped wailing, but though I strained to hear I couldn't make out any sounds from outside that might have been explosions.

The Germans noticed it too, and a discussion started about whether it might be all right to go back upstairs. Some of the women—they seemed to be all women and children—thought they should wait for an all clear. Others weren't sure there would be an all clear. There weren't any bombs dropping, so why sit here in the coal dust? Finally they decided that one of them would go out and look around. When she came back a minute later she said the street seemed normal. Nothing was going on. It wasn't until their footsteps and voices faded up the stairwell that I began breathing normally again.

That was the beginning. After that the sirens sounded more and more frequently, and each time the Germans stormed down to the basement, angry and frightened. The attacks came mainly during the day, when only the families were at home. But sometimes the Russians bombed in the evening, after the Gestapo husbands had come back from work. Then I'd hear the curses loud and sharp, as though the flimsy coal bin walls weren't there at all. It sounded to me as if they hadn't expected the Russians to come bombing this soon, or this often.

From the talk I learned that certain parts of the city were being hit hard, but I never heard any bombs go off, no matter how hard I listened. I was getting more and more nervous anyway. If a bomb did fall nearby and the blast knocked my door open, I'd be lost. I could just imagine, the door flies open and I'm sitting there with a dozen Gestapo men, women, and children staring at me.

When I discussed the situation with Katy Wowkowa we decided the best thing would be to dig a bunker. The coal bin floor was just wooden planks laid down over bare earth. With her help I could dig a pit, which I could get into whenever the sirens started. That way even if the door did blow open, there'd be nothing to see except an empty stall.

That night Katy brought me a shovel and I started digging. The earth was moist and a little loose, easy to scoop out. With Katy carrying the soil out to the backyard I finished the hole in a couple of hours. It looked like a shallow grave, six feet long and several feet deep, just big enough for me to slip into and pull the floorboards back on top of me.

From then on, each time the sirens wailed, which by now was three or four times a day, I'd scramble into the bunker and slide the boards into place. In the dark I'd listen to the Germans cursing the Russians and bemoaning their fate, while I silently urged the Russians on, praying that they would drop bombs by the truckload until the Germans disappeared in a vast whirling cloud of dirt and smoke.

Up until the Russian planes arrived Katy used to make food for me and slip it into the stall whenever it was convenient. Since no one ever came into the basement there was no danger that we'd be caught. Occasionally she would even invite me to share dinner in her room. But after the bombing started, it became riskier. The sirens would go off unpredictably, and a moment after they did the Germans would come rushing down the stairs. The safest time was after dark, when the city was blacked out. Only rarely did the Russians fly at night.

One evening I was in Katy's room having something to eat. It had been a day full of raids, with the Germans in and out of the basement and I in and out of my bunker. I remember thinking that it must be Sunday because the men were home as well as the women. Now it was pitch black outside and I was enjoying the small dinner Katy had made, relaxing after all the tension. Suddenly the sirens started, much louder in Katy's apartment than they were in the stall. I jumped up, thinking I would run back to my place, but already the Germans were hurrying out of their apartments and down the stairs. I looked around quickly for someplace to hide. Katy's door was locked, but I felt exposed. I thought about crawling under the bed, but anybody who came in was likely to see me. The only other place was a shaky wooden cabinet that Katy used as a closet. I ducked inside and she pressed the door closed behind me. There wasn't room to stand, but if I scrunched myself up the cabinet was just wide enough for me to sit down.

I waited, getting more uncomfortable by the minute. They never sounded an all-clear siren; you just had to wait until you felt it was safe. It could be fifteen or twenty minutes, or maybe a half-hour. As long as there were no bombs falling it depended on how you felt. I thought about getting out. Who was going to come into Katy's room anyway? Then I decided against it. Better to put up with the discomfort than take a chance.

At long last I heard muffled voices, the Germans going back to their apartments. I was just about to push the cabinet open when there was a knock on Katy's door. "*Wowkowa*," it was a man's voice. "*Ich will eine weil bei ihnen bleiben.*" One of the Gestapo was coming in and he was going to stay. The closet was really no more than a few boards knocked together. I could hear everything, exactly as if I was out in the room. A chair scraped along the floor just inches from my hiding place. The man sat down. "*Ein andere angrif kommt, ja? Ich will hier bleiben, ja?*" He expected another raid. He was going to wait here for it instead of going all the way upstairs then having to come down again.

He was so close I could hear his heavy breathing as well as his voice. "*Ja.*" said Katy. Suddenly my throat was itching. I had to stifle a cough. The Gestapo was trying to talk to Katy in German, throwing in a few words of Ukrainian. A halting conversation, about nothing. Katy saying a word here, a word there, "*ja*," "*nein*," "*ach so*." Just passing time, waiting for the sirens to start up again. I felt a powerful urge to urinate. With all the raids I hadn't been able to get to the toilet all day. I clenched the muscles tight, but the need grew. After a few minutes I didn't know if I could hold it. The Gestapo just sat there and blathered on. I knew that Katy couldn't possibly understand most of what he was saying. I thought about hiding in that barn out on Janowska, Chaim, his niece, her careless boyfriend and me. The urine trickling down from the loft, as mine was going to start trickling out of this closet any minute. Without thinking about it I realized I was praying. "My, Lord, open my lips that my mouth shall declare your praise." The *Shmoneh Esray*, the Eighteen Blessings, the "standing" prayer, always said standing, feet together, the way the angels are supposed to stand, not scrunched up in a closet. "Blessed art Thou, O Lord...who will bring a redeemer" "Blessed art Thou, O Lord...who revivest the dead." "Blessed art Thou, O lord, who gatherest the dispersed of Thy people Israel." How many times had I said this prayer, three times a day. For how many years? "Blessed art Thou, O Lord, who breakest the enemies." The unbelievable German bastard was still talking. "Blessed art Thou, O Lord, who healest the sick." I dug my fingernails into the skin on my forearm. "Blessed art Thou, O Lord..." I was getting near the end of my rope. "O my God, guard my tongue from speaking evil, my lips from speaking falsehood." I clenched tighter and felt a spasm in my kidney. "He who maketh peace in his high places..." The chair scraped the floor. "May He make peace for us and for all Israel..." Yes, he was getting up. "*Ach so, nichts mehr Kommt, Wowkowa.*" "I guess they're not coming." "And say ye, Amen." Wowkowa's door banged shut. I crawled out of the cabinet and listened, just in time to hear his footsteps disappearing up the stairs.

———————

July, 1944

For a time the raids went on almost non-stop, which meant a constant, nerve-wracking coming and going of Germans. Then, on July 27—I learned the date later—Katy came to my stall and told me that all the Germans had run away. There were none left in the building. I came out warily, not that I didn't believe Katy, but I thought the news was too good to be true. If the Germans were really gone, that meant the Russians must be in the city, or they would be very soon. I wanted to look outside, but I was afraid to go out the front door; instead I went through the back into the yard behind the building. The light was dazzling. It was a brilliant, warm day. Flowers were blooming everywhere. I felt faint from the aroma. I had last been outside more than ten months ago, the day I escaped from Janowska.

Off to the east the tower of the Polytechnic jutted into the blue sky, and atop the tower I saw the flags, four of them, the red Soviet flag, the American, the British and the French tricolor. The allies had definitely arrived.

Without another thought I set out for the Polytechnic. I needed to find out what was going on. I didn't think the Americans and the others were really there, the Russians were just flying their allies' flags. But the Red Army was definitely in town. And if they were, maybe I could get some news about what had happened to the Jews. If any of my friends were still alive they'd probably be heading for the Polytechnic as well.

Hardly anyone was on the streets. Some Russian soldiers here and there, a civilian or two standing outside a doorway and looking around, but that was all. From the west came the distant chatter of small arms, barely audible. It must have just happened, I thought. The Russians haven't even completely pushed them out yet.

Ten minutes of fast walking took me to the massive iron gates of the Polytechnic. Since Hapsburg times the school had been "extra-territorial," off limits to civil authorities. Even the police weren't allowed inside the gates unless specifically invited by the chancellor. But now they were wide open. The guard booth outside was unmanned. Beyond the courtyard with its trees and shrubs I could see people moving in and out through the big front doors.

The first thing I noticed when I came into the main hallway was that the Polytechnic had been turned into a hospital. Nurses were tending to patients on stretchers while two white coated doctors conferred animatedly. Just to the right was a desk behind which sat a man in what looked like an old Polish army uniform.

"What's going on?" I asked, wondering about the uniform.

"We're registering people for military service," he said.

"What, in the Polish army?"

"Yes, friend. In the Polish army. We're fighting alongside our Soviet comrades. We're going to chase the German bastards back to Berlin."

"Soviet comrades." That had to mean a Polish army organized by the Russians. The Polish army I fought in had been dispersed by the Soviets in 1939. But I was happy to hear it. Just at that moment I was experiencing a surge of gratitude toward the Russians for what they had done. They were the ones who had freed me from the cellar. Before I had even thought about it I heard myself saying, "Well, if that's the case I want to volunteer."

After liberation, June 1944
Ready to join the Polish Army in the fight against the Germans.

"Excellent, friend. What's your name?"

I was feeling absolutely elated. Ten months in the coal bin and now I was alive again. The officer was smiling at me, the first friendly face other than Katy's I'd seen in ages.

"My name? Well, my Polish name is Edward Wawer." He started to write. "But my Jewish name is Wilo Ungar." He stopped writing and looked up. The smile was gone.

"Your Jewish name is Wilo Ungar?" An edge came into his voice. I knew instantly I had let myself get carried away. This is a Jew? I could hear him saying it to himself, I could always hear them. This is a Jew? Telling me he's a Pole? What the hell is that supposed to mean? And if he's a Jew, what the hell business does he have being alive?

"I can't register you here." The words were cold, flat. "Go up to the second floor and see the colonel."

I turned away, feeling as if someone had just poured cold water on me. That was when I heard it. "Wilo, Wilo," sounds so weak it seemed scarcely a voice. "Wilo, help me. They're killing me, Wilo." I turned around and there was a stretcher just being carried in. I took a step or two forward and saw that it was Rabbi Bartfield, my old friend from the Korkis faculty. Bartfield had taught Jewish studies, then when the Russians came in Horazi Horowitz had hidden him in an administrative job. He had even stayed on under the Germans, who of course hadn't known he was a rabbi. I hadn't seen him since the end of the semester in June of '42, two years ago, just before the Germans sent everyone off to the HKP. Chaim told me that he had disappeared and after that no one had heard anything about him.

When I came up to the stretcher Bartfield looked at me with big round eyes. "Wilo," he said, "they're trying to kill me."

I tried to calm him down. Blood stained his pants and shirt under his hands, which he had spread across his stomach as if he were trying to clamp something down.

"Rabbi," I said, "what happened?"

"I was hiding in Sheptytsky's palace," his voice was a hoarse whisper. "When I saw the flags on the Polytechnic I decided to go over to Korkis. I thought maybe some of the others would come there. There were two Poles on St. Teresa in uniforms. When they asked for my documents I told them I was Jewish. They shot me, Wilo."

I walked alongside Bartfield, my hand on his shoulder, as the orderlies carried him into a room and lifted him onto the bed. "Wilo," he said, "is this a hospital now?"

"Yes. There are doctors here."

"Wilo, get me a surgeon. I can feel one of the bullets in my stomach. Please, Wilo."

I turned to go, but I felt his hand touch my arm.

"Wait," he said. "Before you go I have to tell you something. I might die here, and somebody has to know about the children."

With that Bartfield told me how his sister who lived in Palestine had come to visit their father in the summer of 1939, bringing her two young daughters. At the end of August she was ready to go back and asked her father to join them. But he wanted to stay in Lvov for the High Holidays. She went back alone, leaving the children with their grandfather to come to Palestine when the holidays were over. Of course then the war had started, and there was no way to get out. Her father and Bartfield had kept the children, and when the Germans announced that the school's Jewish teachers would be sent to the labor camp, Bartfield had taken the girls with him to Sheptytsky. The old Metropolitan had hidden Bartfield in his palace and had sent the girls into hiding in a convent. Bartfield was the only one who knew what had happened. "You have to see to them," he said, "in case I die."

"All right," I said, "I'll make sure the right people know. But you're not going to die, so don't worry about it. Now let me get you a surgeon." I wasn't just cheering him up. By this time he didn't look like he was dying. There wasn't any more bleeding and his voice had gotten stronger as he told me about the two girls. His color looked better, too. If they had shot him at close range and the bullet was still in his stomach, it couldn't have been a very powerful pistol. Outside the room I told a nurse that my friend needed help, and asked her where would I be able to find a surgeon. "Up on the second floor," she said. "I'll look in on him and see what I can do."

More medical people were on the second floor and someone directed me to a surgeon. I explained to him that Bartfield had been shot in the stomach and gave the room number. When he said he'd go right down, I thought that as long as I was up here I'd try to find the colonel. Then I'd go back to check on Bartfield.

It only took a few minutes to find the colonel's office, but when I went in his assistant kept me waiting while he finished doing some paperwork. When he finally acknowledged my presence and heard what I wanted, he told me the colonel had gone out for lunch. If I wanted to see him I could come back in an hour.

By the time I got back to Bartfield's room, maybe ten or fifteen minutes had gone by. The door was open and when I went in Bartfield was alone in the room lying in bed. Blood was everywhere. The sheets were soaked with it. Little pools were collecting in the bed and dripping onto the floor. The headboard and the wall behind the bed were spattered with it. Bartfield lay there motionless, his eyes wide opened and staring sightlessly. He had been massacred.

I stood there paralyzed. I had never seen anything like this. It was hard to believe a body could have so much blood in it. Bartfield was riddled with wounds. At some point, it might have been a minute, it might have been five, I noticed that the window was wide open. I walked over and looked out. There was nothing, just shrubbery and lawn.

At the end of the hallway I found the nurse, the one who had told me she would look in on him. She was trembling so badly she could hardly speak. "The surgeon came in to look at your friend," she said. "When he began examining him two men came in with guns. They started shooting and the surgeon jumped out the window. I ran. I don't know what happened after that. I'm afraid to go back in there. I think they were from the AK."

I was reeling. Poor Bartfield. Can you imagine, I thought, the man hides from the Nazis for years. Finally he's liberated, then this. I couldn't believe I had been so careless, casually telling the registering officer I was Jewish. That was the kind of slip that could be fatal. There still were people around, searching for Jews. The ones who shot Bartfield weren't here by accident.

Suddenly I knew I was in danger. The AK was the right-wing Polish underground, real Jew-haters. This had just happened a few minutes ago, they could still be in the building. It wouldn't take much for me to end up like Bartfield, especially if I was foolish enough to be blurting out that I was Jewish to everyone I met. Forget about the army, I thought. They can wait. The first thing to do is get out of here alive.

I walked out the front door and through the courtyard, looking back over my shoulder and ready to take off in an instant. Once I got through the gates, I felt my fear turning to anger. More Russian soldiers were on the streets now than there had been earlier. The Russians were no friends of the AK; they'd probably shoot them on sight. I'm not going to just let this go, I thought. I'll tell the Russians and maybe they can find those bastards.

I walked up to the first Russian I saw who looked like an officer and began telling him what had happened. But just as I started the roar of planes filled the sky and a few blocks off bombs began exploding. The Germans were bombing the city. Together the Russian and I ducked into the closest building and crouched down behind a stairwell. "You're Jewish?" he said. "I'm also Jewish. Listen, you were hiding? You have a good place? Take my advice. You survived this long, go back and hide a few more days. We're still fighting, it's going to take a while to get them out of here. Don't take any chances with your life, please. You can tell the civil authorities what happened to your friend when they get here."

I followed his advice. I went back into hiding, though not in the basement. I had enough experience with the Soviet system to know that if you already lived someplace there was a good chance you'd stay there. If you waited for them to assign you a place, you could wait forever. At Nabielacka 12, I took possession of a second floor apartment the Gestapo had just vacated.

That morning I had wakened in a coal bin. Now I had a spacious apartment with two bedrooms, a living room, a dining room and balconies in front and back. But my spirit was heavy. After Michael was born Wusia and I used to dream about getting a larger place. And now I had one, by myself. I still clung to the shreds of hope that they would come back to me, that they would emerge from some unknown hinterland somewhere in the east. But in the depths of my heart I knew what those chances were.

I sat at the table in my new dining room lost in reverie, fiddling with a pen I had found in my new desk. I had sat down intending to write my name on a piece of paper to insert in the nameplate on the apartment door, to claim it for myself. Instead I was overwhelmed by a tidal wave of sorrow. I sat there almost comatose, my head flooded with black thoughts. Bartfield's death was like a boulder crushing my chest. I tried to imagine him at Sheptytsky's. Where did he hide there? In a cellar, like me? An attic? Maybe in some little crawlspace behind a wall. Hiding out for two years, evading the searchers. There had to have been searchers— the Germans knew Sheptytsky. And at last the glorious, long awaited day arrives, liberation day, with the Red Army in the streets of Lvov. So he comes out, this mild, gentle, scholarly man. To what welcome? To be shot down, then massacred in his bed. What did that Gestapo tell me in Lublin station so long ago? That they would shoot me like a dog. That's exactly what those AK did to Bartfield. They shot him like a dog. This lovely, lovely Jewish man.

My left hand took the little square of paper, pressing it to the table with my forefinger and thumb. With the pen I wrote my name, bearing down hard to impress the letters on the surface of the paper. Not WILO UNGAR, but EDWARD WAWER. Tears streamed down my cheeks as I opened the door and inserted it into the bracket.

That night I lay awake. From far away came the tap tap tap of machine gun fire and now and then a muffled explosion. It sounded as if the Germans were making a fight of it on the outskirts. I hardly cared. I was finished with my suffering. All I wanted to do was forget it, consign it to hell and move on from it. I felt as if this day I had stood at a crossroads. Who needed to live a life like this when some other kind of life was available? Who needed to live with such hatred, from these people who had sucked the milk of anti-Semitism from their mothers' breasts? What possible virtue was there to have your life end like Rabbi Bartfield? After all, what did I have but this one fragile life, which I had miraculously managed to preserve, not once but half a dozen times? Why, when it would mean peace and finally a chance for happiness by giving up this unbearable burden, which I hadn't chosen anyway but which had been thrust upon me? My nameplate read Edward Wawer. My birth certificate read Edward Wawer. So be it, I thought. From now on I would be Edward Wawer.

At dawn I was still awake. Having made the decision was so simple and, in a way, so right. What could be more logical for someone in Poland than to be a Pole? But instead of a peaceful, dreamless sleep, I was kept awake by what seemed a multitude of insistent voices and images. They crowded in, one after the other, among them the cheerful, cracked voice of my grandmother. "Remember, Wolce"— she said this to me every time we visited her in Postulufka. "Remember your grandfather whom you are named after. Remember your good name, Wolce, your *shem tov*." In some odd way, her words conjured up memories of my Bar Mitzvah. I had such detailed recollections of my childhood, but for some reason my Bar Mitzvah wasn't very clear. What I mainly remembered was the subject of the little speech I gave after reading my Torah part. The portion had been about wearing *tefillin*, the small leather boxes Jewish men bind onto their left arms and their foreheads each morning as a sign of their devotion to the Torah. My text was the words said while wrapping the strap around the middle finger of the left hand, like putting on a wedding ring. "I will betroth You to me forever." Like the sacredness of a marriage vow. And suddenly

I realized, with the sky barely lightening outside my window, what I had known all along. That I was the sum of my memories. From the forests of my childhood, to my mother's lilting voice, to the endless hours pouring over the sacred books. To the prayers, and the music, and my father's devotion to my mother, these memories were my life. Wusia and my baby lived in my memory. Mine. No one else's. And what I had witnessed, and what I survived. I had to accept it all, this life that was mine. This one Jewish life. The words of my Bar Mitzvah speech seemed just beyond my grasp, but it didn't matter. The words that mattered were engraved on my heart. "I will betroth You to me forever." I knew that when I got up the first thing I would do would be to reclaim my good name. Now I needed to close my eyes and sleep.

EPILOGUE

Sam Kleiner was one of my oldest and dearest friends, from Sadzawky, the next village over from Krasne. Like me, he was in Lvov when Hitler attacked the Russians. Unlike me he fled to the east, eventually ending up in Moscow.

In the summer of 1944 Sam was an engineer with the Red Army as it pushed the Germans out of the Ukraine and into the Carpathians. He saw what the Nazis had done in Grzymalov, Sadzawky, and Krasne. He was in Tarnopol with his unit, then followed the front into Lvov just a few days after I took Edward Wawer's name off my front door and replaced it with my own.

When he arrived in Lvov, Sam went to Nabielacka Street looking for me; he knew the apartment house well from his many visits before the war. Outside the building he paced back and forth for a long time, unable to summon the courage to go in. He had marched through enough cities and towns so that he knew what to expect, and he didn't want to face the possibility that I too had disappeared. When he finally did go in he found the apartment where Wusia and I used to live empty. Then he came to the second floor, saw my name on the door, and knocked.

Sam found me alive, but what he told me about was death. In Krasne he had learned that the Germans executed all the Jewish men and Jewish boys they found there. Among them were my brother Max with his son Jonah, my brother-in-law David and his son Herman, David Hersh Zeftel, his son Abraham and his grandson. Krasne's women and the rest of the children were also gone, transported to the Grzymalov ghetto. Mama had died there. But Esther, Dvorah and her children Henia and Michael, Zeftel's wife Sarah, Abraham's wife Judith, Max's wife Henia, and their children Ceil and Mundek, and Blima, in whose hair I had once put a frog, had been murdered later in Skalat. Sam made further inquiries in Postolufka and Czortkow, Choroskow and Kopyczynce. As far as he could tell, all of them had perished, all of my mother's family and all of my father's. Among my close relatives he knew of only one who had survived, Max's daughter Manya. She had escaped to the east and had ended up as a worker on a mink farm deep inside Russia. Sam had somehow managed to locate her and he gave me the address.

Of Wusia and Michael he had heard nothing. Nor had other survivors who slowly began reappearing, each of whom I searched out and interrogated. I talked to hundreds of people, but no one remembered them from that June *Aktion*.

No one had seen them in Janowska. They had vanished into thin air.

But their trail led only toward one place—Belzec, the mysterious death factory near which I had seen the corpse-strewn tracks. It was there that most of Lvov's 160,000 Jews ended their lives. But it seemed that not a single witness had been left to testify. If anybody had escaped from there, no one in Lvov had heard about it. Long before the Red Army arrived, the Germans had closed Belzec down and destroyed it, erasing the evidence of what they had done.

But an enormity on that scale can't be completely hidden. People living in the vicinity knew, as did the Polish railroad workers who manned the transport trains. They talked and the word spread. The Polish railroadmen brought people in, but they never saw anybody coming out. They had driven their trains onto a special spur surrounded by barbed wire. From there they could see the chimneys and the smoke. They smelled the stench. The Poles took the train to the spur, then a German crew came on to drive it the rest of the way. We heard that later the camp buildings had been razed, that a multitude of bodies had been disinterred from the great burial pits, burned, then the skeletons ground up and buried again. We heard that on the site, already covered by vegetation, one could still find traces of buildings and scattered bits of charred bone.

As hard as I tried to block them from my mind, I began seeing pictures of Wusia in the boxcar, clutching Michael as the train moved toward its destination. I imagined it pulling onto the siding in the woods outside of Belzec. I could feel the desperation that must have come over her when the train stopped and the German crew came on. I tried not to imagine the barracks where they were ordered to take off their clothes, or their final march to the gas chambers. But I couldn't help myself. For a long time I couldn't rid myself of these images. I saw them every night while I was trying to sleep. When I finally did drop off, they appeared in my dreams. Their faces came to me during the day too. They were always there. When I started teaching again I'd be in the middle of a class and suddenly I'd see Wusia and Michael as I imagined they must have been as they went to meet their fate. On the surface I carried on, but deep in my heart I mourned for them. For years anxiety and fear for them had been my constant companions. Now that I knew they were gone, I yearned for them more than ever.

It helped that I was back at school staying busy. With the Russians in charge again many of Lvov's schools reopened, including the technical high school on Snopkowska Street. The principal there, Mikhail Molochko, gave me a job teaching my old subjects, mathematics and mechanics. Molochko was an army officer and party member who had been wounded and reassigned as an educator. A humane, sympathetic man, he and I soon became good friends.

At the end of the school year Molochko gave me a *kommandurofko*, a permit so I could travel back to Krasne. In those days travelling from place to place was permitted only to people on official business, and my *kommandurofko* stated that my presence was urgently required in Podwoloczysk on the Zbrucz, which just happened to be the nearest railroad station to Krasne now that the tracks to Grzymalov were destroyed. I knew what had happened in Gryzmalov and Krasne, but Molochko understood that I was aching to go back to see those places for myself. I needed to know more details of what had taken place.

On the way to Podwoloczysk the train stopped in Tarnopol, which had been the scene of terrible fighting the previous summer. The Russians had liberated the city, and the Jewish survivors came out of hiding. But then the Germans counterattacked and drove the Russians back, leaving the Jews out in the open to be rounded up and killed. The beautiful old station in Tarnopol had been completely demolished, though the two-story building next to it was still standing. I was amazed to see the undercarriage of a locomotive embedded in its roof, blown there by the force of an explosion.

At Podwoloczysk I stayed overnight at an inn, planning to hire a wagon and driver the next day to take me to Krasne. But that night I fell into conversation with a Polish priest. When I mentioned that I was leaving for Krasne in the morning he warned me against it. He knew the area well, he said. It was overrun by the remnants of Stepan Bandera's Ukrainian nationalist army. They were attacking Russian rear guard forces and had even killed a Russian general. They were also murdering every Jew they could find, and I'd be putting my life in grave danger. I was torn. I had a deep need to go home, if only to see it one last time, but I finally decided not to take the risk.

In the train back to Lvov a young Polish soldier came into my compartment and sat down opposite me. When we started talking we were both shocked to find out that we were related. He was Dov Altschuler, a second cousin on my mother's side, whose parents I had known before the war. Among other things, he told me that another cousin, Giza, had also survived. I had never met this young Altschuler before, but Giza was a first cousin, daughter of my mother's sister, and I knew her well. She too was in the Polish army, he told me, as was her husband. They were now stationed in Lublin.

By this time Max's daughter, Manya, was living with me in the big apartment. After Sam gave me her address we had started writing. She told me how miserable she was on the mink farm and asked if there were some way I could get her a permit to come to Lvov so we could live near each other. In the Soviet Union you couldn't just leave your place of work, and without some kind of intervention Manya would have been stuck in central Asia. Once again Mikhail Molochko proved his friendship and wrote an official letter declaring she was needed for work at the technical high school. I took the letter to the local Communist Party secretary for approval and he scrawled in big letters underneath Molochko's name, "Do Not Object." With that "Do Not Object" the mink farm released Manya, and since then we had been sharing my apartment.

Sam had also put me in touch with the Joint Distribution Committee, a Jewish rescue organization based in America. One day a food package unexpectedly arrived from them, along with a questionnaire asking if I had any relatives in the United States. It was through the "Joint" that I established contact with Zalman (who had changed his name to "George"), my older brother who had moved to the United States before I was born. Before long it became clear that the American government would allow me to immigrate to America. But the problem of getting out of the Soviet Union was another matter entirely.

It was my good luck, though, that just then the Soviets had arranged a repatriation procedure, which permitted Polish citizens in the Ukraine to move back into Poland now that Russia was annexing the country's pre-war eastern territories.

It wasn't an easy decision. By then I had a good teaching position, and under Mikhail Molochko's sponsorship I had been attending political meetings and taking courses which eventually would have made me a candidate for party membership. The Soviets had saved my life and had treated me kindly. I was looking forward to resuming my university studies, and as an engineer and a party member my future in the USSR looked bright. But the chance to go to the United States could hardly be ignored. When I talked to Molochko about my mixed feelings, he was blunt. "Don't be a fool," he said. "Go. If I had a chance I'd go myself."

At the end of September 1945 Manya and I were on the last train of repatriates to Poland. In Krakow we saw Sam Kleiner, who had arrived a short time before. Leaving Manya with Sam, I went off to Lublin to see if I could find Giza at the address my young Altschuler cousin had given me. When I arrived the house was full of Polish soldiers having a boisterous party. Giza was sitting at her dining room table in the middle of a card game. When she looked up and saw me she dropped her cards on the floor and almost knocked her chair over in her rush to throw her arms around me. She had been sure I was dead, along with the rest of my family.

Giza was a nurse officer in the Polish Army Medical Corps while her husband Leon Falik was an army doctor stationed in Lodz, where we went to see him the next day. While we were there a messenger appeared with a letter from the United States Army in Berlin. As she read it, Giza's face filled with joy. Then she started crying. The letter was from her sister Mildred whom she hadn't seen since 1934 when

Mildred immigrated to America. Mildred wrote that she was in Berlin with the US Army. She wanted Giza to come to see her immediately.

I knew Mildred as well as I knew Giza. We had all visited each other often while we were growing up. And when it turned out Giza couldn't get leave, we decided that I would go to Berlin to see Mildred in her place.

I had no papers that would get me across the Polish-German border. But I knew that all the Russian military trains shuttling back and forth between Moscow and Berlin stopped in Lodz to water and refuel. After my experiences moving around Poland under the Nazis, I thought, how hard could it be to smuggle myself into Berlin?

Once I had watched a couple of these military trains make their stops, I borrowed one of Leon's army uniforms. Then I cut off the end of a loaf of bread and hollowed out the inside, into which I stuffed a wad of money I had gotten from selling the furniture from my Nabielacka Street apartment. On a train filled with soldiers I thought there was a good chance I wouldn't be noticed. If that failed, I'd try to bribe my way.

When the Moscow-Berlin express stopped for water at Lodz station I was waiting in the shadows with my briefcase ready to swing myself aboard. The train was packed with Russian troops and I just blended in. Nobody seemed to care that I was wearing a Polish uniform. Everything went smoothly until we reached the border and the Russian border police began checking documents. When I couldn't supply any, they took me off the train and handed me over to the local train guards. I knew I had to do something quickly, before they formally arrested me. Explaining as fast as I could that a mistake had been made, I showed them my teacher's identification card, my union membership card, and my apprentice party activist card. But none of the talk seemed to be having any effect until I happened to mention the word "vodka," and would they care to join me in a bottle. With that word the guards turned instantly friendly. A bottle of vodka might be just the thing to relieve the thirst of their difficult workday. Unfortunately, I didn't actually have a bottle with me at the moment. But wouldn't it be equally enjoyable, I suggested, if they were to buy one themselves, with money I could "loan" them for the purpose. They agreed it would and I extricated some bills from my loaf of bread as inconspicuously as I could. After the transfer of funds, they apologized profusely for inconveniencing me and assured me that I would not be disturbed again. Another train to Berlin would soon be coming through, and they'd see to it I got aboard.

The train guards were as good as their word. They put me on the next train, said a few words to the border police, and a few hours later I was in Berlin. My meeting with Mildred was as emotional as my meeting with Giza. Mildred was with an American intelligence unit, which explained how she had been able to locate Giza. Her own parents had perished, she told me, as had Sulio, their brother. Like Giza, Mildred had been sure that I was dead too.

I spent a couple of days with Mildred, who solved the problem of spiriting me back across the border by introducing me to an American war correspondent stationed in Warsaw. He had a car and would be driving back. Mildred thought it unlikely anyone would stop him, and she was right. He dropped me off in Lodz without incident.

Two months later I returned to Berlin, this time with Giza and her husband, who had managed to acquire travel permits ostensibly to buy medical equipment. Now I had more time to study the situation. At Schlachtensee, just outside the city, the UNRRA had set up a camp for displaced persons waiting to be resettled. Moreover, the German civil authorities were making travel documents available for refugees searching for family members. When I again returned to Lodz I had travel permits for myself, Manya, and her cousin Andzia. I also had a permit for Max Heller, a close friend of mine from our time in *Kvutzah Barzel* in 1935. Max had been mobilized into the Soviet Army after the German attack, which is how he had survived. Now, like Manya and me, he had repatriated to Poland. We were all sure that once we got to the UNRRA camp we'd eventually be able to immigrate to the United States.

By this time, the situation in Europe was changing fast. It was 1946 and all over Eastern Europe the Soviets were taking control. Borders were closing and it was becoming more difficult to move. Poland was nominally independent, but everyone knew that real power was in the hands of the NKVD. The iron curtain was beginning to descend.

Under these circumstances, as the weeks passed our travel documents lost their value. I was pretty sure that if I were alone I'd still be able to get into Berlin. But smuggling a group was a different matter. Looking around for a way to do it, I learned that controls in the Polish border city of Szczecin were still relatively loose. From there it might be possible to get all of us to Berlin, and once in Berlin I was sure we'd somehow be able to get into the American sector.

We traveled to Szczecin by train, Manya, Andzia, Max and I. Scouting for the most likely way over the border, I found there was a steady traffic of big Russian military trucks carrying supplies to Soviet troops in Germany. Before long I made the acquaintance of a Russian driver who said he had room to take ten or twelve people who would hide in his truckload of furniture. He had already lined up six; our four would make ten. His fee was high, but I agreed to it. He seemed to know what he was doing and I wanted to minimize the chances that anything would go wrong.

It was just past twelve o'clock on a cold winter night when the big truck pulled in front of the building where we were staying. In the dim light of the street lamps the four of us slipped out the door and into the truck's cab, where the driver showed us into the rear compartment through a little entranceway behind the seat. There we found ourselves in a confined space already occupied by six other people, including a mother and her young son. Stacked around us were large cabinets and wardrobes, desks, tables, and chairs.

The gloom in our hideaway was relieved only by the faint light from the little door to the cab. "Make sure you keep absolutely quiet," the driver said. "They stop these trucks all the time at the checkpoints. If they hear anything they'll send you all to Siberia." Then he closed the door, leaving us in utter darkness.

As the truck rumbled off, I could sense the people sitting on either side of me. I couldn't see anything, but the space was filled with tension. The driver's warning had set my heart pounding. I had been fantasizing the last few days about how it would be to arrive in America, to see the Statue of Liberty and the New York skyline. But the truth was that Siberia was much closer than New York. When you make a bargain like this you understand the risks, but you're willing to take them. Once in the middle of it, though, that changes. All your fears about what could go wrong spring to life. I didn't know this driver at all. We had paid him, but that didn't mean anything. He could do whatever he liked, including turning us over to the police. I knew how these things worked. He could easily have a deal with the police to stop the truck, rob us of everything, then ship us off to prison. It didn't even have to be the police. He could just as easily be working with ordinary robbers. Szczecin was crowded with people wanting to get across the border. For an enterprising person with a truck, preying on refugees could be a lucrative pastime.

Mulling over thoughts like these, I couldn't even think about sleep. The truck rumbled along and the cold began to seep into my bones. Hours passed. Nobody spoke. The only sounds were the growl of the engine and a disconcerting creaking when the furniture shifted. Suddenly the truck slowed down, pulled toward the right, and jerked to a stop. We had been travelling for a long time, we must be well into Germany, I thought. But there were no noises from outside. Wherever we were, it wasn't Berlin.

A moment later the door opened and the driver's head appeared. "Everybody out," he said. "Come on, everybody out. Something's happened. Take your things with you." I could imagine what happened, I'd been imagining it since we got in the truck. I felt all my senses coming alert as they always did in these situations. I ducked into the cab, trying to see the conditions outside, expecting to see men with guns. But nobody seemed to be around, only silence of the snow-covered woods.

"This is it," the driver said when we were all out of the truck. "Berlin's not too far off. I can't take you any further. It's too risky. I'm sure they'll check the truck, and if they find you we'll all be goners."

"Wait a minute," I said. "We paid you a good price to take us to Berlin. Why did you take our money if you weren't going to keep your word? You must have known the risks when you made the deal. So why are you changing your mind now?"

"Look, friend," he said. "Don't talk so much. This way is much safer for you and me both. There's a railroad station right around here. There's no point in arguing, just take the train to Berlin." With that he went around to the other side, hoisted himself up into the cab, and pulled out onto the road. We stood there in shocked silence, our little pile of baggage making a pathetic display on the snowy shoulder.

To the right of the highway the woods fell away into a valley. To the left in the distance we could make out what looked like lights from a window of a house. This was the first good look I had of our fellow passengers—the mother and her son, a frail looking six year old with big frightened eyes; two girls in their twenties; a boyfriend of one of them; and an orthodox man in a black hat and coat fidgeting nervously and praying softly to himself. They were all hunched up against the cold. They seemed to be waiting for someone to tell them what to do.

"Let's get off the highway," I said. "We don't want to be seen. Once we get ourselves out of sight we can decide what to do."

The crust on the foot-deep snow crackled as we trudged into the valley. Walking was slow, but not impossible, nothing like it usually was in the woods around Krasne. The only one I was worried about was the little boy, so after a few minutes, Max, the boyfriend, and I began taking turns carrying him.

Fifteen minutes or so later we found a small hollow that gave some protection from the wind and shielded us completely from the line of sight of anybody who might be looking from the roadway. There we made a camp, huddling next to each other for warmth. After a few minutes of talk, the group elected me leader and it was agreed that I should try to find out if the people in the house we had seen in the distance might be willing to help us.

When I finally found the building, the night sky was already turning gray on the horizon. As I got closer I could see it wasn't a house at all, but the railroad station the truck driver had mentioned. As early as it was, the waiting room was already crowded with Russian soldiers and Germans awaiting the first train to Berlin. Checking the schedules, I bought ten tickets, then headed back through the woods to find my friends.

When I got back to them they were overjoyed by what I had managed to do. I gave out the tickets and told them how we should conduct ourselves to lessen the chances of being noticed. A group was likely to attract attention, so the trick would be to keep our distance from one another and travel as individuals. That way, even if one person was caught, it wouldn't necessarily mean that everyone else would be. At the same time we had to keep an eye on each other. I knew Berlin, so they should watch me and follow what I did, but inconspicuously.

We plodded through the woods together, but entered the station separately and mixed with the waiting room crowd. When the train came, it was full of soldiers and German civilians heading into Berlin to work. We all got into the same car, everyone doing their best to fit in. Our orthodox comrade was the only one who was a real concern, but I was experiencing more than enough apprehension for us all. I had smuggled myself through enough situations so that I didn't panic easily, but being responsible for a group was a fearful business.

To my vast relief, the train made its stops in Berlin without incident. We passed through the Russian zone uneventfully, then headed into the American sector. There we got off, and before long we were checking in at the Schlachtensee refugee camp. In the lavatory I looked at myself in the mirror and was startled to see that my hair had started to turn gray. The last time I had looked in a mirror it had been the same blond as always.

It took four months before the Americans processed my application and Manya's and issued us entry visas. Given that the only worthwhile piece of identification I possessed was my identity card from the technical high school in Lvov,

I was struck with gratitude that they did it at all. A few days later Manya and I were on our way to Bremenhaven to sail on the SS Marine Flasher. We were among the first boatloads of Holocaust survivors to leave Europe for the United States. Before we boarded I bought a large round loaf of dark bread and hid it under my jacket. We had been told not to take food aboard, that all our meals would be provided. But I didn't think it would hurt to bring along some insurance. It was going to be a long trip, and I was determined to start my new life with body and soul intact.

Manya Ungar Landau and I after repatriation from Russia to Poland in the DP camp of Schlachtensee. October 1945

That life started on May 19, 1946. Late that night Manya and I were standing together on the deck of the

Marine Flasher as the lights of New York twinkled dimly in the distance. As we drew closer Manhattan emerged from the night, a surreal fairyland, unimaginably wondrous. Magisterial and gigantic, the Statue of Liberty loomed in front of the city, bathed in light. We knew Emma Lazarus's poem was inscribed on her somewhere, "Give me your tired, your poor, your huddled masses yearning to breathe free." As the ship glided by we strained to find the words. We weren't able, but it didn't matter. We knew them by heart.

A little while later the Marine Flasher nudged into a berth in this incredible city. The crew told us that no one would be allowed to disembark until morning, and that we should all get some sleep. But I doubt that anyone did.

Early the next day Manya and I walked down the gangway onto a pier packed with people desperate to catch sight of relatives who had miraculously escaped the cataclysm. In our pockets each refugee carried fifteen dollars, a present from the Joint Distribution Committee. Among those waiting were my mother's brother Sol, her cousin Frieda, and my brother George, whom I had never seen. They welcomed me with hugs and kisses, letting me know that I was no longer alone. I was riding a tidal wave of emotion, overwhelmed by the sights and sounds, and by a towering optimism that here in this place I could build my future.

Looking back on that moment and the years that followed I can see that in many ways mine was a typical immigrant story. For a while I lived on the generosity of my family. I studied English and attended evening school (some were open only to returning veterans. I had told the authorities that I was a veteran too, of the Polish army, America's ally). I found a job, and when my English was good enough I enrolled in the City College of New York (CCNY) night school, eventually graduating with a degree in mechanical engineering.

My first and only job was on the assembly line at the F.L. Smithe Company, which manufactured envelope-making equipment. I was lucky there. The Smithe family knew I was a refugee and they and their employees, Abe Novick, Bruno Faust and others, treated me with kindness. Something of the American entrepreneurial spirit must have infected me at Smithe. I had never in my life thought of myself as a businessman, but when the opportunity presented itself I bought three antiquated envelope machines and started my own company in a loft in Chinatown.

It took a number of years before I had settled down to the point where I was able to think about a family. Wusia and Michael were still entrenched in my heart, where they would always be. But in time I found that despite the wounds, my emotional life was still basically whole and that my desire for companionship had come back to life.

One reason was that I had met a most attractive girl. Her name was Jerry Schweitzer, the daughter of parents who had immigrated in the early part of the century from southeastern Poland. Though an American, she had grown up in a Yiddish-speaking house, with the food and customs that were such a part of my own life. She also shared my love of Israel, and she wasn't afraid of acting on her beliefs. After the war she had worked closely with Haim Slavin, who was in charge of equipping the Jewish community in Palestine with arms and was running a large covert operation in the United States. At one point a crateload of TNT had broken open on a dock and as the FBI began closing in on Slavin's American office Jerry left for Florida where she lived until it was safe to come back.

I had first met Jerry a year or so after arriving. It was a time when I was so numbed by what had happened that I thought I might never again be capable of feelings. But I noticed, and when we met again in 1949, I found myself deeply attracted. It wasn't just her good humor and sincerity that drew me to her, nor the things we had in common. There was something more, a feeling between us that startled me as it grew. To my amazement, I found that I was in love. I didn't understand it then, and fifty years later I still don't—how the ashes of my heart, which I had thought dead forever, came alive again. It felt as if I had been reborn. When I proposed I gave her a little diamond ring, one of the few items I had brought with me from Germany.

Jerry Schweitzer and myself. 1949

*Our marriage—January 1, 1950
"The ashes of my heart, which I
had thought dead forever, became
alive again."*

The four Ungar daughters—
Florette, Joan, Denise, Rita

The Ungar Family—photo courtesy of Nick Del Calzo, displayed in the rotunda of the
U.S. Senate Office Building. May 8, 1997

Jerry and I were married on January 1, 1950. It was a joyous occasion, though she said later that she had seen a momentary shadow on my face. She didn't know about Wusia and Michael then; I still found it too painful to talk about that part of my past. While I was struggling to establish my business during the day and attending City College of the City of New York in the evening, Jerry supported us with her salary as an office manager at the Inland Machinery and Metals Company. At night she did my books and helped me face innumerable problems. I was in the envelope making business, although I knew almost nothing about envelopes, or business. But with her advice on how to deal with Americans and my knowledge of machinery, the business began to grow.

Jerry and I with our friends Dina & Chaim Rosen after the business began to grow

When we were successful enough, Jerry resigned from her job to make a home for our children and me. That was in 1953. Over the next six years Florette, Joan, Denise, and Rita were born. Being a father to them, bringing them up and watching them grow, I felt blessed far beyond the usual blessings of parenthood. With wonder I saw them through school, college and beyond. Together with Jerry they gave me a world I had never dared hope for. Our daughters too have married and have given us seventeen wonderful grandchildren. Two generations come into being, of all the potential generations of a family destroyed almost to the root by the Nazis.

Through all my years in America I felt the need to go back, to set my eyes one last time on the places where I grew up and came of age and see where it was that my dear ones had lost their lives. I needed to do that, if only to give the past a chance to rest in peace. I had tried to go in 1945, when Mikhail Molochko gave me the travel permit, but Bandera's guerrillas stopped me. And, of course, the summer after that I left for Poland, then for Germany to emigrate to the United States. During the Cold War the western Ukraine was a closed region, off limits to travelers. It wasn't until after the Ukrainians declared their independence and the political dust had settled that I began thinking seriously about returning.

In 1992 Jerry and I went to Eastern Europe, part of a group from the United States Holocaust Memorial Museum in Washington, D.C. charged with bringing back soil from each of the German death camps. At Auschwitz, which is outside of Krakow, we decided to separate from the group and go to Lvov. From there we would try to get to Krasne. When we learned that the Lvov airport was closed for repairs, we hired a Polish driver to take us.

At Przemsyl on the River San we drove over the same narrow bridge I had tried to cross on crutches in 1939. A long, unmoving line of trucks waited for the unhurried attention of the border guards. Remembering what had worked for me more than once in the past, I bribed the guards, this time with chocolate and cigarettes, and we left the trucks behind. We arrived in Lvov late that night. In the cold rain the city looked dreary and broken down. We had a hard time finding our hotel; in the dark I wasn't sure I could recognize the building, and Russian street names had replaced the old Polish and Ukrainian ones.

Early the next morning we left for Krasne, taking a hotel security guard with us for protection. Tourists who want to see the countryside usually go in groups, but we were the only two and we were told the roads weren't safe. Six hours later we were in Tarnopol where I went to the Jewish cemetery in hopes of finding my father's grave. But the cemetery held only the ruins of tombs and gravestones. For an instant I saw myself as I had been in the Lvov cemetery after I escaped from Janowska, watching the prisoners pounding the Jewish gravestones into gravel. From the look of the place, that had happened here too.

From Tarnopol we drove to Skalat. My mother had died in Grzymalov. She had starved to death in the ghetto—I had learned that from the Bernsteins, friends who had been there with her but who had escaped and eventually had come to the United States. Later the surviving Jews of the Grzymalov ghetto had been taken to Skalat where they were executed, my sisters Esther and Dvorah, Max's wife Henia, and her children, and Dvorah's young children among them. But there was no time to stop and we drove straight through to Grzymalov, another hour south.

My niece—Henia Freiberg—born in 1933, perished along with her family at the hands of the Nazis in 1943.

In Grzymalov I made inquiries about the Jewish cemetery, hoping that by some chance my mother's resting place might be intact. An old man showed me where the graveyard had been. But here too the markers were crumbled or missing. My guide remembered that the Germans had used the cemetery as a garbage dump. When the Russians came, he said, they cleaned it and planted some trees, making the grounds into a small garden. Looking around I found a jagged piece of a stone with two Hebrew characters on it: *pay nun*— "here is buried." I put the stone in the car and dug up a little soil for the museum. Then I said *Kaddish*, the prayer for the dead. But we didn't linger.

It used to take two hours to get from Grzymalov to Krasne by wagon. By car it's about twenty minutes. On the road outside the village we passed a sign, "Krasne," spelled out in Cyrillic. Beyond the sign we stopped for a driver herding his cows down the middle of the road. I tried to get my bearings. The flourmill was still there, on the right. Here was the Ukrainian church, down there was the Roman Catholic. The roads were still unpaved. The houses looked dilapidated, uncared for. The place seemed poverty-stricken, so different from the village I remembered.

As we drove slowly along the main street I noticed a woman standing alone in front of the Roman Catholic Church. When I got out to talk she curtsied and introduced herself. Wasn't I the priest, she asked, who had been sent to

Return to my birthplace. Krasne, 1992

Return to Nabielacka 12, where I had been hiding in the basement a half-century ago.
Lvov, 1992

The former house of my brother, Max, and his family, 1992

Posing with friends of Olga, third from left, in Krasne, 1992

In front of the church in Krasne with the Ukranian woman, 1992

talk with her about restoring the church? When I explained who I was, tears came to her eyes. Yes, she said, she knew what had happened during the war, although she had been a little girl then and had no memories of it herself. But there was an elderly woman, Olga, a neighbor, who remembered everything. She could tell me more about it.

A short walk took us down the street to the neighbor's house. But it was the house next door that caught my attention. It was my brother Max's, looking exactly as it had a half-century earlier, except shuttered and locked. No one lived there, the woman said, no one had for a long time. Olga, the old neighbor woman would know more.

I never would have recognized Olga, a stout, bright-eyed individual in her seventies, but I remembered who she was. I had known her father, the town barber. They had been Max's neighbors forever. Olga knew my whole family, the way village people always know each other. She could hardly believe it when I told her who I was. Her face seemed a changing mask of emotions as she looked at me. Warmth and concern played across her features, but mostly, I thought, sorrow. She invited us in and instantly set about preparing dinner, although we tried our best to decline. Her voice choked as she told us how horrified she and her family were over what had happened, how badly it had affected them. Her memory was utterly clear about the events of those days. She would remember them forever.

David Zeftel was first, she said. She hadn't seen it herself, but everyone knew. His house was on the road that led east out of Krasne, and the first German patrol to arrive stopped there to ask for something to drink. Remembering the Germans from the First World War, Zeftel was friendly. He brought them not just water, but a pitcher of sourmilk. The Germans drank the milk, and as they left one of them turned and shot him, "because he was Jewish." Zeftel's wife dragged him inside where he suffered until nightfall. Then— Olga apologized profusely—Ukrainian militiamen came into town. Among the houses they went to was Zeftel's. They killed him in his bed.

Worse happened the next day when the *Einsatzgruppen* arrived. Olga told us how they rounded up all the Jewish men and took them out to the forest on the outskirts of the village. They forced them to dig a pit, then they shot them all. When she finished her story the room was silent. Outside it had started raining. Drops pattered on the windows. "I'll come with you," she said. "I'll show you where it happened."

We stopped first at the other end of the main street, where my house had stood. In its place there was now a food co-op. When we went in we saw only bare shelves. There was very little to buy, no food, only a sheaf of propaganda bulletins by the door. The only person in the store was a dispirited clerk, with an abacus lying on the counter next to him. To make room for the empty co-op they had torn down our house. All but a few trees of our beautiful orchard were also gone. Nothing was left, only my memories of how it had once been.

Olga took us north of town, off the road to Grzymalov opposite the flourmill. I knew the beautiful pine woods here intimately. As a child the place had been one of my favorite haunts. I remembered how the trees filled the air with the delicious, sharp scent of pine resin. You could play in the deep shadows or hide out and spy on the wagons lumbering down the road to Grzymalov, the gravel surfaced "Kaiser Road"—as distinguished from the dirt "field road" that ran to the south.

A little way into the woods Olga stopped. "Here," she said. "It was here." I looked at the ground. It was indistinguishable from the rest of the forest floor. Yet I felt their presence somehow, standing at the spot, that grave, knowing that my dear ones were here, and others I knew so well. There was none of the remoteness that I had felt through all the years. This was the very place they had died.

I felt the helplessness wash over me of those who had been here, faced with the unspeakable and unable to act. Today we think about these situations with hindsight, analyze them, consider the alternatives that might have been. Couldn't they have run? Fought? But at that moment they could do nothing. It had come so suddenly upon them. They didn't expect it. They didn't know where they were being taken, or what the Germans were capable of doing, what they had in mind. It took years before people understood and would try to escape by any means. At the beginning nobody understood. Nobody could imagine. So they weren't prepared. Just as I had not been prepared. Had I been in Krasne I would have been here with them, at the edge of the muddy pit. Face to face with my last moments on earth.

It was when the Germans told them to start digging that they must have understood. It was only then that they realized what was about to happen here. But too late. They had shovels in their hands, looking around, maybe not accepting it. Looking for a way out, but covered by rifles and submachine guns.

The village had kept a tenuous memory of the place. No marker had been erected, but for a long time the villagers knew where it was. The place where the Jews were killed. North of town, off the Kaiser road. Across from the flourmill. Fifty three years later some still knew, but now it was only the old ones, like Olga, who had taken the tragedy to their hearts.

Here, too, I took up a little soil and said *Kaddish*. For the second time during our trip I was hammered by the thought that such precious lives could just disappear, unhonored and uncommemorated. In Belzec too, incredibly, there had been no marker. The Russians had put up a monument declaring what the Germans did, but never mentioning that they had done it to Jews. At Belzec I had walked away from the

Holocaust Museum group to the back of a little park the Russians created. I had sat on a bench by myself and conjured up what it had been like for Wusia walking her last steps, purposely summoning images which for years I had done everything I could to suppress. Here the Germans had excavated the bodies and ground the bones, spreading them over the area. They called to you, those bones. The park soil had an unnatural, brittle feel which was not some psychological aberration. You felt it with the soles of your feet, stepping on those shards and slivers, the bony detritus of half a million souls. Two of whom were my own.

In Belzec I had thought about Edward Wawer, whose name had saved my life so many times. I thought about that night so long ago when I had wrestled with myself over who I was going to be: A new man insisting on his right to live life free of an intolerable burden of suffering. A new man abandoning the terrible confines of his people's inheritance and his own pain, boldly making his unfettered way into the future. I remembered how fierce that struggle had been inside myself. And I thought, sitting there in Belzec, how puerile such a life would have been, and how devoid of the meaning that comes with grasping your people to your heart no matter what and accepting the full weight of your own history, and theirs.

At Belzec, 1992
Behind me the inscription on the monument erected by the Soviet Union reads as follows:
"In memory of the victims of Hilter's terrorism, murdered during the years 1942–1943."

Collecting soil at the site of the 1941 massacre of the Jews by the Nazis. Krasne, 1992

Monument dedicated to baby Michael Ungar at Yad Layeled, The Living Memorial to the Children of the Holocaust, established by the Ghetto Fighter's House in Israel.

ETERNAL GRATITUDE

During the darkest days in my life, unexpectedly, a ray of hope appeared that in time not only saved my life, but also gave me an insight into human behavior. Surrounded by conditions of hatred, atrocities and annihilation implemented by the Nazi government and its collaborators, there were remarkable individuals who at the risk of their own lives undertook to save Jews during the Holocaust. They believed in human values and acted accordingly regardless of consequences.

I was fortunate that two of them had an impact upon my life. Katherine Wowkowa and Edward Wawer, two righteous gentiles who had the courage independently to put their own lives at risk for me, knowing that I was unable to repay their kindness.

In 1950 Edward Wawer, while trying to cross from Russia to Poland illegally, was shot and killed by a Russian border guard.

In the years after I came to the United States, I continuously sent packages to Katy Wowkowa in Lvov, enabling her to sell their contents and thereby improve her standard of living. Later on, through Russian immigrants, I sent money. We corresponded with one another until the late 1970s when, unfortunately, she passed away.

Deep in my heart, I often think about my two saviors whose humane deeds will always evoke eternal gratitude.

TRIBUTE

To our father, from your loving daughters.

Silence…For many years we waited to hear your story. For many years we wished to be told the untold. To hear of your past, of your family, of your life during another time…

We, your daughters, understood your story long before it was written. For our lives were shaped by it. Despite the grief and pain, you succeeded to create again a life, a family, a future. To build a future for us, your daughters, and for many others whose lives have been touched by your goodness and courage.

Without words, you have taught us. You have given us your majestic example of man's ability to say no to circumstances, to strive and succeed, despite doom and horror, to build a life of beauty and goodness.

And yet, it is a story that we somehow always knew. For silence speaks louder than words. Pain and suffering, tears and torment, can be conveyed perhaps, only through silence.

Your silence merged with the eternal silence of those dear to you who perished...whose silence is the echo of a cry, a scream. It was the silence of a home once occupied, suddenly empty...of a cradle suddenly bereft of its cries... of a family, a people, who are no more.

And so, we knew. We knew the story behind the words, which was also the story of your spiritual strength. For, without words, you transmitted to us your belief and courage. Despite the horror and the pain, you maintained faith. Faith in God and in Judaism, which those who would destroy the spirit of our people could not touch. Faith in man's goodness, and in your own ability to resist evil. A faith which defies cruelty, and which cruelty could not diminish. To quote Tschernichovsky:

> *For my soul has not been sold*
> *To the golden calf of scorn*
> *And I still believe in man*
> *And the spirit in him born*

You witnessed and endured what no human being ever should, and rebuilt your life with integrity.

We, your children, lived our lives, and will continue to do so, steeped in the responsibility of transmitting your message and example to the generations that follow. There is a certain daily awareness that is ours, to live life in a worthwhile way, to try to make up somehow for the lives that were lost, among them our own aunts, uncles, grandparents, cousins. We dream of the faces we never saw and never shall see, the hours from them, from you, from us. We wonder at the generations of children, forever lost to us, to the world, to our people. Your life echoes a resounding cry of "No" to Hitler's attempt to annihilate the Jewish people. Your bitterness has become sweetness; you have spread goodness in your wake, strengthening the Jewish people with all your being and ultimately, by imbuing your four daughters and now seventeen grandchildren with your shining examples of loving kindness.

Your story is the story of the triumph of the spirit above circumstances that would destroy it. The triumph of humanness above inhumanity and cruelty. You have a vision, a belief in man's ability to rise above his surroundings, which we understood.

We are forever grateful to you for this tremendous labor of love you have undertaken. To wade through the dark morass of memories, ridden with terror and sorrow, has surely been a monumental task. You have now bequeathed us with the legacy of knowledge, one that is precious beyond words.

You are forever an inspiration to us. Our pledge of remembrance, continuity, dedication and love endures forever, to the generations that follow. In your footsteps we walk.

This tribute would be incomplete were we not to express our deep love, admiration, and gratitude to our mother, Jerry Ungar. You are not only the most harmonious partner and helpmate to your husband, but you are the most incredible living example of generosity, courage, vitality, and kindness to your children and indeed, the world, with whom you have shared your largesse of spirit. You have made a difference in the lives of so many and we, your children, love you beyond words.

FLORETTE, JOAN, DENISE *and* RITA